SUFI BOOK OF

SPIRITUAL ASCENT
(AL-RISALA AL-QUSHAYRIYA)

ABU 'L-QASIM
AL-QUSHAYRI

TRANSLATED BY
RABIA HARRIS

EDITED BY
LALEH BAKHTIAR

ABC INTERNATIONAL GROUP, INC

Library of Congress Cataloging in Publication Data
Qushayri, Abu 'l-Qasim
    Sufi Book of Spiritual Ascent (*al-Risala al-Qushayriya*)
    abridged translation by Rabia Harris.

    Includes biographical reference and index.
    1. Sufism—Early works to 1800. 2. Psychology, Religious.
    3. Consciousness. 4. Ethics. 5. Counseling. I. Qushayri,
    Abu 'l-Qasim. II. Title
    BP189.Q7313   1992   92-82685
    197'.4—dc20   CIP
ISBN: 1-871031-53-2

Cover Design by Liaquat Ali
Manufactured in the United States of America

Published by
ABC Group International, Inc.

Distributed by
KAZI Publications, Inc.
3023 W. Belmont Avenue
Chicago IL 60618
Tel: 773-267-7001; FAX: 773-267-7002
email: info@kazi.org; web:http://www.kazi.org

CONTENTS

Handwritten annotations:

bd al-Karim ibn Hwazin ibn Abd al-Malik ibn
Talha Abu 'l Qasim al-Qushayri
which means a "princely" title ↙
born in July AD 986
of mixed Arab and old Iranian aristocracy.

also known not just for his poetry and prose but for his courage as a rider and swordsman.

buyutat - old Iranian aristocracy.

↳ This is important for he is not just a man of the mind but one of action equally important.

TRANSLATOR'S INTRODUCTION

QUSHAYRI'S SPIRITUAL ENVIRONMENT

Abd al-Karim ibn Hawazin ibn Abd al-Malik ibn Talha Abu 'l-Qasim al-Qushayri[1] was born in the town of Ustuva near Nishapur in July AD 986 (AH Rabi l-Awwal 376, ten years after the Ghaznavids won the rulership of Khurasan. His *nisbah* derived from Qushayr, one of the Arab tribes who settled in Khurasan after the first conquests. Through his mother he was also related to the important Arab tribe of Sulaym, and his mother's brothers were local landlords. He was, therefore, born into the mixed Arab and old Iranian aristocracy known as the *buyutat*, who in Nishapur "were very preoccupied with Islamic solidarity and its great intellectual activity."[2]

As a child he received a thorough Arabic literary education which included memorization of the Koran as a matter of course. He was known not only for his beautiful writing in poetry and prose but also for his courage as a rider and a swordsman. His father died when he was still quite young. He inherited a village and from the income of that village he moved into Nishapur, where he studied mathematics with the hope of a job in the Ghaznavid financial administration. Mahmud of Ghazna had only been in power a few years.

Shah-nama (Book of Kings) → written and known as the foundation of Persian literature.

Asharism → pre-cursor to Sufism it seems.

Nishapur was a city just coming into its own as "the capital of the East (*mashriq*) and even the center of Sunni Islam."[3] Its intellectual life was now glorified by Ghaznavid military exploits. Mahmud made Sunnism his banner, and his Indian conquests in its name gained him enormous prestige. A Turk himself, his patronage was instrumental in bringing Persian language and culture to a point where it would soon be of international importance. The *Shah-nama* (*Book of Kings*), the foundation of Persian literature, was written during his reign.

Balkh had been the intellectually dominant city in the Samanid period, but Nishapur's influence had been growing among both legal and theological scholars and Sufis for perhaps fifty years.[4] Hallaj had preached there and been well received.[5]

Some years before Qushayri's birth in AD 970/AH 359, the Hallajians of the city had split with those of Bukhara by abandoning an "incarnationist" (*hululi*) interpretation of his teaching[6] for a more centrist one. This view was very compatible with the Ashari theology which also found a home in Nishapur. In the days of Hallaj, the city's younger followers of Hadith had been less conservative than those in Baghdad[7] and had accepted intellectual arguments parallel to those of Muhasibi. This trend, though persecuted at first, eventually led to Asharism finding a firm position in Khurasani intellectual life and to Ashari-trained Sufis becoming the inheritors of Hallaj.

Asharism was basically "a rational defense of a non-rationalistic kerygmatic position."[8] It logically supported many difficult Koran and Hadith statements concerning the attributes of God, divine omnipotence, and other thorny topics by adopting a very subtle and seemingly counter-intuitive model of the universe. This model first contested the reliability of sense perception as an ulti-

SHARISM

(handwritten top margin)
① God is a word, a vision to put an attachment to it. Our senses [are] not reliable. How can we name what is unnamable hence is the First Cause in which everything secondary to it is effect. the First Cause.

② This power, being a free creative adaptation unlimited by law higher then itself can be altered.

②

mate criterion. Next, by tracing all secondary causes back to the First Cause, it denied the secondaries true causality, seeing them instead as means for the manifestation of the effects of the First Cause, which alone was genuinely active. The obvious uniformities visible in nature, then, were not the result of independent and unbreakable "natural laws," but instead were the traces left by the habitual action of the First Cause itself. This action, being a free creative adaptation unlimited by any law higher than itself, could be altered. Hence, miracles were possible. Finally, the action of the First Cause was not distanced from its effect, the universe, by any chain of intermediaries, but each instant, each event, was an immediate direct creation.[9]

(handwritten margin, left: direct creation)
(handwritten margin, right: THIS IS A VERY INTERESTING PARAGRAPH!)
(handwritten after footnote: → see this footnote at the end of this chapter)

Though Asharite theologians came in the course of time to be more and more bound up with the niceties of logical argumentation and less and less concerned with substance, the basic view itself was hadith-derived and congenial to the Sufis. According to Wensinck, a typical Asharite creed stated: Faith is believing in God and His Messengers in accordance with what Tradition reports concerning them, and this belief is not sound unless it rests on knowledge (*marifah*) of God.[10]

While thoroughgoing theologians may have held this knowledge to be the result of theology (*kalam*), Asharite Sufis took it rather another way. By chance, it appears, while pursuing his financial studies in Nishapur, young Qushayri found himself at one of the sessions of just such an Asharite Sufi, Abu Ali al-Hasan ibn Muhammad al-Daqqaq. Abu Ali, according to Hujwiri, was "the leading authority in his department (of science) and had no rival among his contemporaries. He was lucid in exposition and eloquent in speech as regards the revelation of the way to God."[11]

Under the impact of that lucid and eloquent discourse, Qushayri changed his plans and attached him-

self to the shaykh as a Sufi novice. Abu Ali al-Daqqaq
had been the student of the master-teacher Nasrabadhi.
Nasrabadhi himself, "like a king in Nishapur, save that
the glory of kings is of this world,"[12] had sat with Shibli
(Junayd's student and perhaps Hallaj's sincerest friend).
Through him the writings of Hallaj had been carefully
preserved.[13] Abu Ali received these influences and
passed them on to his student, four generations from the
time of Abu Uthman al-Hiri and Junayd.

The shaykh took a special interest in Qushayri. He
did not, however, call him out of worldly life but had him
intensively educated as a scholar. On al-Daqqaq's advice,
Qushayri began to read jurisprudence with Abu Bakr
Muhammad ibn Bakr al-Tusi, then Asharite theology
with the famous Abu Bakr Muhammad ibn al-Hasan Ibn
Furak (d. AD 1015/AH 406), and then jurisprudence,
again on an advanced level of independent reading and
questioning with Abu Ishaq al-Isfaraini (d. AD 1027/AH
417). Daqqaq undoubtedly occupied himself personally
with the young man's inner education. When all seemed
at a satisfactory level, he married Qushayri to his
daughter, Fatima, who was herself independently
known as a scholar, a Sufi, and a transmitter of
hadiths.[14]

On the death of Abu Ali al-Daqqaq (in either AD
1021/AH 412 or possibly AD 1014/AH 405), Qushayri sat
briefly with the master of Daqqaq's master, Abu Abd al-
Rahman al-Sulami (d. AD 1021) who was then about
eighty-five years old. If Daqqaq formed Qushayri as a
teacher, Sulami formed him as a writer.

Sulami was a famous author. Among other works, he
had composed the first comprehensive biographical history of Sufism, originally written in two volumes. The
first volume, on the years between the Prophet and the
generation of Sari al-Saqati, has been lost.[15] The second
volume, the *Tabaqat al-sufiyah* (*Grades of Sufis*),

remains and has been extremely influential. An authoritative compilation of Sufi lives, it is distinguished by the careful attention it gives to transmission (*isnad*) documentation.[16] Qushayri quotes Sulami often in the *Risalah*.

Sulami was the product of a change in policy that had resulted from the Baghdad disaster. Schimmel observes, "The case of Hallaj had confronted the Sufis with the danger of persecution, and even without his magic death one might well have felt that the path had to be made accessible to people who could never reach the abysses of mystical experience Hallaj had reached, or who could not be compared in sobriety to Junayd, in burning love to Nuri, or in paradoxical speech to Shibli. It was left to men like Ibn Khafif of Shiraz (d. AD 982, at about 100 years of age) and similar mystics to teach the path, to make it understandable—at least in part—to the intellectuals, and to set an example to larger groups of the faithful."[17]

Ibn Khafif, Asharite, ascetic, and testifier to the truth of Hallaj, was an associate of all the old masters of the Baghdad School. He became the teacher of Abu Nasr al-Tusi al-Sarraj (d. AD 988/AH 378),[18] author of the first of the Sufi "manuals," *Kitab al-luma li-l tasawwuf* (*Glimmers of Sufism*)." Both Sarraj[19] and Ibn Khafif himself[20] had been teachers of Sulami.

Qushayri, heir to all the major forces in Sufism in his time, was gradually "elevated to the position of the greatest teacher of Sufism not only in the city of Nishapur, but in all of Khurasan."[21]

QUSHAYRI AND THE SELJUKS

When Qushayri was fifty-one and at the height of his maturity and influence (he had already written his *Great Commentary on the Quran, al-Tafsir al-kabir*

Toghril Bey → leader of the Seljuk Turks,
followed by
Alp Arslan

lataif al-isharat bi tafsir al-quran,[22] Toghril Bey, leader of the Seljuks, first captured the city of Nishapur. He held the city a year, lost it again to the Ghaznavid Masud, then recovered it two years later, in AD 1040/AH 432, when his control of all of Khurasan became firm. The Seljuks were already Muslim and fervently Hanafi when they came to power. They also (under an influence dating perhaps from the days of Hallaj) favored the Sufis. This tendency did not in itself, however, prevent them from intolerance and especially fierce anti-Shism. In this they continued the attitude of the Ghaznavids. The great Seljuk vizier, Nizam ul-Mulk ,would later write, "In the days of Mahmud, Masud, Tughril, and Arp-Arslan (may God have mercy upon them) no Zoroastrian or Jew or Rafidi [Shia] would have had the audacity to appear in a public place or to present himself before a great man. Those who administered the affairs of the Turks were all professional civil servants and secretaries from Khurasan who belonged to the orthodox Hanafi or Shafii sects. The heretics of Iraq were never admitted as secretaries and tax collectors. In fact, the Turks never used to employ them at all. They said, 'These men are of the same religion as the Dailamites [Buyids] and their supporters. If they get a firm footing they will injure the interests of the Turks and cause distress to the Muslims. It is better that enemies should not be in our midst.'" Consequently they lived free from disaster.[23]

Such an attitude was certainly understandable when the Sunnis felt threatened by fragmentation on every side and needed, at all costs, to maintain themselves as a coherent unit. It was, in fact, very politically effective. Yet it activated the shadow side of consensus, the maintenance of conformity by force. Mahmud had vented his wrath on the Shias of Rayy. Nizam ul-Mulk records that even in the intellectual life of Nishapur, in many ways a far more liberal city than for instance Baghdad, Hanafi and Shafii legal scholars joined to prevent other opinions from being heard.[24] Hodgson makes such motivations clear, ". . . if the safety and good order of society depended on the strength and coherence of the religious community, then everything else must, at need, be sacrificed to this. Even pity for an honest but misguided man should not divert one from one's duty to prevent him from corrupting society with his misguided ideas."

In such an atmosphere even personally magnanimous men, able to resist the impulse to protect their own intellectual security by silencing a threatening voice, might become persecutors. For they might feel it their duty to support intolerance for the sake of others who could not endure the threat so easily.[25]

Toghril Bey was one such personally magnanimous man who felt it his duty to protect the orthodox Sunnis. The dangerous element brought to his attention was not the Sufis per se, as had been the case in the Baghdad disaster. It was the Asharites.

Amid ul-Mulk al-Kunduri, Toghril Bey's vizier, on the advice of the head of Nishapur's Shafii jurists, received permission from his prince to have the Shia and instigators of innovation publicly cursed from the *min-bars* of the mosques of Nishapur. He then had this permission extended to Abu 'l-Hasan al-Ashari.

This was a provocative move as the Asharites were numerous and well established in the city, especially among the Shafiis. Quite possibly some internal Shafii power struggle was involved. The curse was an extension of the cursing of the Shia, and given the predominance of the surrounding Shia regimes, the action has a resounding political ring: it as much as called the Asharis agents of subversion. The connection was probably taken to be the theologians, for the Shia sect at that time was essentially Mutazili. The old argument against theology as innovation reappeared.

[handwritten annotation: A law was passed in AD 1044 to bring Asharism legitimacy, and protection from Turkish rulers by equating Asharism ≟ the Sunni creed.]

Yet what underlay this argument was now different. In Ahmad ibn Hanbal's time, combating theology had involved, on the one hand, resisting the power of an absolutist state and, on the other, defending the supremacy of revelation. Now, the transcendence of revelation was not in question. It was the state itself that was attacking theology. A coercive manipulation of Sunnism was being attempted, and this the Sufis, and many others, could not accept.

Qushayri responded to this state of affairs. As Hasan al-Basri had done centuries before, he assumed the duty of admonition, "commanding the right and forbidding the wrong." In AD 1044/AH 436 he passed an edict arguing that Ashari was a great leader of the followers of Hadith whose creed was Sunni and entirely congruent with the faith of the Sunnis. He and his followers could not be cursed. Still pressure on the Asharis continued and in AD 1054/AH 446 or a little earlier, Qushayri wrote a long letter addressed to all the scholars of the Islamic world entitled "Complaint of the People of the Sunna with Reports of the Trials That Have Afflicted Them." Within a short while the situation appeared threatening to the regime and the crackdown came. Kunduri received an order from Toghril Bey to have several of the leading scholars of Nishapur arrested and deported. The names specified were al-Rais al-Furati, Abu Sahl ibn al-Muwaffaq (who had succeeded to the leadership of the Shafiis and was well-known at court), Juwayni (the later theological teacher of Ghazzali), and Qushayri. Juwayni fled to Makkah whence he would attain wide renown. Qushayri and Furati were arrested and imprisoned in the old citadel of Nishapur.

They did not stay there long. Abu Sahl, who had been out of Nishapur when the arrest order arrived from Rayy, put his influence to work. He gathered a body of men. With them, he demanded Furati and Qushayri from the governor of the city. When their release was not forthcoming, he entered Nishapur, dispersed the governor's soldiers by force of arms, and rescued the prisoners. In a surprising gesture—seemingly for the sake of the unity of the Sunnis—he then proceeded to Rayy and surrendered himself to Toghril Bey.

Qushayri could not stay in Nishapur. He went on the pilgrimage. He took the Baghdad road and apparently reached the old capital just after the Buyids finally lost it. According to Ates, Khatib al-Baghdadi's contemporary history places him in Baghdad in AD 1056/AH 448. The triumphant Toghril Bey had been invited into Baghdad as protector of the caliph in AD 1055/AH 447.

The current caliph was al-Qaim bi-Amrillah (AD 1031-75/AH 422-467). Under the Buyids, the caliphate had worked at developing what little power was left to it by playing upon its moral authority as the symbolic center of the Sunni community. The residual prestige of the office was still strong and the Seljuks, as its liberators from the Shias, received unprecedented honor and acceptance in the Islamic world. A new political theory was introduced—namely, Mawardi, AD 1058/AH 450), whereby the caliph was seen as the source of legitimacy of the military regimes that served as his executive lieutenants (and held the actual power).

This retrieval of the caliphate's spiritual existence by giving temporal power to the Turks had been engineered by al-Qaim's vizier, Ali ibn al-Muslimah. At his investiture in 437/1046—still under the Buyids—this vizier had stopped the official procession to pray at the site of Hallaj's martyrdom.[26] This was the first public official recognition of the center of so much controversy. It marked a change of feeling in the caliphal court.

Thus when Qushayri arrived in the city, he found al-Qaim well-disposed. Though Toghril Bey was master of Baghdad, the caliph stubbornly maintained his local authority. It was Toghril Bey's vizier—the persecutor of the Asharis, Kunduri—who was instrumental in keeping the caliph subordinate to the Turks.[27] Those fleeing from Kunduri's action were good candidates for caliphal protection. Al-Qaim built Qushayri a school where he received a wide audience. According to Massignon, it was in Baghdad that he published the *Risalah*, which had been written in AD 1046/AH 437, at the beginning of the persecutions.[28]

Qushayri apparently stayed in Baghdad about seven years—through the temporary Fatimid seizure of the capital in AD 1058/AH 450 and its recapture a year later[29]—not completing his pilgrimage until AD 1063/AH 455.[30] While he was in Makkah, some 400 *qadis* and religious scholars arrived, also escaping from the persecution. They were in turmoil as to their future. It is said that Qushayri received a mystical insight that Kunduri would die and advised them to go home. He himself started back on the Baghdad road. That same year Toghril Bey died and Alp Arslan came to the throne. He promptly (AD 1064/AH 456) had Kunduri executed. The great Nizam ul-Mulk became vizier.

Qushayri lived eight peaceful years in Nishapur, writing and transmitting hadiths. Some twenty works are credited to him. Fatima, who lived on until 481/1088[31] had borne him six sons, all called Qushayri like their father. One became a scholar (as did a grandson). Another wrote of the Sufis. A student of his, Shaykh al-Shuyukh Abu Ali al-Farmadi (who sat with several other important teachers of the time) later was the master of Ghazzali.[32] He died on 31 December AD 1072/16 Rabi I AH 465. The tomb of his shaykh and father-in-law, Abu Ali al-Daqqaq, was in his *madrasah* (traditional school), and he was buried there. His *Risalah*—written two years before the *"Complaint"* as an affirmation of Islamic spirituality in the midst of

The Sufis ... ascetics who have developed through self-examination and an interiorization of the acts of worship, a method of guidance capable of morally purifying the life of society by spreading recollection...[11]

Translator's Introduction   xv

political abuse—became the most widely disseminated handbook of Sufism in the Islamic world.[33]

THE MANUALS

Massignon, listing futile early efforts toward Islamic universalization, includes the Sufis. "The third attempt was that of the Sufis, those ascetics who from Muhasibi to Hallaj developed through self-examination and an interiorization of the acts of worship, a method of guidance capable of morally purifying the life of society by spreading recollection and communal centers of spiritual and fraternal mutual aid. This attempt collapsed too, since it was caught in a vice between the large banking capitalism of the Imamite Shiite businessmen and the urban bedouin communism of the Ismaili revolutionaries, both the declared enemies of the universal Sunni caliphate."[34]

While this analysis is probably correct, what it actually describes is the political dimensions of the Baghdad disaster. The Sufis, as has been shown, existed as such well before Muhasibi, are still in existence, and were pivotally active in the generations after Hallaj. Their "attempt," rather than collapsing, decentralized. After the disaster and the fall of the Abbasids, Sufi meeting-houses (*khanaqah*), began to be founded in numbers throughout Iraq, Transoxania, and, as already discussed, Khurasan.[35] In them the life of "spiritual and fraternal mutual aid" was maintained. From them, it would spread.

As has also been shown, even before Hallaj action began to be taken by Yahya ibn Muadh and Abu Uthman al-Hiri in Khurasan to draw the general populace into connection with the Sufi life. The Karrami "evangelists" in the same region widened the base of interest. One impact of Hallaj was to make the nature of sincerity a popular issue.

a new science of Sufism took form. Like todays Scientology? This science of Sufism was called
↳ ilm al-tasawwuf
↳ it indicated directions for real self-attainment.

In the AD 10th/AH 4th century, paper, which previously had been an expensive Chinese import, began to be manufactured in Iraq, Syria, Egypt, and even Arabia.[36] Further, by the AD 11th/AH 8th century Arabic had become the common tongue of culture and exchange from Spain to Persia, superseding the old local languages.[37] Wide dissemination of written work began to become practical.

The old AD 9th/AH 3rd century mosque curriculum started to be organized and recorded in books. A new science, the science of Sufism or *ilm al-tasawwuf*, took form. Pedersen describes it in his introduction to Sulami's *Tabaqat*.[38]

The science of Sufism served to aid Sufi aspirants in testing the soundness of their practice and their state. Its criteria and comparisons help deflate fantasies of attainment that vitiate moral and spiritual character, while indicating directions for real development. This approach, made accessible in written form, can be valuable not just for geniuses of the spirit, but for all those who take their inner integrity seriously. Qushayri received from Sulami the importance of the transmission of this knowledge.

Sulami's teacher, Sarraj (d. AD 988/AH 378), had belonged to the generation in which this type of transmission began to be undertaken by the so-called "manual writers." Among his contemporaries were Kalabadhi (d. c. AD 990/AH 380), author of the *Kitab al-taarruf li madhhab ahl al-tasawwuf* (*Book of Familiarization with Sufi Doctrine*), and Abu Talib al-Makki (d. AD 996), who produced the comprehensive *Qut al-qulub* (*Food of Hearts*). Sulami's *Tabaqat* found a companion-piece in the ten-volume compilation of Abu Nuaym al-Isfahani (d. AD 1037/AH 428), *Hilyat al-awliya* (*Ornament of Saints*). Qushayri's fellow in the undertaking was Hujwiri of Lahore (d. AD 1074/AH 466), whose *Kashf al-*

The writers of the science of Sufism are particularly concerned to show the unbreakable relationship that must exist between the outward manifestation of form and the inward realization of being in order for religion to be real,

Translator's Introduction xvii

Mahjub, (Unveiling of the Hidden), has often been quoted here.

The manuals emerged to argue for what Islamic spirituality was intended to be. They based their authority on the Quran and Hadith, proof-texts for the transmission of the unitary and non-discursive attitude of Madinah. It was precisely this that the Sufis claimed to be preserving. The manual writers did not see themselves as the mouthpiece of a sect but as guardians of the heart of the whole Islamic enterprise. This is made particularly explicit by the inclusion in several of the manuals[39] of many of the Companions, the four rightly-guided caliphs, the Shia Imams, and the four founders of Sunni law among the founders of the Sufis.

The writers on the science of Sufism are particularly concerned to show the unbreakable relationship that must exist between the outward manifestation of form and the inward realization of being in order for religion to be real. Hujwiri comments, "Two parties err in this matter: firstly, the formal theologians, who assert that there is no distinction between Shariah (law) and Haqiqah (truth), since the Law is the Truth and the Truth is the Law; secondly, some heretics, who hold that it is possible for one of these things to subsist without the other, and declare that when the Truth is revealed the Law is abolished."[40]

These are the twin poles that threaten the Islam of an individual or a community with disintegration: the reduction of religious responsibility to a shell of procedure maintained by force and the rejection of concrete duties owed to God and humanity in favor of imaginary epiphanies.

Both these heterodoxies calling themselves orthodoxies had come into focus in the days of Junayd, with the Sufis, accused as heretics for the first time, caught in the middle. The situation was then complicated by the appearance of new sects taking the name of Sufi for themselves. Hallaj's magnetism and his growing legend had merged with the millenarian atmosphere to produce antinomian groups. They still existed in Qushayri's time. Hujwiri records, "I have seen at Baghdad and in the adjoining districts a number of heretics who pretend to be the followers of al-Hallaj and make his sayings an argument for their heresy and call themselves Hallajis. They spoke of him in the same terms of exaggeration as the Rafidis [extremist Shias] apply to Ali."[41]

He speaks of another such group attached to the figure of Abu Hulman of Damascus, whom he exonerates, as he does Hallaj, from personal responsibility for the beliefs attached to his name.[42] Further, his "Rafidis" must include not just the Ismailis, whose doctrine was spreading on every side, but the Nusayris of Khurasan, another Shia splinter, who believed Ali to be the incarnation of God.[43] Many more exotic doctrines could be described.

Amid so much mythologizing enthusiasm and so much violent reaction, a spirituality of discipline and balance had to be actively affirmed. The old goods had to be put back on public display. The manual writers and the generation of Qushayri struck the return blow. It has become common place among modern writers in Islamic studies to see Ghazzali as having achieved for the first time a meeting or fusion of Sufism with orthodoxy. Because of this, nearly every influential earlier Sufi writer is likely to be tagged as the "precursor of Ghazzali"—for instance, Qushayri, Sulami, Kalabadhi, Junayd, and even Muhasibi.[44] In point of fact, however, the Sufis never stopped being orthodox. Whether in terms of maintaining the solidarity of the Community (*ummah*), holding to the primacy of the Quran and Hadith in the definition of Muslim life, or clinging to the spirit of the Prophetic example and the impulse of the

Tariqahs → the Sufi orders

the most effective Sufi manual was the Risalah.

community of Madinah, they were orthodox from the very beginning. Ghazzali was simply in a unique position to give authority to this recognition. His success was really the success of a 150 years of Sufi effort. That universalizing effort—which did not fail in Baghdad as Massignon describes—was to have substantial social effects.

THE SOCIAL IMPACT OF THE SUFIS

Sufism, Fazlur Rahman notes, was an urban phenomenon until the AD 10th/AH 4th century, but from the AH 11th/AH 5th was the "religion of the masses."[45] This expansion was simultaneous with the consolidation of Sunnism, and the Seljuk domains were its cradle.[46] The *madrasah*s, the international network of schools which helped to unify the forming Sunni society, grew from the model of Karrami spiritual schools (where Yahya ibn Muadh had taught) already established in Khurasan. The integration of theology—which had been fought for by Qushayri at the head of the Asharite Sufis and which alone would make theological consensus and consequent peace possible—was also first achieved in Khurasan.[47] The Sufi orders (*tariqahs*), the teaching lines that would carry the culture and attitudes of the great shaykhs through the whole of the Islamic world, originated here as well. The manuals would be their textbooks. The most effective of these, for purposes of broadening general understanding, was the *Risalah*. "It was accounted such a blessing for the Muslims," Ates quotes Subki, "that a copy was found in every home."[48]

After the manuals, the consensus of the community recognized the Sufi inheritance as its own. It is likely that the existence of Sufism as a tolerated aspect of Islamic life gave strong support to Sunnism in the process of establishing itself. The existence of Sufism and its toleration implied the validity, at least in certain

The majority of the Seljuk Turks like Alp Arslan were Sunni and gave respect to the Sufi.

cases, of the religious experience of individuals, and Sunnism was largely based on ordinary men.[49] The Seljuk rulers were aware of this legitimizing function of Sufism and encouraged it, while simultaneously fostering the legal and theological scholarship of the religious scholars (*ulama*), giving the latter an unprecedented institutional basis and state support.

Nizam ul-Mulk, the vizier of Alp Arslan, was the architect of these arrangements. It was he who founded the great universities, the Nizamiyyahs, centers for the study of the divine law (Shariah) in the two cities of Qushayri, Baghdad and Nishapur. According to Muhammad ibn Munawwar, who wrote his *Asrar al-tawhid* in the latter half of the 8th/12th century,[50] Nizam ul-Mulk had been, as a youth, a student of Abu Said ibn Abil-Khayr (b. 356/967)—another illustrious disciple of Sulami and the first Sufi to draw up a rule for his pupils, marking the formative stage of that other great unifying institution, the *tariqah*s.[51]

The body of opinion that insists on invoking a separation between Sufism and orthodoxy finds this policy of the Seljuks a remarkable rather than a natural development and perhaps even slightly suspect: "The Turkish sultans, although outwardly zealous patrons of orthodoxy, nevertheless paid real homage and honor to the Sufi shaykhs."[52] The Seljuks' devotion to Sunnism can scarcely be doubted, and it is significant that Fazlur Rahman would rather hesitate over their orthodoxy than admit that of the Sufis. His reluctance to recognize how intrinsic the Sufis were to the Sunni synthesis stems from his distaste for situations that were to develop in India half a millennium later, when the name of "Sufi" was taken up by late inheritors of the Ismaili pattern of thought.[53] But the spiritual outreach of the Sufis was probably instrumental in limiting the spread of this pattern in the era of Qushayri. The Sufi shaykhs could

The tolerances of the sufis could bridge differences and build unity.
If Sunni & Shia had this Sufism as a bridge to end their mutual annihilations, they would be an unstoppable force against U.S. and western forces in Iraq, Iran, Syria, etc.

do this in a way that the partisans of legal or theological uniformity could not—by insisting on the spirit of the Shariah animating its letter, making the consensus of faith and practice attractive rather than insistent, a way of life rather than a dogmatic structure. Where the persecutions of a Mamun or a Kunduri could never create consensus, the tolerance of the Sufis could bridge differences and build unity. In this they materially aided the work of the religious scholars by bringing the popular religious consensus to assent to the theoretical one. Hodgson notes, "It is probable that without the subtle leaven of the Sufi orders . . . the mechanical arrangements of the Shariah would not have maintained the loyalty essential to their effectiveness."[54]

It was this loyalty that made the international Sunni society outlast its competitors. The seemingly formidable Fatimid state was based on allegiances that were unstable at best. From the late AD 11th/AH 5th, through the AD 12th/AH 6th centuries, group after local Ismaili group withdrew support deciding that the Imam at Cairo was not the real Imam—first the Berbers, then the Druzes in Syria and Egypt itself, then the Iranians, and finally the Arabians and Indians withdrew.[55] The Qarmathian republic of townsmen in Bahrain was destroyed in the latter half of the AD 11th/AH 5th century by the surrounding peasants it had exploited. The Shariah was put back into force.[56] The most powerful of the local Ismaili factions, the famous Nizaris or "Assassins," in AD 1090/AH 482 seized the fortress of Alamut and surrounding towns in the south of Khurasan from which it conducted campaigns of strategic terror and led piecemeal uprisings against the Turks. It too was overthrown in AD 1107/AH 500,[57] and the movement withered to a handful of supporters.

Yet though the Nizaris had succeeded in assassinating Nizam ul-Mulk and demoralizing the Seljuk regime

* The most powerful of the local Ismaili factions, the famous Nizaris or "Assassins" seized their famous fortress of Alamut in AD 1090 and led campaigns of terror against the Turks *

(which began to collapse in AD 1092/AH 485 and finally fell, some twenty-five years later, into a series of transient military governments without structure or ideas)[58] the network of relationships which underlay what was now Sunni society did not fail. The last outbreak of Ismaili force, in fact, only cemented it and brought into the consensus even the Shias.[59] The orthodox Sunnis found their form, and the religion found its proper agent.

During the three centuries following the initial spread of Muslim rule, the boundaries of Muslim territory had varied little. In the many centuries after 945, on the contrary, there was an almost constant expansion of the area in which the religion and even the civilization flourished, often with no dependence on any previously Muslim state. This expansion has indeed continued, in some sense, down to our own time.[60] Islam is like a banquet to which everyone is invited, and when the Community (*ummah*) shows its universality, many accept the invitation. But the feast is found in the point of gathering together, and not in the mere gathering itself. It is for the service of God that the Community was constituted. That the believers should be enabled to dine at the table of the Prophet, rather than eating scraps in a cellar, was the whole object of the *Risalah*.

NOTES TO
TRANSLATOR'S INTRODUCTION

[1] Where not otherwise noted, biographical facts are drawn from the article "Kusheyri" by Ahmad Ates, in *IslamAnsiclopedisi* (Istanbul: Milli Egitim Basimevi, 1977), s.v .(hereafter IA.)

[2] Massignon, 1:170.

[3] *Ibid.*

[4] Massignon, 1:173.

[5] *Ibid.*, 1:170-72.

[6] *Ibid.*, 1:39.

[7] *Ibid.*, 1:172.

[8] Hodgson, 2:178.

[9] The essentials are laid out in Goldziher, p. 112, with rather a different understanding. Orientalists have tended to see Asharite cosmology as preposterous, and certainly "anti-scientific." But in light of major questions of contemporary physics-quantum and probability theory, and the provocative issue of the origins of physical laws-it would seem to hold up rather well.

[10] Baghdadi, *Usul*, p. 248, quoted in Wensinck, p. 134.

[11] Hujwiri, p. 162.

[12] Hujwiri, p. 159.

[13] Massignon, 1:641.

[14] Schimmel, p. 427.

[15] Pedersen, p. 50.

[16] *Ibid.*, p. 25.

[17] Schimmel, p. 83.

[18] Schimmel, p. 84

[19] Tosun Bayrak, Foreword, Muhammad b. al-Husayn al-Sulami, *The Book of Sufi Chivalry: Futuwwa*. Tosun Bayrak, trans. (New York: Inner Traditions International, 1983), p. 5

[20] Pedersen, p. 24.

[21] *IA.*

[22] In about AD 1016/AH 410 according to Ates. Reputed to be one of the best, not a copy survives.

[23] Nizam al-Mulk, *Siyasat-namah*, quoted in *Camb. Iran.*, 5:292.

[24] Hodgson, 2:194.

[25] *Ibid.*, 2:193.

[26] Massignon, 1:40.

[27] Hodgson, 2:43.

[28] Massignon, 2:104.

[29] According to Massignon (1:40-41), Ibn al-Muslimah was captured and executed by the Fatimis during this year. His family was saved along with the caliph's grandson and on this account a cenotaph was erected on the spot where he had honored Hallaj with a prayer. This marker stood in 1945 and may still stand.

[30] The chronology of these events is reconstructed from indications in Ates and Massignon.

[31] Schimmel, p. 427.

[32] *Camb. Iran* 5:287.

[33] Schimmel, p. 88.

[34] Massignon 1:379.

[35] Camb. Iran, 5:296.

[36] Lewis, p. 87.

[37] Lewis, p. 132.

[38] Pedersen, p. 23.

[39] Hujwiri is the best example in translation.

[40] Hujwiri, p. 383.

[41] *Ibid.*, p. 152.

[42] *Ibid.*, p. 260.

[43] *Camb. Iran*, 5:290.

[44] Qushayri, according to *IA*; Sulami, according to Pedersen, p, 23; Kalabadhi, according to Arberry, p. xii; Junayd, according to Abd al-Kader, p. 34; Muhasibi, according to Rahman, p. 164.

[45] Rahman, *Islam*, pp. xxi-xxii.

[46] Hodgson, 2:203.

[47] *Ibid.*, 2:210-11.

[48] Subki 1:246, quoted in *IA*.

[49] Watt, pp. 264-5.

[50] *Camb. Iran* 5:301.

[51] Schimmel, p. 241

[52] Rahman, p. xxii.

[53] In fact, Hindu-Muslim syncretism and the abandonment of *shari* practice in some regions appear to have been mediated precisely by the Ismailis (who established one of their last few strongholds in India), according to Annemarie Schimmel, *Pain and Grace:. A Study of Two Mystic Writers of Eighteenth Century India* (Leiden: E. J. Brill, 1976), p. 24. It is interesting that just as in the earliest days the terms *zuhhad* and *ubbad* were abandoned as they lost the mean-

ing they were intended to convey, eminent 18th century Indian Sufis like Shah Waliullah, Mazhar Janjanan and Mir Dard began to refuse the "Sufi" label. (Schimmel, *Pain and Grace*, p. 10-18.)

54 Hodgson, 2:125.
55 Hodgson, 2:26-28.
56 *Ibid.*, 1:491.
57 *Ibid.*, 2:58-59.
58 *Ibid.*, 2:53.
59 *Ibid.*, 2:61.
60 Hodgson, 2:272.

Repentace (Tawba)
↳ it's root meaning is
taba → "to come back"

Thus repentance is to return from what
is blameworthy in the divine law to what
is praiseworthy in it.

1

ON REPENTANCE (*TAWBA*)

God Most High said, *"Turn to God together, O believers, that you may be successful"* [24:31].

Abu Bakr Muhammad ibn al-Husayn ibn Furak reported to us . . . from Anas ibn Malik, that the Messenger of God (ﷺ) said, "One who repents from sin is like one who has not sinned at all. When God loves a servant, a sin will not persist in him." Then he recited, *"God loves the repentant and loves those who purify themselves"* [2: 222].

Someone asked, "Messenger of God, what is the sign of repentance?" He replied, "Remorse." Ali ibn Ahmad ibn Abdan al-Hawari reported to us . . . from Anas ibn Malik that the Prophet (ﷺ) said, "There is nothing dearer to God than a repentant youth."

Tawba, repentance, is the first station for spiritual travelers and the first stage of development in seekers. The root meaning of *tawba* in the Arabic language is "return"—its associated verb, *taba*, is used to mean "to come back." So repentance is to return from what is blameworthy in the divine law to what is praiseworthy in it.

The Prophet said, "Regret is an act of repentance."

1

" there is a piece of flesh in the body; if it is sound, the whole body is sound, and if it is corrupt, the whole body is corrupt. It is the HEART."

2 *Sufi Book of Spiritual Ascent*

Sunni scholars of the Koran and Hadith have said that three things form the conditions for the authenticity of repentance: regret for violations committed against the divine law, immediate abandonment of the error, and the resolve never to go back to the act of disobedience that was performed. And these, indeed, are undoubtedly the prerequisites for the soundness of one's repentance.

These scholars say that the Hadith, "Regret is an act of repentance," is only pointing out the most important element of repentance. When the Prophet said, "The pilgrimage is Arafa," he meant its most important element is Arafa or rather standing in prayer there. He did not mean that there was no other necessity of pilgrimage except standing at Arafa, but that to stand and pray there was of greatest significance. Just so, his saying "Regret is an act of repentance," means that the greatest foundation of repentance is regret.

However, one among the people of realization said, "Regret is sufficient for the authenticity of repentance because the consequence of regret is the other two conditions. An evaluation that would count regret to truly exist while one persisted in similar acts or was resolved to pursue them is absurd." This is the definition and general meaning of repentance.

From an analytical perspective, repentance has causes, degrees, and parts. First comes the heart's awakening from the sleep of heedlessness and the servant's recognizing his negative condition. He will attain this if he manages to pay attention to the reprimands of God, the Truth within him, by listening to his heart. This is found in the hadith, "God's counselor is in the heart of every Muslim," and in the hadith, "There is a piece of flesh in the body: if it is sound, the whole body is sound, and if it is corrupt, the whole body is corrupt. It is the heart."

When the servant has reflected in his heart on the evil of what he is doing and has seen the ugliness of his actions, the wish for repentance and for leaving his negative behavior will form in his heart. God will help him by confirming his resolution, his starting to return to good deeds, and his readiness for the steps to repentance. These steps begin with his leaving bad company—that is, people who would entice him to turn back from his purpose and confuse him about the rightness of his decision. Perfection at this level only comes with the diligent practice of witnessing that increases the servant's longing for repentance and with the dedication of his efforts to accomplish his resolve through the strengthening of his fear and hope of God. Then the knot of his persistence in negative actions will be loosened from his heart. He will stop running after dangerous things. He will rein in his ego from pursuing passions or desires of the flesh. Then he will immediately abandon his sin and confirm his resolution never to return to the like of it in the future. If he proceeds according to his intention and acts in conformity with his will, he has been granted true sincerity in his repentance. But even if his repentance has weakened once or many times and only his force of will induces him to renew it—and this sort of thing occurs very frequently—he must not give up hope of repentance on account of such incidents because "*Surely to each period is a decree established*" [13:38].

It is related that Abu Sulayman al-Darani said, "I attended the meeting of a judge. His words made an impression on my heart. When I rose to go, nothing remained in my heart of it. I went back yet again and the effect of his words stayed in my heart until I returned to my house. I shattered the means of my disobedience and became attached to the Way." When this story was told to Yahya ibn Muadh, he remarked, "A sparrow captured a crane!" By the sparrow he meant the judge and by the crane, Abu Sulayman al-Darani.

It is related that Abu Hafs al-Haddad said, "I left the action so many times and I returned to it. Then the action left me, and I did not return to it again." It is said that at the beginning of his wayfaring, Abu Amr ibn Nujayd attended the sessions of Abu Uthman [Said ibn Salam al-Harani], whose words affected his heart so that he repented. Then his first enthusiasm faded and he fled from Abu Uthman whenever he saw him and avoided attending his meetings. One day Abu Uthman met him in the street. He turned aside and took another path. Abu Uthman followed him and kept following him until he caught up with him. "My dear son," he said, "you are not in the company of someone who only loves you when you are sinless. And only Abu Uthman can help you in a case like this!" Abu Amr ibn Nujayd repented and returned to his intention and fulfilled it.

I heard Abu Ali al-Daqqaq say, "A spiritual seeker repented and then his feelings cooled. He lapsed from his repentance. One day he was wondering what the decision on his case would be if he were to repent again. A voice from the unseen spoke to him and said, 'O so-and-so! You obeyed Us and We thanked you; then you abandoned Us and We gave you time. If you return to Us We will accept you.' The youth returned to his resolve and completed it."

When the servant abandons disobedience and the knot of persistence in it is loosened from his heart, genuine remorse will come into his heart. He will regret his behavior and begin to grieve for what he has done to himself and for the ugly acts he has committed. His repentance is complete and struggle sincere when he has exchanged society for solitude and changed his association with bad friends into alienation and withdrawal from them, when his night passes into day with longing, and when in all his states he is embraced by real sad-

awba... whoever repents out of respect for the divine order, neither from desire of reward nor terror of punishment, possesses awba.

ness. Then the rightness of the lesson he has learned will cancel the effects of his having slipped. The goodness of his repentance will heal the wounds inflicted by his offense. He will be distinguished from those like him by how emaciated he is which bears witness to the soundness of his state.

The servant will never be able to carry through any of this until he has cleared himself by satisfying those he has wronged and has left behind what still attaches to him from his misdeeds. Certainly the first stage of repentance is the satisfaction of those who have been wronged insofar as the servant has power to give them their due or until their feelings change and they declare the thing lawful and themselves free of it. When this is not possible, the resolve in the servant's heart must be to give them their rights as soon as he can and he must turn to God with sincere supplication and prayer for them.

The characteristics of the repentant include various attributes and states. All of these are counted as within the compass of repentance, for its soundness makes their different qualities shine. The differing remarks of the masters on the meaning of repentance point to this.

I heard Abu Ali al-Daqqaq say, "Repentance has three parts. the first of these is *tawba*, in the middle is *inaba*, and the last is *awba*." He makes *tawba* a beginning and *awba* an end, with *inaba* between them. Everyone who repents from fear of the consequences of his actions possesses *tawba*. Whoever repents from hope of reward possesses *inaba*. And whoever repents out of respect for the divine order, neither from desire of reward nor terror of punishment, possesses *awba*.

It is also said that *tawba* is the attribute of the believers—God Most High said, "*So turn (tubu) to God together, O believers*" [24:31], *inaba* is the attribute of the Friends of God and those who are brought close to

Repentance means to stop procrastinating.

Him. God Most High said, "*Come with a repentant (munib) heart*" [50:33], and *awba* is the attribute of the prophets and Messengers. God Most High said, "*The best of servants is the repentant one (awwab)*" [38:30, 44]. I heard Abu Abd al-Rahman al-Sulami say... Junayd said, "Repentance has three meanings. The first is to feel regret. The second is to give up going back to what God has forbidden. The third is to make an effort to repair the wrongs that have been done." Sahl ibn Abd allah al-Tustari said, "Repentance means to stop procrastinating. I heard Muhammad ibn al-Husayn say . . . that Harith al-Muhasibi said, "I have never said, 'My God, I ask You to turn to me,' but I say, 'I ask You for the desire to turn to You [in repentance].'"

Abu Abd Allah al-Shirazi informed us that Junayd said that one day he went to Sari al-Saqati. Seeing he was disturbed, he asked him what had happened. Sari said, "A young man came to me and asked me about repentance. So I told him, 'It is that you not forget your sins!' He contradicted me, and said, 'No, rather repentance is that you do forget your sins.'" Junayd said that in his opinion the young man was correct. Sari asked why. Junayd said, "When I was in a state of estrangement from God, He transported me to a state of fidelity and to remember estrangement in a state of purity is itself estrangement." Sari was silent.

I heard Abu Hatim al-Sijistani say that he heard . . . that Sahl ibn Abd Allah al-Tustari was asked about repentance and said, "It means not to forget your sins." Junayd was asked about repentance and said, "It means to forget your sins." Abu Nasr al-Sarraj said, "Sahl was referring to the state of disciples and novices which are constantly changing. As for Junayd, he pointed to the repentance of those who have reached the state of truth. They do not recall their sins because the majesty of God Most High has dominated their hearts and they are in

continual remembrance of Him." He also observed that
this is like when Ruwaym was asked about *tawba* and
said, "It is to repent from repenting," or when Dhu 'l-
Nun was asked about *tawba* and said, "The repentance
of the majority is from sins, while the repentance of the
elect is from forgetfulness."

Abu Husayn al-Nuri said, "Repentance is to turn
away from everything other than God Almighty and
Glorious." I heard Muhammad ibn Ahmad ibn
Muhammad al-Sufi say that he heard Abd Allah ibn Ali
ibn Muhammad al-Tamimi say, "What great differences
there are among those who repent from their sins,
among those who repent for moments of heedlessness or
forgetfulness, and among those who repent from awareness of their own good deeds!" Al-Wasiti said, "Pure
repentance does not allow any trace of disobedience, hidden or manifest, to remain in the one to whom it comes.
If someone's repentance is pure, it does not matter
where he spends the night or where he spends the day."

I heard Abu Abd al-Rahman al-Sulami say . . . that
Yahya ibn Muadh used to pray, "My God, because I know
my nature, I cannot say, 'I have repented and will not go
back on my repentance.' With what I know of my weak-
nesses, I can take no responsibility for abandoning sin.
Instead I say, 'I am not going back to my old ways
maybe I will die before I do!'" Dhu 'l-Nun said, "To ask
forgiveness from God without leaving the sin is the
repentance of liars."

I heard Muhammad ibn al-Husayn say that he heard
al-Nasrabadhi say that Ibn Yazdanyar was asked,
"When the servant abandons the world for God, what
should be the principle of his departure?" He said, "Not
to return to what he has left, nor to pay attention to anything but the One for Whom he has left, and to protect
his inner awareness from giving any notice to the things
from which he has freed himself." Someone remarked,

"This is the case of someone who is leaving something behind. What about someone who has nothing to leave?" He said, 'Sweetness in the future is compensation for bitterness in the past."

Asked about repentance, al-Bushanji said, "When you remember the sin and do not find pleasure in the recollection, it is repentance." Dhu 'l-Nun said, "The reality of repentance is that the world with all its vastness will become narrow for you until you find no rest in it; and then your own self will become narrow for you, as God Most High said in His Book, *'Their selves became narrow for them and they bethought themselves that there was no refuge from God except in Him; then He turned to them so they would turn to Him '* [9:18]."

Ibn Ata said, "There are two sorts of repentance: the repentance of penitence and the repentance of response. The repentance of penitence is when the servant repents for fear of His punishment. The repentance of response is when he repents out of shame at His generosity."

Abu Hafs al-Haddad was asked, "Why does a repentant person hate this world?" He replied, "Because it is the place in which his sins were committed." Someone objected, "But it is also the place in which God honored him with repentance!" "Sins are certain," he returned, "but there is risk in his repentance being accepted!" Al-Wasiti said, "The joy of Prophet David and the sweetness he experienced in obedience to God caused him to fall into a long and deep sadness of repentance. But in this second state his condition was more perfect than it had been before, when his true level was unknown to him." A Sufi there said, "The repentance of liars is on the edge of their tongues," that is, merely saying 'May God forgive me.'" Abu Hafs al-Haddad was asked of repentance. He said, "The servant has no part in repentance! Repentance is extended to him, not obtained from him."

It is said that God Most High revealed to Adam, "O

Adam, you have bequeathed to your offspring hardship and disease and you have also bequeathed to them repentance. Whoever among them calls to me as you have, I will respond to him as I have responded to you. O Adam, I will resurrect the repentant from their graves smiling and laughing and their prayer will be answered."

A man said to Rabia, "I have so many sins and acts of disobedience. If I were to repent, would He also turn to me?" "No," said she. "Rather, if He were to turn to you, then you would repent!"

Know that God Most High said, "*God loves the repen - tant and loves those who purify themselves*" [2:222]. When someone yields to a sin, but sincerely believes that he has sinned and has repented, he is in doubt as to the acceptance of his repentance. This is especially so when he knows that the acceptance of his repentance depends on his being worthy of God's love, for there is a long interval between the time of the commission of the sin and the time when he will find signs of God's love for him in his nature. When the servant becomes aware that he has done something requiring his repentance, constant contrition, with persistent renunciation of the fault and asking of forgiveness, is a necessity. In fact, it is said that he should be continuously worried untill his time comes. God said [speaking of and through His Prophet], "*Say: If you love God, follow me: God will love you*" [3: 31].

Continuous asking of forgiveness was part of the way of life of the Prophet. He said, "Something comes over my heart so that I ask forgiveness of God seventy times a day."

I heard Abu Abd Allah al-Sufi say . . . that Yahya ibn Muadh said, "One slip after repentance is uglier than seventy before it." I heard Muhammad ibn al-Husayn say . . . that Abu Uthman said concerning the word of

God Almighty and Glorious, *"Certainly to Us is their return"* [78:25] that it means "they will be brought back [to God], even though wandering in opposition has given them respite."

I heard Abu Abd al-Rahman al-Sulami say . . . that Abu Amr al-Anmati said, "The vizier, Ali ibn Isa, rode in a great procession. It made strangers ask, 'Who is that? Who is that?' A woman standing by the roadside said, 'How long are you going to ask, "Who is that, who is that?" That is a servant who has fallen from God's favor so God is trying him with what you see!' Ali ibn Isa heard this. He returned to his house, freed himself of the vizierate, and went to Mecca and remained there."

2

ON STRIVING (*MUJAHADA*)

God Most High said, "*Those who strive for Us we will certainly guide in Our ways; God is with the doers of good*" [29:69].

Abu 'l-Husayn ibn Ahmad al-Hawari informed us . . . from Abu Said al-Khudri, "The Messenger of God was asked about the most excellent war for religion and said, 'A word of justice in the face of despotic power.' When he related this, tears came to Abu Said's eyes."

I heard Abu Ali al-Daqqaq say, "If someone beautifies his outer being by struggling against the passions of his ego, God will beautify his inner being with the vision of Him. God Most High said, "*Those who struggle for Us we will certainly guide in Our ways*" [29:69].

Know that whoever does not strive from the beginning will never find the slightest trace of this Way. I heard Abu Abd al-Rahman al-Sulami say that he heard Abu Uthman al-Maghribi say, "If anyone supposes that something of this Way will be opened to him or that something of it will be revealed to him without the necessity of struggle, he is in error." I heard Abu Ali al-Daqqaq say, "Whoever does not stand up in the beginning will not sit down in the end." I also heard him say, "Their saying, 'Movement is a blessing' (*al-harakah*

11

barakah)'—means to bestir oneself outwardly brings on
the bestowal of grace inwardly."
I heard Muhammad ibn al-Husayn say . . . Abu Yazid
al-Bistami said, "For twelve years I was the blacksmith
of my ego and for five years the mirror of my heart. One
year I was looking between the two of them and there
around my waist was an obvious belt of dualism! So for
twelve years I worked to cut it. Then I looked again, and
inside me was another belt of dualism. So I worked to
cut that. For five years I looked for how it could be done
and it was revealed to me. Then I looked at the people
and saw them to be dead. So I said 'God is Greater'
(Allahu *akbar*) over them four times [as at the funeral
prayer]."
I heard Abu Abd al-Rahman al-Sulami say . . . that
Sari al-Saqati said, "O assembly of young men! Be serious before you reach my age and become feeble and incapable as I have." At that time none of the young men
were anywhere near comparison to him for divine service. I heard him say . . . that al-Hasan al-Qazzaz said,
"This undertaking is built upon three things: that you do
not eat except for need, that you do not sleep except
when you are overpowered, and that you do not talk
except as necessary." And I heard him say . . . that
Ibrahim ibn Adham said, "A man is never granted the
degree of the righteous before six difficult things become
possible for him: the first, that he close the door of ease
and open the door of difficulty; the second, that he close
the door of honor and open the door of humiliation; the
third, that he close the door of comfort and open the door
of effort; the fourth, that he close the door of sleep and
open the door of wakefulness; the fifth, that he close the
door of wealth and open the door of poverty; the sixth,
that he close the door of imagining the future and open
the door of readiness for death."
I heard Abu Abd al-Rahman al-Sulami say that he

heard his grandfather Abu Umar ibn Nujayd say, "Anyone whose ego has been honored has had his religion debased!" And I heard him say . . . that Abu Ali al-Rudhbari said, "If a Sufi said after five days [without food], 'I am hungry,' they would order him to the market and command him to earn a living!"

Know that the foundation and rationale of struggle or striving (*mujahada*) is to wean the ego from what is familiar to it and to induce it to oppose its desires (passions) at all times. The ego (animal soul) has two traits that prevent it from good: total preoccupation with cravings (attraction to pleasure) and refusal of obedience (avoidance of pain/harm). When the ego is defiant in the pursuit of desire, it must be curbed with the reins of awe of God. When it stubbornly refuses to conform with God's will, it must be steered toward opposing its desires. When it rages in anger [at being opposed], its state should be controlled—no process has a better outcome than the breaking of the power of anger by developing good character traits and by extinguishing its fires by gentleness. And if the soul finds sweetness in the wine of arrogance, it will have become incapable of anything but showing off its great deeds and preening itself before anyone who will look at it and notice it. It is necessary to break it of this habit, dissolving it with the punishment of humiliation by means of whatever will make the soul remember its paltry worth, its lowly origin, and its despicable acts.

The struggle of the majority of people is to bring their works to full development. The struggle of the elite is to purify their status because the endurance of hunger and wakefulness is simple and easy. The cure of character and the cleansing of its impurities is extremely difficult.

One of the thorniest problems of the soul is its inclination to find great pleasure in praise. Anyone who drinks a mouthful of this wine bears the weight of the heavens and the earths on his eyelids! A sign of the weight of this burden is that when this drink of praise is withheld from such a soul, its state reverts to laziness and cowardice in its striving.

There once was a shaykh who had prayed in the first [and most honorable] row of his mosque for many years. One day an obstacle hindered him from arriving early at the mosque, so he prayed in the last row. After that he was not seen for awhile. When asked the reason, he said, "I had performed my prescribed prayer for so many years and while doing so I held that I was devoting myself exclusively to God. The day that I was late to the mosque, a sort of shame came over me because people saw me in the last row. So I knew that my whole lifetime's zeal had derived only from offering my prescribed prayer where I could be seen. I had to redo all my prescribed prayers."

It is told that Abu Muhammad al-Murtaish said, "I used to perform the pilgrimage on foot without taking any provisions with me. I realized all of my effort was defiled by the sense of pleasure I received in the way that I performed it. One day my mother asked me to draw a jar of water for her and my ego found that hard. I knew then that my ego's compliancy on the pilgrimages had been for the sake of show and was in fact a blemish in it. For if my ego had truly passed away from itself, it would not have found difficult something that was a duty according to the divine law."

A woman who had grown very old was asked about her situation. She replied, "When I was young I found liveliness in my self and conditions which seemed good to me. I thought it was due to the power of my state. But when I grew old this left me, so I knew that it had been the strength of youth, while I had imagined it to be spiritual states." One of the shaykhs could never hear this story without feeling sympathy for this old lady. He said, "She was certainly a woman of principle."

I heard Muhammad ibn al-Husayn say . . . Dhu 'l-Nun al-Misri said, "God honors a servant with no greater honor than to show him the vileness of his ego. He humiliates a servant with no greater humiliation than to hide from him the vileness of his ego." I heard him say . . . that Ibrahim al-Khawwas said, "There was not a thing that horrified me which I did not commit." And I heard him say . . . that Muhammad ibn al-Fadl said, "Rest is liberation from the ego's demands."

I heard Abu Abd al-Rahman say that he heard Mansur ibn Abd Allah say that he heard Abu Ali al-Rudhbari say, "Disaster comes upon people through three things: diseased constitution, attachment to habit, and bad company." I asked him, "What is diseased constitution?" He said, "Eating the forbidden." I asked, "What is attachment to habit?" He said, "To look and listen for forbidden things and slander." I asked, "And what is bad company?" He replied, "Whenever the ego is roused by a desire, you go and pursue it."

I heard him say that he heard al-Nasrabadhi say, "Your ego is your prison. When you have escaped from it, you find yourself in eternal ease." I heard him say . . . that Abu 'l-Husayn al-Warraq said, "Our most sublime principles in the beginning of our undertaking are: [to act as] if the mosque of Abu Uthman al-Hiri were to prefer to give to others whatever gifts were given to us; not to pass the night knowing what our sustenance would be; and, if someone were to confront us with a distasteful action, not to avenge ourselves but to excuse him and behave humbly towards him. If disdain for someone came into our hearts, we would involve ourselves in serving him and doing good to him until it passed."

I heard Abu Hafs say, "The self is entirely darkness. Its lamp is its secret (*sirr*). The light of its lamp is inner direction from God. The result of success is prayer (*taw-fiq*). Whoever is not accompanied in his secret self by such direction from his Lord is in total darkness."

Saying, "Its lamp is its secret," alludes to the secret (*sirr*) between the servant and God Most High that forms the center of the servant's sincerity by means of which he knows that events take place through God and not through nor from himself so that he is free at all times from pretensions to divine power and strength. Then, by the success that God grants, the servant is preserved from the evils of his ego. If this gift of success does not reach someone, neither his knowledge of himself nor his knowledge of his Lord will profit him. Because of this the shaykhs have said, 'He who does not have the secret (*sirr*) will be insistent on following his own desires.'"

Abu Uthman al-Maghribi said, "As long as a person finds anything good in the self, that person will never be able to see his faults. Only one who blames the ego at all times will be able to see his faults." Abu Hafs al-Haddad said, "How swift is the destruction of the one who does not know his own faults! Disobedience is the high road to unbelief." Abu Sulayman al-Darani said, "I did not find a single good work coming from my ego. Why should it count for anything with me?" Sari al-Saqati said, "Beware of those who visit the rich, those who recite the Koran in market places, and those who act as scholars for princes."

Dhu 'l-Nun al-Misri said, "Corruption only comes upon the people through six things. First, weakness of intention in working for the next world; second, their bodies' captivity to their lusts (attraction to pleasure); third, elaborate anticipation of the future despite the shortness of life; fourth, choosing to please creatures rather than the Creator; fifth, following their own whims and casting the Sunna of their Prophet behind their backs; sixth, basing excuses for themselves on tiny slips of our noble predecessors, while burying many of their wonderful deeds."

3

ON RETREAT AND SECLUSION (*KHALWA* AND *UZLA*)

Abu 'l-Hasan Ali ibn Ahmad ibn Abd Allah told us . . . from Abu Hurayra that the Messenger of God said, "The best of all human modes of life is that of a person who takes hold of the reins of his horse in the way of God. If he hears an alarm or an uproar, he is on his horse's back looking for death or battle wherever it is to be found. Or it is that of a person living on what he has won by warfare on the top of some mountain or at the bottom of some valley, who stands in prayer, gives charity, and serves his Lord until the certainty of death overtakes him. He comes not among people except for good."

Khalwa, retreat, belongs to the purified, while *uzla*, withdrawal from the world, marks the people of union. The seeker needs to withdraw from his own kind in the beginning stages. Then, in the last stages, he needs to retreat in order to confirm himself in intimacy with God.

If the servant chooses to withdraw, his intention must be to separate himself from people so that they will be safe from his evil—he must not be looking to protect himself from their evil. For the first of these attitudes comes from thinking little of one's own ego, while the

17

second comes from making oneself out to be better than other people. A person who thinks little of himself is humble, while a person who sees himself as better than anybody else is arrogant.

A Christian monastic was asked, "Are you a monk?" He replied, "No, I am the guardian of a dog. My ego is a dog that injures people, so I have taken it out from among them so that they may be safe from it."

A man passed by one of the righteous and that shaykh gathered his garment away from him. The man said to him, "Why are you pulling your clothes away from me? My clothes are not defiled!" The shaykh answered, "I thought that you would think that my clothes were defiled so I pulled them away from you—in order not to defile your clothes, not so that you would not defile mine!"

One of the rules of withdrawal is that whoever goes into seclusion must acquire the knowledge that makes his commitment to unity (*tawhid*) firm, so that satan cannot seduce him through the imagination. Then he should acquire enough knowledge of the divine law that he is able to fulfill his religious duties so that his undertaking may be built on definite and sure foundations.

Withdrawing from the world does not mean going away from inhabited places. The essence of seclusion is to isolate blameworthy traits in order to substitute the divine names for them. Thus it was asked, "Who is the gnostic (*arif*)?" and they replied, "A creature distinguished," that is, someone who appears to be together with people, but is inwardly separated from them.

I heard Abu Ali al-Daqqaq say, "When you are with people, wear what they wear, eat what they eat and be separated from them by what is within you." I heard him say, "A man came to me and said, 'I have come to you from far away.' I said, 'That is not the way it is done. To really cross distances and endure the difficulties of travel, leave yourself. If you are successful, you will attain your object."

It is related that Abu Yazid al-Bistami said, "I saw my Lord Almighty and Glorious in a dream and asked, 'How shall I find You?' He said, 'Leave yourself and come!'" I heard Abu Abd al-Rahman al-Sulami say that he heard Abu Uthman al-Maghribi say, "Whoever chooses retreat over companionship must be free of every recollection but the remembrance of his Lord, free of every wish but the pleasure of his Lord, and free of every variety of the ego's demands. If he does not have these qualities, his retreat will plunge him into inner conflict or disaster."

It is said, "Solitude in retreat contains all one could ask of comfort." Yahya ibn Muadh said, "Look and seek whether your intimacy with God is through retreat or whether your intimacy is through Him, but in retreat. If your intimacy is through retreat, it will vanish when you leave the retreat. But if it is through Him, in retreat, then any place you may be, in the desert or on the plains, will be the same to you."

I heard Muhammad ibn al-Husayn say . . . he heard that Muhammad ibn Hamid say, "A man paid a visit to Abu Bakr al-Warraq. When he wanted to go back home, he asked him, 'Advise me.' Abu Bakr said, 'I found the good of this world and the next in retreat and having little, while [I found] evil in this world and the next in having much and mixing with people." And I heard him say . . . that he heard al-Jurayri say when asked about seclusion, "It is to go among the crowd, while your secret prevents them from crowding you and to withdraw your ego from sins while your inner awareness is bound to the Real."

It has been said, "Whoever prefers seclusion has attained seclusion." Sahl al-Tustari said, "Retreat will not work unless one's sustenance is lawful. Eating lawful sustenance will not work unless one carries out one's duties to God."

Dhu 'l-Nun al-Misri said, "I see nothing more productive of purity of faith than retreat." Abu Abd Allah al-Ramli said, "Make retreat your companionship, hunger your food, and intimate prayer your conversation until you either reach God or die." Dhu 'l-Nun said, "Someone who is concealed from the people by retreat is not like someone who is concealed from them by God."

I heard Abu Abd al-Rahman al-Sulami say Junayd said, "The suffering of seclusion is easier to bear than the sociability of mixing with people." Makhul said, "There is some good in associating with people, but in seclusion there is safety." Yahya ibn Muadh said, "Solitude is the table companion of the truthful."

I heard Abu Ali al-Daqqaq say he heard Shibli cry, "'Bankruptcy! Bankruptcy, O people!' They asked him, 'Abu Bakr, what is the sign of bankruptcy?' He replied, 'One of the signs of bankruptcy is familiarity with people.'"

Yahya ibn Abi Kuthayr often said, "Whoever mixes with people tries to influence them, and whoever tries to influence them attempts to impress them." Shuayb ibn Harb said, "I went to see Malik ibn Masud in Kufa. He was in his house by himself. I asked, 'Why do you isolate yourself here alone?' He answered, 'I do not think of anyone as isolated who is together with God.'"

I heard Abu Abd al-Rahman al-Sulami say . . . that Junayd said, "Whoever wants to secure his religion and rest his body and his heart, let him withdraw himself from people. This is a difficult time and the intelligent person will choose solitude in it." And I heard him say . . . that Abu Yaqub al-Susi said, 'Only the strong have the strength to manage separation from people. For the likes of us, community is more fortunate and more useful. Some will work because of seeing the efforts of others."

And I heard him say . . . that Abu Abbas al-Damghani said that Shibli advised him saying, "Cling to solitude. Efface your name from among the people and face the prayer niche until you die." A man went to Shuayb ibn Harb. "What brings you here?" he asked. The man said, "I want to be with you!" "My brother," Shuayb told him, "Worship should not depend on companionship. Someone who enjoys no closeness with God will not be brought close by anything external." Some people asked a Sufi, "What is the strangest thing you have encountered in your travels?" He told them, "Khidr came to meet me and sought my company, but I was afraid that it would spoil my trust in God alone." Another Sufi was asked, "Is there anyone here with whom you would be close?" "Yes," he said. He stretched out his hand to his copy of the Koran and placed it against his heart. "This." With this meaning they have recited,

> Your Book is my strength; it does not leave my couch,
> And in it is healing for that which I conceal.

A man asked Dhu 'l-Nun, "When will withdrawing from the world be the right course for me?" He answered, "When you are capable of withdrawing from yourself." Ibn al-Mubarak was asked, "What is the remedy of the heart?" He replied, "Few encounters with people."

It is said that when God wants to transport a servant from the humiliation of disobedience to the honor of obedience, he makes him familiar with solitude, enriches him with contentment, and brings him to see the shameful deeds of his own ego. So whoever has been given this has been given the best of this world and the next.

4

ON GOD-WARINESS (*TAQWA*)

God Most High said, "*The noblest of you in the sight of God is the one who is most God-wary*" [49:13].

Abu 'l Husayn Ali ibn Ahmad ibn Abdan reported . . . that Abu Said al-Khudri said that a man went to the Prophet and said, "O Prophet of God, advise me." He said, "'*Be wary of God*' [3:102] for in it is gathered all good." Take upon yourself war for God's sake, for it is the monasticism of a Muslim. Take upon yourself the remembrance of God, for it is a light for you."

Ali ibn Ahmad ibn Abdan reported . . . that Anas said that someone asked, "Prophet of God, who are the Family of Muhammad?" He said, "Everyone who is God-wary, for in the fear of God is gathered all good."

The basic meaning of *ittiqa* (or *taqwa*), fear of God, is protection, by obedience to God, from His punishment. In ordinary usage it is said, "So-and-so was protected (*ataqqa*) by his shield." The foundation of this fear or awe is to guard yourself from attributing equals to God. After that, it manifests in guarding yourself from acts of disobedience and offenses, then in guarding yourself from doubtful situations, and later still in guarding yourself from omitting to do what is good.

Thus I heard Abu Ali al-Daqqaq say, "To every part of

23

God-wariness there is a door. This has come to us in the explanation of His saying, *'Be wary of God with the respect that is due Him'* [3:102], which means that the servant obey and not revolt, remember and not forget, give thanks and not be ungrateful."

I heard Abu Abd al-Rahman al-Sulami say . . . that Sahl ibn Abd Allah al-Tustari said, "There is no helper but God, no guide but the Messenger of God, no provision but being wary of Him, and no work but patience in worship." And I heard him say . . . that al-Kattani said, "The share of this world is trouble. The share connected to the next world is God-wariness." And I heard him say . . . that al-Jurayri said, "No one who fails to institute fear and inner attention as the principles of his relations with God will arrive at the disclosure of secrets and the contemplation of Him."

Al-Nasrabadhi said, "Fear means that the servant fear what is other than God Almighty and Glorious!" Sahl al-Tustari said, "Whoever wants fear of God as his proper state must abandon sins altogether." He also said, "Someone who adheres to God-wariness yearns for separation from this world, for God Most High has said, *'In the next world is good for those who fear Him—do you not understand?'* [6:32]."

A Sufi said, "When someone makes God-wariness a reality, God makes avoidance of this world easy on his heart." Abu Abd Allah al-Rudhbari said, "Being wary of God is to shun what distances you from God." Dhu 'l-Nun al-Misri said, "The one who is God-wary is the one who does not stain his exterior with acts of resistance nor his interior with delusions and who stands in a position of agreement and conformity with God."

I heard Muhammad ibn al-Husayn say he heard Abu 'l- Hasan al-Farisi say, "God-wariness has an outside and an inside. Its outside is to preserve the limits set by God on behavior. Its inside is intention and sincerity."

Dhu 'l-Nun said:

> There is no living except with people
> Whose hearts long for God-wariness
> And who are happy in remembrance
> Content are they with the spirit of certainty
>   and its goodness
> Like the nursing infant in its mother's arms.

It is said that a person is judged to possess God-wariness on the basis of three things: the beauty of his trust in God for what has not been granted; the beauty of his satisfaction with what has been granted; the beauty of his patience toward what has passed him by. Talq ibn Habib said, "God-wariness is to work in obedience to God with light from God, wary of the penalty of God."

I heard Abu Abd al-Rahman al-Sulami say . . . that Abu Hafs al-Haddad said, "'God-wariness means the lawful alone and nothing else." And I heard him say . . . that Abu 'l-Husayn al-Zanjani said, "If someone's capital were fear of God, tongues would grow tired describing his profit." Al-Wasiti said, "God-wariness is that one be wary of being wary—that is, of seeing one's own fear of Him."

The one who respects God's right over him is like Ibn Sirin. He bought forty jars of butter. His servant took a mouse out of one of them. Ibn Sirin asked, "Which jar did you take it from?" The man replied, "I don't know!" So he dumped all of them onto the ground. Or he is like Abu Yazid al-Bistami. He bought a measure of oats in Hamadan, and a little of it was left over. When he returned to Bistam he spied two ants in it so he returned to Hamadan and set down the ants.

It is said that Abu Hanifa used to avoid sitting in the shade of a tree that belonged to someone to whom he had loaned money. He would say, "This derives from the hadith, 'Every loan drawing interest is usury.'"

It is told that Abu Yazid al-Bistami washed his robe in the desert. He had a companion with him. The man said, "Let's hang up your robe to dry on the wall of this vineyard." He answered, "No, don't drive a peg into somebody's wall." His companion said, "Then we'll hang it on a tree." "No," he returned, "it may break the branches." "We'll spread it out on the grass." "No, the animals eat it. We will not block it off from them." So he turned his back to the sun, with his robe on his back, until one side of it dried. Then he turned it until the other side dried.

Abu Yazid al-Bistami went into the congregational mosque one day and drove his staff into the ground. It slipped and rested on the staff of an old man next to him who had also stuck his staff in the ground and knocked it down. The old man leaned over and picked up his staff. Abu Yazid went to his house and asked his forgiveness. He said, "The reason you bent over was my negligence in driving in my staff which made it necessary for you to do so."

He was once seen at the doorstep of a bathhouse server. When asked why, he answered, "It is the place where I disobeyed my Lord!" On being questioned further, he said, "I removed from this wall a bit of clay with which a guest of mine cleaned his hand and I did not ask the permission of its owner so that it would be lawful."

Ibrahim ibn Adham said, "I spent a night under the Rock in Jerusalem. When part of the night had passed, two angels descended. One of them said to his fellow, 'Who is here?' 'Ibrahim ibn Adham,' answered the other. 'That is the one whom God, glory be to Him, lowered by a degree!' 'Why?' 'Because he bought some dates in Basra and one of the dates belonging to the grocer fell in among his dates. He did not return it to its owner.' Ibrahim said that he went back to Basra, bought dates from that man and let fall a date into the man's dates and then returned to Jerusalem and spent the night at the Rock. When part of the night had passed, suddenly he found himself with two angels descended from heaven. One of them said to his companion, 'Who is here?' 'Ibrahim ibn Adham,' the other replied, and added, 'He is the one whom God returned to his place and whose degree was raised!'"

It is said that God-wariness has various aspects. For the common people it is to guard against attributing equals to God. For the elect it is to guard against acts of disobedience. For the saints, it is to guard against attempting to gain things through actions. For the prophets, it is to guard against the attribution of actions to themselves, since their fear of Him is from Him and towards Him.

Ali, the Commander of the Faithful said, "The most noble of humanity in this world are the generous, and the most noble in the next world are the God-wary."

Ali ibn Ahmad al-Ahwazi reported . . . from Abu Umamah from the Prophet, "If someone has looked upon the beauty of a woman and lowered his eyes without looking again, God has created an act of service for him whose sweetness he will find in his heart." I heard Muhammad ibn al-Husayn say . . . he heard Muhammad ibn Abd Allah al-Farghani say, "Junayd was sitting with Ruwaym, al-Jurayri and Ibn Ata. Junayd said, 'No one who is saved is really saved except by sincerity in taking refuge. God Most High said, *"And upon three who were opposed until the earth with its expanse became narrow for them . . ."* and so on, to the end of the verse [9:118].

Ruwaym said, "No one is saved except by sincere carefulness of the rights of God. God Most High said, *'God will rescue those who have been careful with their gains'* [39:61]." Jurayri said, "No one who is saved is really saved except by the respect which comes of loyalty. God Most High said, *'Those who are loyal to the covenant of God and do not violate the pact, for them is the final abode'* [13:20-22]."

Ibn Ata said, "No one who is saved is really saved except by actualizing the shame that comes from real awareness of one's state. God Most High said, *'Does he not know that God sees?'* [96:14]."

No one who is saved is really saved except by the judgment and decision of God. God Most High said, *"Those to whom good has come from Us previously will be removed far [from hell]"* [21:101]." No one who is saved is really saved except by being chosen beforehand. God Most High said, *"We chose them and guided them to the straight path"* [6:87].

5

ON ABSTAINING (*WARA*)

Abu 'l-Husayn Abd al-Rahman ibn Ibrahim ibn Muhammad ibn Yahya al-Mazaki reported . . . from Abu Dharr that the Messenger of God said, "Part of the beauty of Islam is that a person leaves what does not concern him."

As for *wara*, abstaining from unlawful acts,, it means to leave everything whose rightness is doubtful. Thus Ibrahim ibn Adham said, "Abstaining from the unlawful is to leave every doubtful situation and to leave what does not concern you. It is the abandonment of the superfluous."

Abu Bakr al-Siddiq said, "We used to pass by seventy lawful situations for fear that we would find ourselves in one situation that was forbidden." And the Prophet said to Abu Hurayra, "Be heedful of the lawfulness of your acts. You will be the most worshipful of people."

I heard Abu Abd al-Rahman al-Sulami say . . . that Sari said, "The people who abstained from unlawful acts in their era were four Hudhayfah al-Murtaish, Yusuf ibn Asbat, Ibrahim ibn Adham and Sulayman al-Khawwas. They looked into how to care for the lawful and when matters became difficult for them they took refuge in needing little."

And I heard him say . . . that Shibli said, "Abstaining

29

from the unlawful means to refrain from everything other than God Most High." And I heard him say . . . that Ishaq ibn Khalaf informed us, "To be scrupulous in speaking is harder than to be scrupulous with gold and silver. To renounce social position is harder than to renounce gold and silver because you spend both of them in search of social position."

Abu 'l-Sulayman al-Darani said, "Abstaining from the unlawful is the beginning of renunciation of the world, just as contentment with one's lot is a branch of satisfaction with the will of God."

Abu Uthman said, "The reward for abstaining from the unlawful is an easy accounting on the Last Day."

Yahya ibn Muadh said, "Abstaining from the unlawful means to stop at the limit of religious knowledge without making interpretations."

I heard Muhammad ibn al-Husayn say . . . that Abd Allah ibn al-Jalla said, "I knew someone who stayed in Mecca thirty years and would not drink any other water than Zamzam which he drew himself with his own pitcher and a rope and would not eat food imported from an outside city." I heard him say . . . that Ali ibn Musa al-Tahirati said, "A small coin belonging to Abd Allah ibn Marwan fell into a polluted well. He paid thirteen dinars to have it brought out. When asked about this, he said, 'The name of God Most High is upon it.'" And I heard him say . . . that Yahya ibn Muadh said, 'Abstaining from the unlawful has two aspects: Exterior abstaining, which is not to make a move except for the sake of God Most High and interior abstaining, which is not to admit anything other than God Most High into your heart."

Yahya ibn Muadh said, "Whoever does not look into the fine points of abstaining from the unlawful will not attain the sublimity of the gift." And it is said, "The one whose attention to religion is meticulous is the one whose importance at the resurrection will be great."

Ibn al-Jalla said, "Someone who takes up the dervish life unaccompanied by fear of God eats what is totally unlawful." Yunus ibn Ubayd said, "Abstaining from the unlawful is to leave the doubtful and to call the ego to account for its every glance."

Sufyan al-Thawri said, "I never saw anything easier than abstaining from the unlawful. Leave everything that makes a mark upon you conscience." Maruf al-Karkhi said, "Guard your tongue from praise as you have guarded it from blame." Bishr ibn al-Harith said, "The hardest works are three: to be generous when you have little, to be scrupulous about what is lawful when in retreat from the world and to tell the truth before someone from whom you hope for benefit or fear harm."

It is told that the sister of Bishr al-Hafi went to Ahmad ibn Hanbal and said, "We spin on our terrace while torches pass by us outside and their beams fall upon us. Is it permissible for us to spin in their rays?" Ahmad asked, "Who are you? May God Most High forgive all your sins!" She answered, "I am Bishr al-Hafi's sister." Ahmad wept and said, "From your house issues true care for the divine law! No, do not spin in their rays."

Ali al-Attar said, "I passed through the streets in Basra. Old men were sitting there while boys played around them. I asked, 'Aren't you ashamed to show so little respect for these elders?' One of the boys answered, 'These old men had little care for the lawful, so they have inspired little respect.'"

It is said that Malik ibn Dinar made his home in Basra for forty years, but it never felt right to him to eat any of the dates of Basra, dry or fresh. He died without having tasted them. Each time the date harvest would pass, he would say, "People of Basra! This stomach of mine has not shrunk any. Has anything of yours increased?"

Ibrahim ibn Adham was asked, "Don't you drink

Zamzam water?" He answered, "If I had a bucket of my own, I would drink it."

I heard Abu Ali al-Daqqaq say, "When Harith al-Muhasibi passed his hand over food whose lawfulness was in doubt, a vein in his fingertip would throb and he would know it was not permissible." Bishr al-Hafi, it is told, was invited to a banquet. Food was placed before him. He tried to stretch his hand out to it, but his hand would not reach. This happened three times. A man who knew something about him said, "His hand will not stretch towards food that has anything doubtful in it! What use is it for the one who is holding this dinner to invite this shaykh?"

Ahmad ibn Muhammad ibn Yahya al-Sufi reported . . . that Ahmad ibn Muhammad ibn Salim said in Basra that Sahl ibn Abd Allah al-Tustari was questioned about the purely lawful. He said, "It is that in which there is nothing producing disobedience to God Most High." Sahl also said, "The purely lawful is that in which there is nothing producing forgetfulness of God Most High."

Hasan al-Basri entered Mecca and saw a young man, one of the children of Ali ibn Abi Talib, who was resting his back against the Kabah while preaching to the people. Hasan got hold of him and asked, "What is the foundation of religion?" The youth replied, "Abstaining from the unlawful." Hasan asked, "And what is the disaster of religion?" He said, "Ambition!" Hasan marveled at him. Hasan said, "An atom's measure of sound abstaining from the unlawful is better than a thousand measures of fasting and prayer."

God, glory to Him, revealed to Moses, "Those who draw near do not come near to Me with anything that can compare to abstaining from the unlawful and renunciation of the world."

Abu Hurayra said, "Those who will sit with God Most High tomorrow are the people who abstain from the unlawful and practice renunciation." Sahl ibn Abd Allah al-Tustari said, "A person unattended by the ability to abstain from the unlawful could eat the head of an elephant and not be full!"

It is said that Umar ibn Abdul-Aziz was brought some musk that had been taken as spoils of war. He held his nose closed. He said, "The only benefit of this is its scent. I would hate to discover its scent without the rest of the Muslims."

Abu Uthman al-Hiri was questioned about abstaining from the unlawful. He said, "Abu Salih Hamdun al-Qassar was with a friend of his at his last moment. The man died. Abu Salih blew out the lamp. Asked why, he replied, 'Up until now the oil in the lamp was his. From now on, it belongs to his heirs.' So they looked for other oil."

Kuhmus said, "I committed a sin for which I have wept for forty years. A brother of mine visited me. I bought some fried fish for him. When he had finished, I took a bit of clay from my neighbor's wall so that he could clean his hand with it. I did not ask my neighbor to make it lawful."

It is said that a man wrote a note while he was living in a rented house. He wanted to blot what he had written with dust from the wall of the house. It occurred to him that the house was rented, but then it came to his mind that it was of no importance, so he blotted the letter. Then he heard a voice from the unseen say, "The one who thinks little of dust shall learn what a long accounting he will face tomorrow!"

Ahmad ibn Hanbal left a copper pot as security with a grocer in Mecca. When he wanted to redeem it, the grocer took out two pots and said, "Take whichever of them is yours." Ahmad said, "I am not sure which is my pot, so it is yours, and the money is also yours." The grocer said, "This one is your pot. I wanted to put you to the test!" He replied, "I will not take it." And he went away and left the pot with the grocer.

It is said that Ibn Mubarak let loose a horse of great value while he prayed his noon prescribed prayer. The animal pastured in the field of a village whose revenues belonged to a king. Ibn Mubarak abandoned the beast and would not ride it. It is said that Ibn Mubarak returned from Merv to Damascus because of a pen he had borrowed and not returned to its owner.

Al-Nakhai hired a riding animal. His whip dropped from his hand. He descended, tied the animal and went back and picked up his whip. It was said to him, "If you had ridden your mount back to the place where you dropped your whip in order to pick it up, it would have been easier for you." He answered, "I only hired it to travel from such-and-such a place to such-and-such a place!"

Abu Bakr al-Daqqaq said, "I was lost in the desert of the Children of Israel for fifteen days. When I found the road, I encountered a soldier who gave me a drink of water. Because of this, a covering came over my heart from which I suffered for thirty years."

It is said that Rabia al-Adawiyyah mended a tear in her shirt by the light of a sultan's lamp. For awhile she lost knowledge of her heart. Then she remembered, ripped her shirt, and found her heart.

Sufyan al-Thawri was seen in a dream. He had two wings with which he was flying from tree to tree in paradise. He was asked, "By virtue of what were you granted this?" and said, "By abstaining from the unlawful."

Hasan ibn Abi Sinan stopped with the companions of Hasan al-Basri and asked, "What thing is most difficult for you?" He replied, "To be scrupulous about the lawful." "Nothing is easier than that for me," he said. "How can that be?" they asked. "I have not drunk from this river of yours for forty years," said he.

Hasan ibn Abi Sinan used never to sleep reclining nor to eat any sort of oil nor to drink cold water for sixty years. After he died he was seen in a dream and asked, "How has God treated you?" "Well," he said, "but I am veiled from paradise by a needle I borrowed and did not return."

Abd 'l-Wahid ibn Zayd had a slave who had waited upon him for many years and spent forty years in worship. In the beginning he [the salve] had been a grain measurer. When he died, he was seen in a dream and asked, "How has God treated you?" "Well," he replied, "except that I am veiled from paradise. I measured forty measures of grain and did not clean the dust that collected at each measure. This giving of short measure was counted against me."

Jesus son of Mary passed by a grave and called a man out of it. God Most High brought him back to life. Jesus asked, "Who are you?" The man said, "I was a porter who carried things about for people. One day I carried firewood for someone. I broke off a splinter and used it as a toothpick, and I have been paying for it since I died."

Abu Said al-Kharraz was discoursing on abstaining from the unlawful when Abbas ibn al-Muhtadi passed by. He said, "Abu Said, aren't you ashamed? You sit under the roof of a miserly sultan, drink from the well of a queen, do your business with false coin, and you talk about abstaining from the unlawful?"

6

On Renunciation (*ZUHD*)

Hamzah ibn Yusuf al-Sahmi al-Jurjani related to us . . . from Abu Khilad, who sat with the Prophet, that the Prophet said, "If you see a man who has been gifted with renunciation of the world and who has eloquence, seek to approach him, for wisdom has been instilled in him."

The Sufis have differing opinions in the matter of renunciation (*zuhd*). Some of them say that one need only renounce the unlawful, because the lawful has been made permissible by God Most High. When God benefits His servant with lawful property and the servant in turn worships Him with gratitude for it, it is not preferable for him to leave it with his own will rather than keeping it with God's permission.

Other Sufis say that renunciation of the unlawful is an obligation, while renunciation of the lawful is a virtue. From this point of view, as long as the servant is patient with his state of little property, satisfied with what God Most High has apportioned for him, and content with what he has been given, he is more perfect than one who lives richly and comfortably in the world. God Most High has urged people to abstain from the world by His saying, "*Say: The provision of this world is but small, while the next is better for whoever is God-*

wary" [4:77] and in many other verses that may be cited disparaging the world and recommending abstention from it.

Some of them say that if the servant spends his wealth in works of obedience, his state being marked by patience and, in difficult times, by not raising objections to what the law forbids, then his renunciation of lawful property is the more preferable.

Others say that the servant must neither attempt to abandon the lawful by his own effort nor to seek superfluous wealth, but that he should respect his apportioned share. If God Exalted and Glorified has provided him with the sustenance of lawful income, he should thank Him. If God Most High has appointed to him enough to take care of all his needs, he should not strive to seek out excess property. Patience is the better course for the poor man. Gratitude is more suitable for the possessor of lawful wealth.

They have discoursed on the meaning of renunciation. Each of them has spoken of his own time and pointed to its particular character. I heard Abu Abd al-Rahman al-Sulami say . . . that Sufyan al-Thawri said, "Renunciation of the world means to give up placing your hope in it, not to eat coarse food or wear the robe of an ascetic." And I heard him say . . . Sari al-Saqati said, "God strips the world from His Friends, denies it to His purified ones, and removes it from the hearts of those He loves because He is not satisfied with that for them."

It is said that the principle of renunciation derives from His Word, *"So that they may neither mourn over what has escaped them, nor exult over what has been granted them,"* [57:23] because the renunciater does not exalt in what he has of the world nor grieve over what he does not have.

Abu Uthman said, "Renunciation is to give up the world and then not care who gets it." I heard Abu Ali al-

Daqqaq say, "Renunciation is to leave the world as it is and not to say, 'I will construct a shelter,' or 'I will build a mosque.'" Yahya ibn Muadh said, "Renunciation makes one generous with property, while love makes one generous with spirit."

Ibn al-Jalla said, "Renunciation is to look at the world with an eye for its transience, so that it becomes small in your eyes and avoiding it becomes easy for you."

Ibn Khafif said, "The sign of renunciation is that ease exists when wealth departs." He also said, "When the heart has forgotten apparent causes and the hands have withdrawn themselves from wealth, it is renunciation."

It has been said, "Renunciation exists when the ego genuinely dislikes the world." I heard Abu Abd al-Rahman al-Sulami say that he heard al-Nasrabadhi say, "The ascetic is a stranger in this world, and the gnostic is a stranger in the next."

It is said, "If someone is sincere in his renunciation, the world comes to him despite himself." And about this they say, "If a crown were to fall from heaven, it would only fall on the head of someone who didn't want it."

Junayd said, "Renunciation is that the heart be free of whatever the hand is free of." Abu Sulayman al-Darani said, "To wear wool is a sign of renunciation, but it is not right for a renunciate to wear it if he has three dirhams and the wish for five dirhams is in his heart."

Our predecessors have held varying views in the matter of renunciation. Sufyan al-Thawri, Ahmad ibn Hanbal, Isa ibn Yunus and others have held that to renounce the world is to abandon ambition and be satisfied with one's lot, which they say is one of the signs, motivations and consequences of renunciation.

Abd Allah ibn al-Mubarak said, "Renunciation is trust in God Most High together with love of poverty." So say also Shaqiq al-Balkhi and Yunus ibn Asbat. This is also one of the guideposts of renunciation, for the servant has no strength to renounce except by means of trust in God Most High. Abd al-Wahid ibn Zayd said, "Renunciation is to leave both the dinar and the dirham." Abu Sulayman al-Darani said, "Renunciation is to abandon whatever distracts you from God Glorified and Exalted."

I heard Muhammad ibn al-Husayn say . . . when Ruwaym asked about renunciation, Junayd said, "It is seeing the world as insignificant and erasing its vestiges from the heart." Sari said, "The life of an ascetic is not good while he is distracted from himself. The life of a gnostic is not good while he is distracted by himself."

Junayd, questioned about renunciation, said, "It is that the hand be free of property and the heart of pursuing it." Shibli was asked about renunciation and said, "It is to abstain from what is other than God Most High."

Yahya ibn Muadh said, "No one attains the reality of renunciation until there are three characteristics in him: work without attachment, speech without personal motives, and honor without seeking position."

Abu Hafs said, "One can only renounce the lawful, and there is nothing lawful in the world, so there is no renunciation." Abu Uthman said, "God Most High gives to the ascetic more than what he desires. He gives to the desirous one less than what he desires. He gives to the one on the middle and straight path exactly in accordance with his desires."

Yahya ibn Muadh said, "The ascetic makes you snuff up vinegar and mustard. The gnostic lets you smell ambergris and musk." Hasan al-Basri said, "Renunciation of the world is that you loathe its people, and you loathe what it contains." A Sufi was asked, "What is renunciation of the world?" He answered, "To abandon whatever is in it to whoever is in it."

A man asked Dhu 'l-Nun al-Misri, "When will I

renounce the world?" He replied, "When you have renounced yourself."

Muhammad ibn al-Fadl said, "The predilection of ascetics is for having no needs and the predilection of spiritual warriors *(fityan)* is for being in need. God Most High said, '*And they prefer others over themselves, even though they may be in need*' [59:9]."

Al-Kattani said, "The thing about which the Kufan, the Medinese, the Iraqi, and the Damascene do not differ is abstinence from the world, generosity of nature, and giving good counsel to people. Not one of all those sorts of people would call these traits anything but laudable."

A man asked Yahya ibn Muadh, "When will I enter the tavern of trust in God, don the cloak of renunciation and sit with the ascetics?" He said, "When the secret training of your ego progresses to such an extent that if God cut off your sustenance for three days, you would not be weakened in yourself. Inasmuch as you have not matured to this degree, your sitting on the prayer carpet of ascetics would only be ignorance. And I could not guarantee that you would not be exposed among them!"

Bishr al-Hafi said, "Renunciation is a king who dwells only in a free and empty heart." I heard Muhammad ibn al-Husayn say . . . that Muhammad ibn Muhammad ibn al-Ashath al-Bikandi said, "If someone discourses on renunciation and preaches to the people and then desires what they have, God Most High removes the love of the next world from his heart."

It is said that when the servant has renounced the world, God Most High sets an angel over him who will plant wisdom in his heart. A Sufi was asked, "Why did you renounce the world?" He replied, "It renounced me!"

Ahmad ibn Hanbal said, "Renunciation has three phases. The first is abandonment of the unlawful which is the renunciation of the majority of people. The second is abandonment of excess in the lawful which is the renunciation of the elite. The third is abandonment of whatever distracts the servant from God Most High, which is the renunciation of gnostics."

I heard Abu Ali al-Daqqaq say, "A Sufi was asked, 'Why do you abstain from the world?' He answered, 'When most of the world renounced me, I disdained to take an interest in the rest of it.'"

Yahya ibn Muadh said, "The world is like an unveiled bride. The one who seeks her waits upon her like a maid while the ascetic blackens her face, tears out her hair, and sets fire to her raiment. But the gnostic is occupied with God Most High and does not even notice her."

I heard Abu Abd Allah al-Sufi say . . . that Sari said, "I exercised every aspect of renunciation and was granted what I wished, except for renunciation of other people— I have not attained it, nor am I capable of it." It is said, "Ascetics leave nothing but for their own sake. They give up a temporal benefit for an eternal one."

Al-Nasrabadhi said, "Renunciation spares the blood of the ascetics, but sheds the blood of the gnostics." Hatim al-Asamm said, "The ascetic exhausts his purse before he exhausts his ego. The would-be ascetic exhausts himself before he has exhausted his purse!"

I heard Muhammad ibn Abd Allah say . . . that Fudayl ibn Iyad said, "God put everything bad in one house and made its key the love of this world. He put everything good in another house and made its key renunciation."

7
ON SILENCE (*SAMT*)

Abd Allah ibn Yusuf al-Ispahani informed us . . . through Abu Hurayra that the Messenger of God said, "Whoever believes in God and the last day, let him not trouble his neighbor. Whoever believes in God and the last day, let him be generous to his guest. Whoever believes in God and the last day, let him say what is good, or let him be silent."

Ali ibn Ahmad ibn Abdan informed us . . . that Ukbah ibn Amir said, "I asked, 'O Messenger of God, what is salvation?" He said, 'Keep your tongue to yourself, stay home, and weep over your sins.'"

Silence is security. That is the root of the matter This can be cause for remorse on occasions when keeping quiet is blameworthy. What is necessary is that one choose speech or silence according to the divine law and the obligation of a Muslim to command what is good and forbid what is evil. To say nothing at the proper time is a characteristic of true men, just as to speak at the proper occasion is one of the noblest of qualities. I heard Abu Ali al-Daqqaq say, "Whoever holds back from speaking the truth is a devil without a tongue."

One should be silent in the presence of God. God Most High said, "*When the Koran is recited, hearken to it and give ear so that you may receive mercy*" [7:204]. And

He said, referring to the *jinn* who were in the presence of the Messenger, *"When they were present with him, they said, 'Listen!'"* [46:29], and *"Voices will be lowered for the Beneficent, so that nothing will be heard but a whisper"* [20:108].

What a difference is there between a servant who is silent to protect himself from lying and gossiping and a servant who is silent because he is overwhelmed by the power of the awe he feels! With this sense they recite:

> I ponder over what to say when we are apart,
> And judge myself addicted to proving by the word.
> But when we are together, I lose all from the start,
> And if I say a single thing, say only the absurd.

And they recite:

> O Layla, how many proofs have been my task!
> When I come to you, O Layla, I don't know what that
> means.

And they recite:

> And how many speeches to you!
> But when I was set before you, I forgot them all.

And:

> I realize that speech adorns a noble youth,
> But silence is the better course for one who can keep
> silent.
> On how many an occasion has the alphabet brought
> death,
> And how many a speaker has wished he had been
> quiet?

Silence has two parts, outer quiet and the quiet of heart and mind. Someone who trusts in God stills his heart as a way of laying claim to his sustenance. The gnostic stills his heart in acceptance of destiny through the quality of harmony with God. The one relies upon the fineness of His work. The other is content with the totality of His decrees. With this meaning they have said:

His misfortunes came over you,
And the cares of your inner being were relieved.

Sometimes silence is caused by the amazement of spontaneous understanding. When the unveiling of a divine attribute occurs suddenly, all expressiveness is struck dumb. There can be no explanation or discourse, and all demonstrative evidences are blotted out so that there is neither knowledge nor sensation. God Most High said, *"On the day [of judgment] God will gather the Messengers and ask, 'What answer have you received?' They will reply, 'We have no knowledge'"* [5:109].

As for the predilection of the masters of inner struggle for silence, it is because they know what disasters there are in speech; that is, it involves the pleasure of the ego, the display of qualities for praise, and the inclination to discriminate among people on the basis of how well they speak, and other catastrophes of human nature. Thus silence is a trait of practitioners of inner discipline. It is one of the pillars of the conduct of their campaign and of their training of character. It is said that Dawud al-Tai, when he wanted to seclude himself in his house, decided to attend the sessions of Abu Hanifa, whose student he had been, sit with his fellow scholars, and not discuss a single question. When he had steeled himself by putting this quality into practice for an entire year, he secluded himself in his house and chose solitude. Umar ibn Abd al-Aziz, if he wrote something and embroidered in its expression, tore it up and wrote something else.

I heard Abu Abd al-Rahman al-Sulami say . . . Bishr ibn al-Harith said, "When speech makes you conceited, be silent. When silence makes you conceited, speak." Sahl ibn Abd Allah al-Tustari said, "Silence is not appropriate for a person until his ego has been compelled to retreat. Repentance is not appropriate for a person until his ego has been compelled to silence."

Abu Bakr al-Farisi said, "He whose native country is not silence is excessive even when he keeps quiet. Silence does not pertain exclusively to the tongue but to the heart and all of the limbs." A Sufi said, "The one who does not value silence, when he speaks, speaks nonsense."

I heard Muhammad ibn al-Husayn say . . . that Mumshad al-Dinawari said, "The wise inherit wisdom through silence and reflection." Abu Bakr al-Farisi was asked about the silence of the inner being, the secret (*sirr*), and said, "It is the abandonment of occupation with the past and the future." He also said, "When the servant speaks about what concerns him and about what he must, he is within the bounds of silence."

It is related that Muadh ibn Jabal said, "Speak to people little and speak to your Lord much. Perhaps your heart will see God Most High." Someone asked Dhu 'l-Nun al-Misri, "Who among people best protects his heart?" He replied, "The one among them who best controls his tongue."

Ibn Masud said, "Nothing is worthier of a stay in prison than the tongue." Ali ibn Bukkar said, "God Most High made two doors for everything, but He made four doors for the tongue—the lips are two leaves of a door, and the two jaws are two leaves of a door. It is said that Abu Bakr al-Siddiq, for many years used to hold a stone in his mouth in order to limit his speech. It is said that Abu Hamzah al-Baghdadi was a fine orator. Then a voice form the unseen spoke to him and said, "You have spoken, and you have done it well. He is waiting for you to be silent and to do it well." He did not speak afterwards until he died which was more or less a week after this occurrence.

Sometimes silence will come over a speaker in order to discipline him, because his conduct has been bad in some respect. When he sat with his circle and they did not ask him about anything, Shibli used to say, "*The decree came upon them because of how they had sinned, and they do not speak*" [27:85].

Sometimes silence will come over a speaker because someone with greater right to speak is among those present. I heard Ibn Sammak say that Shah al-Kirmani and Yahya ibn Muadh were friends. Although they lived in the same city, Shah would never attend Yahya's sessions. Asked about this, he would insist that it was the proper course. People continued to pursue him, however, until one day he went to the sessions. He sat on one side so that Yahya ibn Muadh would not be aware of him. When Yahya began to speak, he fell silent. Then he said, "There is someone here who should speak before me," and he remained speechless. Shah said, "I told you that the right thing was for me not to come to his sessions."

Sometimes silence falls upon a speaker for a reason having to do with those present; that is, because there is someone there who is not worthy to hear that discourse. In such a case God Most High restrains the tongue of the speaker out of jealousy, to preserve that discourse from those to whom it does not belong.

Sometimes the reason for silence affecting a speaker is that God Most High knows the state of a member of the audience to be such that, if he were to hear such a discourse, it would become a test for him. Either he might imagine that what he heard applied to his own case, while it did not, or the matter of the discourse might oblige him to take on something of which he was incapable. So God Almighty and Glorious has mercy upon him by protecting him from hearing that discourse, either to guard him or to hinder him from error.

The shaykhs of this Way have said that sometimes the cause may lie in the presence of *jinn* who are not fit to hear, for the sessions of Sufis are not devoid of the presence of a congregation of *jinn*. I heard Abu Ali al-Daqqaq said, "One time I fell ill in Merv. I longed to return to Nishapur. I had a dream in which it seemed a voice was saying to me, 'It is not possible for you to leave this city, for a gathering of *jinn* is enjoying your discourse and is present at your sessions, so for their sake, remain here.'"

A wise man said that the human being was created with only one tongue, but with two eyes and two ears so that he may hear and see more than he says. Ibrahim ibn Adham was invited to a banquet. When he sat down, the guests began to gossip. He remarked, "It is our custom to eat the meat course after the bread, but you have begun by eating the meat!" (He was pointing to the saying of God, "*Would one of you like to eat the dead flesh of his brother? No, you would abhor it*" [59:12]).

A Sufi said, "Silence is the tongue of forbearance." Another said, "Learn silence as you have learned speech. Speech will guide you, and silence will protect you." It is said, "The chastity of the tongue is its silence." And it is said, "The tongue is like a beast of prey. If you do not tie it up, it will attack you."

Abu Hafs was asked, "Which is better for the Friend of God, speech or silence?" He replied, "If the one who speaks knew what disasters there are in speech, he would be silent even if he lived as long as Noah, and if the one who keeps silent knew what disasters there are in silence, he would pray to God Most High twice as much as Noah did until he could speak."

It is said that the silence of ordinary people is of the tongue, the silence of the gnostics is of the heart, and the silence of the lovers is to protect the secrets of their inner selves. A Sufi was told, "Speak!" He said, "I don't have a tongue!" "Then listen!" "There is no place within me where I can listen!"

One of the Sufi's said, "I lived thirty years in which I did not hear my tongue except from my heart. Then I lived another thirty years in which I did not hear my heart except from my tongue." Another said, "Even if you silenced your tongue, you would not be saved from the talk of your heart. Even if you became old and dried up, you would not be purified from the chatter of your ego. Even if you strove with every effort, your soul would not speak to you, for it is the concealer of the inner secret."

It is said, "The tongue of the ignorant is the key of his destruction." And it is said, "When the lover keeps silent, he perishes. When the gnostic keeps silent, he rules."

I heard Muhammad ibn al-Husayn say . . . that Fudayl ibn Iyad said, "Whoever counts his talk as part of his work will talk little except in what concerns him."

8
ON FEAR (*KHAWF*)

God Most High said, *"They call upon their Lord fearing and desiring"* [32:16].

Abu Bakr Muhammad ibn Abd al-Hiri al-Adl informed us . . . through Abu Hurayra that the Messenger of God said, "No one who weeps from the fear of God Most High can enter the fire any more than milk can re-enter the udder. The dust of the Way of God and the smoke of hell will never be mingled in a servant's nostrils."

Abu Naim ibn Muhammad ibn Ibrahim al-Muhrijani related . . . through Qatadah that the Messenger of God said, "If you knew what I know you would laugh little and weep much." Fear is an emotion connected to the future. A person only fears that something hated will befall him or that something loved will escape him and this cannot happen except with future events. Fear does not attach to what exists now.

Fear of God Most High means that one fears that God will punish him, either in this world or in the next. God, glory to Him, has obliged the servants to fear Him. He said, *"So fear, if you are believers"* [3:175] and He said, *"So let it be Me that you are afraid of"* [16:51]. And

He has praised the believers for fear, *"They fear their Lord above them"* [16:50].

I heard Abu Ali al-Daqqaq say, "Fear has degrees: Fear (*khawf*), dread (*khashiyah*), and awe (*haybah*). Fear is a condition and an effect of faith. God Most High said, *"So fear Me (khafuni) if you are believers"* [3:175]. Dread is a condition of knowledge. God Most High said, *"Only those among His servants who know, dread (yakhshi) God"* [35:28]. Awe is a condition of realization. God Most High said, *"Be wary of God Himself"* [3:28].

I heard Abu Abd al-Rahman al-Sulami say . . . that Abu Hafs said, "Fear is the whip of God with which he drives vagrants from His door." Abu 'l-Qasim al-Hakim said, "Fear is of two sorts, fright (*ruhba*) and dread (*khashiya*). The frightened person takes refuge in flight when he has become afraid. The person who senses dread takes refuge in the Lord."

He said, "'To stand in terror' (*rahaba*) and 'to flee' (*haraba*) may properly be said to have a single meaning, like 'he attracted' (*jadhaba*) and 'he drew' (*jabadha*). When someone flees, he has been drawn by his own desires like those monks (*ruhban*) who follow their instincts or desires [in devising a form of religious life that flees from the world]. But when they have been reined in by the reins of knowledge and are established in the truth of the divine law, it is dread (*khashiya*)."

I heard Muhammad ibn al-Husayn say . . . that Abu Hafs said, "Fear is the lamp of the heart by means of which whatever is good and bad in it is made visible." I heard Abu Ali al-Daqqaq say, "Fear is when your ego does not make excuses with 'perhaps' or 'later'." I heard Muhammad ibn al-Husayn say . . . that Abu Umar al-Dimashqi said, "The man of fear is the one who fears his own ego more than he fears satan." Ibn al-Jalla said, "The one who fears is the one who finds security amid fearful things."

The person of fear, it is said, is not a person who

weeps and rubs his eyes. The person of fear is only he who abandons that for which he is afraid he will be punished. Fudayl was asked, "Why do we never see anyone who fears God?" He answered, "If you were fearers, you would see fearers. The fearer is not seen except by those who fear. It is the woman who has lost a child who likes to see another woman who has lost a child."

Yahya ibn Muadh said, "How sad is the case of the son of Adam! If he feared the fire as he fears poverty, he would have entered the garden." Shah al-Kirmani said, "The sign of fear is perpetual sadness." Abd al-Qasim al-Hakim said, "Someone who is afraid of something runs away from it, but someone who is afraid of God Almighty and Glorious runs to Him."

Dhu 'l-Nun al-Misri was asked, "When will the way of fear become easy for the servant?" He replied, "When he assigns himself the position of a sick person and abstains from everything for fear of lengthening his illness."

Muadh ibn Jabal said, "The heart of the believer is not at rest and his alarm is not quieted until he puts the bridge of hell behind him." Bishr al-Hafi said, "Fear of God is a king who will only dwell in the heart of a pious one." Abu Uthman al-Hiri said, "The shame of the fearer in his fear is reliance upon his fear, for it is a hidden affair." Al-Wasiti said, "Fear is a veil between God Most High and His servant." This statement contains an ambiguity. It means that the one who fears looks toward a moment other than the present, while the Sufis, the sons of the moment, pay no attention to the future. "The virtues of the righteous are the flaws of those brought close."

I heard Muhammad ibn al-Husayn say . . . that Nuri said, "The fearer flees from his Lord to his Lord." A Sufi said, "The sign of fear is amazement and standing before the door of the unknown." I heard Abu Abd Allah al-Sufi say . . . when Junayd was questioned about fear, he said, "It is the expectation of punishment with every breath." I heard Abu Abd al-Rahman al-Sulami say . . . that Abu Sulayman al-Darani said, "Fear does not leave a heart without destroying it." And I heard him say . . . that Abu Uthman said, "Integrity in fear is to be scrupulous about faults both outer and inner." Dhu 'l-Nun said, "Fear never leaves people of the Way. If fear disappears from them, they have strayed from the Way." Hatim al-Asamm said, "Everything has an ornament and the ornament of worship is fear. The sign of fear is the cutting short of worldly hope."

A man exclaimed to Bishr al-Hafi, "I find you to be afraid of death!" "To come before God Almighty and Glorious," replied Bishr, "is a serious matter."

I heard Abu Ali al-Daqqaq say, "I went to visit Abu Bakr ibn Furak in his last illness. When he saw me, tears came to his eyes. I said, 'If God Most High wills, He will cure and heal you.' 'Do you believe me to be afraid of death?' he asked to me. 'I am only afraid of what is beyond death!'"

Ali ibn Ahmad al-Ahwazi informed us . . . on the authority of Abd al-Rahman ibn Said ibn Mawhib from Ayisha that she said, "O Messenger of God, *'Those who will bring what they have brought while their hearts are full of dread'* [23:60]—is this the man who steals, commits adultery, and drinks wine?" "No," he said, "Rather the man who fasts, prays, and gives alms, and fears that they will not be accepted from him."

Ibn Mubarak said, "This means the person whom fear agitates until continuous self-observation dwells in his heart in private and in public." I heard Muhammad ibn al-Husayn said . . . that Ibrahim ibn Shayban, says, "When fear dwells in a heart it sets fire to the places of lust within it and drives away from it the wish for the world."

It is said, "Fear is the power of the knowledge of how God's decrees come into effect." And it is said, "Fear moves and troubles the heart because of the majesty of the Lord."

Abu Sulayman al-Darani said, "It is necessary that nothing overpower the heart but fear. When hope overpowers the heart, it becomes corrupted." Then he said [to one of his followers], "Ahmad, it is through fear that they advanced. When they allowed it to perish, they stopped!"

Al-Wasiti said, "Fear and hope are two tethers that hold people back from falling into egotism." And he said, "When the Truth manifests to one's inner being, no space remains in it for hope or fear."

There is an ambiguity in this statement. It means that when the evidences of Truth have torn up the foundations of someone's inner being, they take it over. No possibility remains for the recollection of ordinary things. Hope and fear, however, are signs of the persistence of perception according to the ordinary limitations of mortality.

Husayn ibn Mansur al-Hallaj said, "When anyone fears something other than God Almighty and Glorious, or hopes for something other than Him, the doors of everything are locked against him. Anxiety and imagination are given power over him. He is veiled with seventy veils, the least of which is doubt."

The Sufis feel an intense fear produced by thinking about the consequences of actions and dreading the loss of their state. God Most High said, *"And there appeared to them from God what they never counted upon"* [39:47], and He said, *"Have We not informed you of the greatest losers in regard to works? Those whose efforts go astray in the life of this world, while they hold they are produc - ing well"* [18:103-104]. Who could wish for the state of someone whose condition is reversed, who is afflicted by the taint of ugly actions, who has traded intimacy with God for alienation from Him and presence for absence? I often heard Abu Ali al-Daqqaq recite:

You thought well of the days when things went well,
Had no fear of the evil that destiny brings.
The nights made excuses, and you were fooled.
In the clarity of night, the clouds appear.

I heard Mansur ibn Khalaf al-Maghribi tell of two
men who were spiritual students together for some time.
Then one of them traveled and became separated from
his friend. A long while passed and nothing was heard of
him. In the meantime, the other student entered the bor-
der wars against the Byzantines where a masked man in
armor came out against the Muslims in search of duels.
One of the Muslim heroes engaged with him, and the
Byzantine killed him. Then a second—he killed him.
Then a third arose, and he killed him as well. Finally the
Sufi came out to him, and they fought. The Byzantine
uncovered his face—and it was his friend with whom he
had shared so many years of training and service! The
Sufi asked, "What is your story?" His friend answered
that he had turned away from Islam and mixed with the
Byzantines, that children had been born to him, and
that he had accumulated property. "And all the Koran
that you used to recite?" "I do not remember a letter of
it," he replied. "Do not do this," urged the Sufi. "Come
back!" "That I will not do," he said, "for among the
Byzantines I have rank and wealth. So turn back or I
will certainly do to you what I have done to these others!" "Know that you have killed three Muslims," the
Sufi said. "It is not for you to be disdainful about turning
back! Turn back yourself, and I will give you time!" But
the man turned and fled so that the Sufi followed him,
stabbed him, and killed him. After all that effort and the
endurance of all that discipline, he was killed as a
Christian!"

It is said that when the events involving Iblis took
place, the angels Gabriel and Michael began to cry. They

wept for a long time. Then God Most High asked them, "Why do you cry all these tears?" "O our Lord," they said, "We are not safe from Your plot!" "This whole creation," said God Most High, "is not safe from My plot."

It is related that Sari al-Saqati said, "I look at my nose so many times a day for fear that it will have turned black from the punishment I dread!" Abu Hafs said, "For forty years it has been by private belief that God Most High looks upon me with displeasure, and my works point to that." Hatim al-Asamm said, "Do not be fooled by a sound position, for no place is safer than paradise, and there Adam encountered what he encountered. Do not be fooled by many acts of worship, for Iblis, after the length of his service, encountered what he encountered. Do not be fooled by much knowledge, for Balam used to know the greatest name of God, and see what he encountered! Do not be fooled by the sight of the righteous, for no personality was of greater worth than Prophet Muhammad, but meeting him did not profit his relatives and enemies."

One day Ibn Mubarak went out to his companions and said, "Yesterday I was bold towards God Almighty and Glorious! I asked Him for His paradise."

It is said that Jesus traveled with one of the righteous of the Children of Israel. A sinner notorious among the Jews for corruption, followed after them. He sat down a little away from them and, contrite, prayed to God Most Glorious, "O God, forgive me." The righteous man prayed as well, and said, "O God, do not join me together tomorrow with that disobedient man." God Most High revealed to Jesus, "I have answered the prayers of both of them at once. I have turned back that righteous one from religion, and I have pardoned that sinner!"

Dhu 'l- Nun al-Misri said, "I asked a man of knowledge, 'Why are you called insane?' He told me, 'When I had been held back from Him for a long time, I became mad for fear of permanent separation from Him in the next world.'" With this meaning they have recited:

If what is in me were of rock, He would dissolve it,
So how is a creation of clay to endure Him?

A Sufi said, "I have not seen a man with greater hope for this community or greater fear for himself than Ibn Sirin."

It is told that Sufyan al-Thawri became ill. When his diagnostic sample was presented to the doctor for examination, he remarked, "This is a man whose liver has been disrupted by fear." He came and felt his pulse and said, "I did not know that there was the like of him in the religion."

Shibli was asked, "Why does the sun grow pale when it sets?" He answered, "Because it is being removed from a public place, and it grows pale from fear of the situation. Thus, when his departure from the world draws near, the believer's complexion becomes pale, for he is frightened by the situation. And when the sun rises, it rises radiant. Likewise the believer: when he is resurrected he will come forth from his grave with a shining face."

It is related that Ahmad ibn Hanbal said, "I asked my Lord Almighty and Glorious to open to me a door of fear. It was opened, and I feared for my sanity. So I said, 'O Lord, give to me to the extent that I can bear.' So that passed off from me."

9

ON HOPE (RAJA)

God Most High said, "*Whoever hopes to meet with his Lord—the reward of God is nigh*" [29:5].

Abu 'l Husayn ibn Ahmad al-Ahwazi informed us . . . that al-Ala ibn Zayd said, "I came in to see Malik ibn Dinar and found that Shahr ibn Hawshab was with him. When we left his company, I said to Shahr, 'May God Most High have mercy upon you. Enrich me. God Most High has enriched you!' 'Certainly,' he said. 'My aunt, Umm al-Darda, related to me from Abu 'l- Darda, from the Prophet that Gabriel said, "Your Lord Almighty and Glorious said, 'My servant who has worshiped Me, hoped In Me, and not associated anything with Me, I have for given you for whatever proceeded from you. Were you to meet Me with errors and sins enough to fill the whole earth, I would meet you with the same amount of forgiveness and forgive you and not care."

Ali ibn Ahmad informed us . . . through Anas ibn Malik that the Messenger of God said, "On the day of judgment God Most High will say, 'Bring out of the fire anyone in whose heart is faith to the amount of a grain of barley.' Then He will say, 'Bring out of the fire anyone in whose heart is faith to the amount of a mustard seed.' Then He will say, 'By My Power and Majesty, I will not make anyone who has believed in Me for one moment, night or day, like someone who has not believed in Me at all."

Hope is the attachment of the heart to something loved that may occur in the future. Just as fear falls upon future time, so hope arises because of something to which one looks forward. The livelihood and freedom of hearts is through hope.

The difference between hope and expectation is that expectation causes laziness in the one who has it so that he does not travel the road of effort and endeavor, while the one who has hope is the opposite. Thus hope is praiseworthy, and expectation is condemnable.

The shaykhs have discoursed on hope. Shah al-Kirmani said, "The sign of hope is good obedience." Ibn al-Khubayq said, "Hope is of three kinds. One kind of person will do good and hope for acceptance. A second kind will do evil, then repent and hope for forgiveness. The third kind is the lying person who persists in sin and says that he hopes for forgiveness. If someone knows himself to be doing wrong, his fear must predominate over his hope." It is said, "Hope is trust in the liberality of the Generous and Loving One." And it is said, "Hope is seeing Majesty with the eye of Beauty." Hope is said to be "the heart's nearness to the benevolence of the Lord," and "the joy of the innermost heart at the goodness of the hereafter," and "to regard the breadth of God's mercy."

I heard Abu Abd al-Rahman al-Sulami say . . . that Abu Ali al-Rudhbari said, "Fear and hope are like the two wings of a bird. When they are balanced, the bird is balanced and its flight is perfect. When one of the two is defective, its flight is defective, and if they both go, the bird is at the edge of death."

And I heard him say . . . that Ahmad ibn Asim al-Antaki was asked, "What is the sign of hope in the servant?" and said, "When virtue and excellence surround the servant he is inspired to gratitude, hoping for the perfection of blessing from God Most High upon him in this world and the perfection of His forgiveness in the next." Abu Abd Allah ibn Khafif said, "Hope is to rejoice in the existence of His grace." And he said, "Hope is the heart's finding rest in seeing the generosity of the hoped-for Beloved."

I heard Abu Abd al-Rahman al-Sulami say he heard Abu Uthman al-Maghribi say, "If someone excites hope in himself, he is idle. If he excites fear in himself, he despairs. Best is sometimes some of the one and sometimes some of the other." And I heard him say . . . from Bakr ibn Sulaym al-Sawwaf, "We went to see Malik ibn Anas on the night he died and said, 'Abu Abd Allah, how are you?' 'I don't know what to tell you,' he said, 'except that you will see things beyond reckoning from the forgiveness of God Most High!' We did not leave him then until we had closed his eyes."

Yahya ibn Muadh prayed, "The hope I place in You when I sin almost drowns the hope I place in You when I am performing good works. In the course of good works I find I rely upon sincerity. How am I to preserve that when I am well-known for calamities? But in sin I find I rely upon Your forgiveness. How will You not forgive, when Your quality is generosity?"

They were talking to Dhu 'l-Nun al-Misri during his last illness. He said, "Don't worry about me. I am amazed by how many kindnesses God Most High has shown me!" Yahya ibn Muadh said, "My God, the sweetest gift in my heart is hope of You. The most pleasant word on my tongue is praise of You. My dearest hour is the hour of meeting You."

In a commentary on the Koran it is written that the Messenger of God came in on his Companions from the Gate of Bani Shaybah and saw them laughing. He said,

"Do you laugh? If you knew what I know, you would laugh little and weep much." He left, but then he came back and said, "Gabriel descended to me with the word of the Most High, *'Tell My servants that I am the Forgiving, the Compassionate.'* [15:49]."

Abu 'l- Husayn Ali ibn Ahmad al-Ahwazi related to us . . . that Ayisha said, "I heard the Messenger of God say, 'God Most High laughs at the hopelessness and despondency of the servants when mercy is so near them.' 'By my father and mother, Messenger of God,' I asked, 'does our Lord Almighty and Glorious then laugh?' 'By Him in Whose Hand I am, He certainly laughs!' he said. She said, 'Good things beyond reckoning come to us when He laughs.'"

Know that the laughter used to describe Him is a quality of His action. It means the manifestation of His grace as in the saying, "The earth laughs with vegetation." His laughter at their despondency manifests the reality of His grace by doubling the bounties His servants had awaited from Him.

It is said that a fire-worshipper sought the hospitality of Abraham the Friend of God who said to him, "If you become a Muslim, I will grant you my hospitality." The fire-worshipper exclaimed, "If I become a Muslim? What kind of a favor is that for you to do?" God Most High revealed to Abraham, "O Abraham, will you not feed him unless he changes his religion? For seventy years We have fed him in his unbelief—if you were to show him hospitality for one night, what is it to you?" Abraham went in pursuit of the fire-worshipper and offered his hospitality. The man asked him, "What brought on this change?" So he recounted what had happened. The fire-worshipper marveled, "Is it thus that He deals with me?" Then he said, "Spread Islam before me!" And he became a Muslim.

I heard Abu Ali al-Daqqaq say that Abu Sahl al-

Suluki saw Abu Sahl al-Zajjaj, who used to speak of the threat of eternal punishment, in a dream. He asked him, "How are you? What is your condition?" Al-Zajjaj replied, "We have found the matter easier than we had imagined."

I heard Abu Bakr ibn Ishkib say, "I saw Abu Sahl al-Suluki in a dream in the shape of indescribable beauty. I said to him, 'O Master, through what have you been granted this?' He answered, 'Through my thinking well of my Lord.'"

Malik ibn Dinar was seen in a dream. He was asked, "What has God done with you?" "I was brought before my Lord Almighty and Glorious with many sins," he replied. "My good thoughts of Him made them vanish from me."

It is related that the Prophet said, "God Almighty and Glorious said in a sacred Tradition, 'I am present with My servant's thought of Me, and I am with him when he remembers Me. If he remembers Me in himself, I remember him in Myself. If he remembers Me in company, I remember him in a company better than his. If he draws near to Me by a hand's length, I draw near to him by an arm's length. If he draws near to Me by an arm's length, I draw near to him by a span. If he comes to Me walking, I come to him running.'" Abu Naim Abd al-Malik ibn al-Hasan al-Isfarayani informed us . . . through Abu Hurayra that the Prophet said this.

It is told that once Ibn Mubarak was fighting an idolater when the time for the idolater's prayer arrived. He asked for a respite. It was granted. When he prostrated himself to the sun, Ibn Mubarak wanted to strike him with his sword, but he heard something speaking in the air that said, "*Keep your agreements if an agreement is made*" [17:34], so he restrained himself. When the fire-worshipper had finished praying, he asked, "Why did you hold back from what you had in mind?" Ibn

Mubarak recounted to him what he had heard. The fire-worshipper cried, "What an excellent lord is a lord who will reprove his friend for the sake of his enemy!" So he became a Muslim, and made good his Islam.

It is said that God only involved believers with sin when He had named Himself the Forgiver. If He were to say, "I will not forgive sins," no Muslim would sin at all. Thus as He said, "*God will not forgive that anything be set equal to Him,*" [4:48]. No Muslim will ever set anything equal to Him, but as He said, "*And He will forgive what is less than that to whom He will*" [4:48], they hope for His forgiveness.

It is told that Ibrahim ibn Adham said, "I had waited a long time for the holy precincts of the Kabah to be empty of all but me. One dark night when there was a heavy rain, the precincts were deserted, so I began to make the circumambulation, saying, 'O God, make me free of sin! O God, make me free of sin!' Then I heard a voice from the unseen say to me, 'O Ibn Adham, you are asking Me for freedom from sin. Everybody is asking Me for freedom from sin. If I were to free you from sin, to whom would I be Merciful?'"

It is said that in his last illness, Abu 'l- Abbas ibn Shurayh had a dream. It was as if the resurrection had arrived when the All-Powerful will say, "Where are the people of knowledge?" Abu 'l- Abbas said, "They came," and He demanded, "What have you done with what you knew?" We answered, "O Lord, we have fallen short and done ill." Again the question was asked as if He were not satisfied and wanted another answer. So I said, "As for me, there is no setting of equals to You in my record. You promised to forgive what is less than that!" "Go forth all." He said, "I have forgiven you!" Abu 'l- Abbas died three nights later.

It is said that a heavy drinker gathered a drinking party and gave a young slave four dirhams, ordering him to buy some fruit for the company. The slave passed by the door of one of Mansur ibn Ammar's meetings. The shaykh was asking something for a poor man, and saying, "Whoever turns four dirhams over to me, I will pray for him four prayers." The slave gave him the dirhams. "For what do you wish me to pray?" Mansur asked. "I have a master," he replied. "I want to be free of him! Pray for me about that, Mansur!" "What else?" "That God Most High recompense me for my dirhams. Pray for me about that." "And what else?" "That God turn to my master [so that he might repent]." He prayed. "And what else?" "That God forgive me, my master, you, and this company." So Mansur prayed for that. The slave returned to his master. "What took you so long?" he demanded. The young man told him the story. "For what did he pray?" asked his master. "I asked emancipation for myself." "Go. You are free," his master said. "What was the second?" "That God recompense me for the dirhams." "There are four thousand dirhams for you," he said. "What was the third?" "That God turn to you." "I turn in repentance to God Most High. What was the fourth?" "That God Most High forgive you and me and the gathering and the one I have mentioned." "This alone I cannot do!" he said. That night when he went to sleep he dreamed that a voice said to him, "You have done what you could do. See if I will not do what is for Me to do! I have forgiven you, the slave, Mansur ibn Ammar and all those who were present."

It is said that Raja al-Qaysi made many pilgrimages. One day, while he had stopped under the rainspout of the Kabah, he said, "My God, I give such-and-such a number of my pilgrimages to the Messenger, ten of them to his ten companions, two of them to my parents, and the remainder to the Muslims." He did not retain anything from them for himself. Then he heard a voice from the unseen say, "O you who show Us generosity! We will certainly forgive you, your parents and whoever has made a true profession of Islam."

It is related that Abd al-Wahhab ibn Abd al-Majid al-Thaqafi said, "I saw a funeral in which the bier was being carried by three men and a woman so I took the place of the woman. We went to the graveyard, prayed over the coffin, and buried the person. I asked the woman, 'What relation did this person have to you?' 'He was my son,' she told me.' 'Have you no neighbors to attend the funeral?' I asked. 'Yes,' she said, 'but they thought little of him.' 'Why should that be?' I asked. She said, 'He was effeminate!' I felt pity for her, so I brought her to my house and gave her money, grain, and clothing. That night when I slept I seemed to see a person come to me. Dressed in white clothes, he resembled the moon at its full. He began to thank me. 'Who are you?' I asked. 'I am that effeminate one you buried today,' he said. "My Lord has forgiven me because of people's contempt for me.'"

I heard Abu Ali al-Daqqaq say, "Abu Amr al-Bikandi one day passed by a side street and saw a group of people who wanted to expel a youth from the neighborhood because of his corrupt ways while a woman cried. He was told she was his mother. Abu Amr felt pity for her. He interceded with them for the youth, saying, 'Give him his liberty this time. If he returns to his corruption, then do as you like.' So they let him go, and Abu Amr left. After some days he was crossing that lane again and heard an old woman crying behind the same door. 'Perhaps the youth has returned to his corruption,' he said to himself, 'and they have banished him from the district.' So he knocked on her door and inquired about the youth's situation. The old woman came out and said, 'He has died!' He asked her about his state. She said, 'When his time approached, he said, "Don't tell the neighbors of my death. I have made trouble for them—

they will be glad and will not come to my funeral. But when you bury me, bury with me this ring of mine on which is written, 'In the Name of God,' and when you have finished the burial, make intercession for me with my Lord Almighty and Glorious.'" She continued, 'I did as he wished, and when I turned from the head of the grave I heard his voice saying, "Leave me, Mother—I have come before a generous Lord."'

It is said that the inspiration from God Most High came to Prophet David, "Say to them that I did not create them in order to place My hopes in them—I only created them so that they would hope in Me!"

I heard Muhammad ibn al-Husayn say . . . that Ibrahim al-Utrush said, "We were sitting in Baghdad with Maruf al-Karkhi on the banks of the Euphrates when some young people passed by us in a boat, beating tambourines, drinking, and making merry. We said to Maruf, 'Look at them, how flagrantly they disobey God Most High! Pray to God against them!' He opened his hands and said, 'My God, as you have made them joyful in this world, make them joyful in the next.' 'But we asked you to curse them!' we cried. 'If He makes them joyful in the next world, He will have brought them to repentance,' replied Maruf."

I heard Abu 'l- Hasan Abd al-Rahman ibn Ibrahim ibn Muhammad al-Mazaki say . . . that Abu Abd Allah al-Husayn ibn Abd Allah ibn Said said, "Judge Yahya ibn Aktham was a friend of mine. He loved me, and I loved him. Yahya died and I longed to see him in a dream and ask him, 'What has God Most High done with you?' One night I did see him. I asked, 'What has God Most High done with you?' 'He has forgiven me,' he said, 'except that He rebuked me and then said to me, "Yahya, you confused Me with things in the world." I said, "Yes, Lord." I trusted in a hadith related to me by Abu Muawiyah al-Darir . . . through Abu Hurayra that the

Messenger of God said that You had said, 'I would be ashamed to punish a grey head with the fire.' "He said, 'I have forgiven you, Yahya, and My Prophet spoke the truth. Nevertheless, you confused Me with things in the world!'"

10
ON SORROW (*HUZN*)

God Most High has said, "*And they said, 'Praise be to God Who has made sadness depart from us'*" [35:34].

Ali ibn Ahmad ibn Abdan informed us . . . through Abu Said al-Khudri that the Messenger of God said, "Nothing afflicts a believing servant, whether sickness or fatigue or sadness or pain that troubles him, without God Most High removing some of his evils from him."

Sadness, *huzn*, is a state that contracts the heart from being scattered in the valleys of unconsciousness. Sadness is one of the characteristics of those involved in active search. I heard Abu Ali al-Daqqaq say, "The sorrowful person experiences in the Way of God in a month what, without his sorrow, he would not experience in years."

A hadith says, "God loves every sorrowing heart." And in the Torah, "When God loves a servant, He puts a mourner in his heart and when He is dissatisfied with a servant, He puts a festive flute in his heart." It is related that the Messenger of God was in continuous sorrow and reflection. Bishr ibn al-Harith said, "Sadness is a king who, when he dwells in a place, does not please to have anyone else dwell there." It is said that a heart that has no sadness in it is as a house with no one living in it; it falls into ruins.

Abu Said al-Qarshi said, "The tears of sorrow blind, while the tears of yearning make the sight dim but do not blind." God Most High said, "*And his [Jacob's] eyes grew white from sorrow and he fell into silent melan - choly*" [12:84].

Ibn Khafif said, "Sadness deters the ego from the pursuit of pleasure." Rabia al-Adawiyyah heard a man lamenting, "What great sorrow!" "You should cry, 'What little sorrow!'" she returned. "If you were really sorrowful, you would not be able to breathe!"

Sufyan ibn Uyaynah said, "If a sorrowful person in this community wept, God Most High would have mercy on the whole community for the sake of his tears." Dawud al-Tai was dominated by sadness. He used to say, at night, "My God, concern for You ruins other concerns for me and comes between me and sleep." And he used to say, "How should a person for whom every moment means grave misfortune seek to be distracted from sorrow?"

It is said that sorrow prevents one from eating, while fear prevents one from sinning. A Sufi was asked, "What indicates a person's sorrow?" He replied, "The extent of his groaning." Sari-al-Saqati said, "I would love for the sadness of all humanity to be cast upon me."

Many people have discussed sadness. All of them have said that only sadness for the sake of the next world is praiseworthy. Sadness for the sake of this world is not commendable. Only Abu Uthman al-Hiri disagrees. He said that every sort of sadness that is not the result of a sin has merit and increase in it for the believer. If it does not necessarily make him one of the spiritual elite, still it must purify him.

There was a shaykh who, when one of his companions went on a journey, used to say, "If you see any sorrowing person, send him my greetings." I heard Abu Ali al-Daqqaq say, "There was a Sufi who used to ask the sun when it set, 'Did you rise today upon one who sorrows?'" No one was able to see Hasan al-Basri without thinking that he had been newly afflicted by troubles. Waki said when Fudayl died, "Today sorrow has left the earth."

One of our predecessors said, "The majority of the good deed the believer will find in his record on the last day will be care and sorrow." I heard Abu Abd Allah al-Shirazi say . . . that Fudayl ibn Iyad said, "Those who came before us used to say that everything owes a tithe and the tithe of the mind is long sadness."

I heard Abu Abd al-Rahman al-Sulami say . . . that Abu 'l-Husayn al-Warraq said, "One day I asked Abu Uthman al-Hiri about sorrow. He said, 'A sorrowful person has no leisure for questions about sorrow. Strive to find sorrow—then ask!'"

11

ON HUNGER AND THE ABANDONMENT OF LUST (*JU* AND *TARK AL-SHAHWA*)

God Most High has said, "*And We shall try them with something of fear and hunger*" [2:155], and at the end of the verse, "*and give good news to the patient.*" So He sent them good news of a beautiful reward following patience in the endurance of hunger. And He has said, "*And they prefer [others] over them - selves even though they may be in need.*" [59:9].

Ali ibn Ahmad al-Ahwazi informed us . , that Anas ibn Malik said, "Fatima went to the Messenger of God with a bit of bread. 'What is this morsel, Fatima?' he asked. 'A piece of flat bread [or barley bread] I baked,' said she. 'I could not feel at ease in myself until I had brought it to you.' 'It was the first food that had entered your father's mouth for three days,' he told her."

On this account hunger is one of the characteristics of the Sufis. It is the first pillar of spiritual struggle. Travelers on the Way are graded according to how habituated they have become to hunger and forsaking food. They have found springs of wisdom in hunger and there are many stories told of them about this.

I heard Muhammad ibn Ahmad ibn Muhammad al-Sufi say . . . that Ibn Salim said, "The proper conduct with regard to hunger is for a person to diminish what he is accustomed to eating by an amount no larger than a cat's ear." It is said that Sahl ibn Abd Allah ate food only once every twenty-five days. When the month of Ramadan came he did not eat until the next new moon and broke his fast every evening only with water.

Yahya ibn Muadh said, "If hunger were a thing sold in the marketplace, it would not have been right for people who hope for the hereafter to buy anything else there."

We have been told that Muhammad ibn Abd Allah ibn Ubayd said . . . that Sahl ibn Abd Allah said, "When God Most High created the world, he placed sin and ignorance in satiation and knowledge and wisdom in hunger." He also said, "For novices, hunger is an act of discipline. For the repentant, it is an experiment. For ascetics, it is a policy. For gnostics, it is a gift."

I heard Abu Ali al-Daqqaq say, "A Sufi visited a shaykh and found him crying. He asked, 'What makes you weep?' The shaykh replied, 'I am hungry.' 'How could someone like you cry out of hunger?' the dervish exclaimed. 'Be silent!' returned the shaykh. 'Don't you know that His object in my hunger is for me to cry?'"

I heard Abu Abd Allah al-Shirazi say . . . that Mukhallad said, "Hajjaj ibn Farafisah, who was with us in Damascus, would go fifty nights without drinking or satisfying his hunger with something to eat." And I heard him say . . . that Abu Abd Allah Ahmad ibn Yahya al-Jalla said, "Abu Turab al-Nakhshabi left to go to Mecca through the desert. Afterwards we asked what he had eaten on the way. He answered, 'When I left Basra I ate once at Nabaj and once in Dhat Irq. From Dhat Irq I came to you.' He had crossed the desert eating only twice."

And I heard him say . . . that Abd al-Aziz ibn Umayr said, "A certain type of bird would fly forty mornings without eating anything. When these birds came back after many days, the fragrance of musk would emanate from them." Sahl ibn Abd Allah used to gather strength when he was hungry and weaken when he ate. Abu Uthman al-Maghribi said, "The one who attaches himself to divine Lordship will not eat for forty days. The one who attaches himself to Absolute Plenitude will not eat for eighty days."

I heard Abu Abd al-Rahman al-Sulami say . . . that Abu Sulayman al-Darani said, "The key of this world is satiation and the key of the next world is hunger." I heard Muhammad ibn Abd Allah ibn Ubaydullah say . . . that Abu Muhammad al-Istikhari said, "Sahl ibn Abd Allah was asked the state of a person who eats one meal a day. "It is the meal of the sincere." And two meals a day? "It is the meal of the believers." And three? "Tell your family to build a trough for you!" said he." And I heard him say . . . Yahya ibn Muadh said, 'Hunger is a light while satiation is a fire. Desire is like the firewood from which the conflagration is generated. Its flame will not be extinguished until it burns the one who keeps it." I heard Abu Hatim al-Sijistani say that he heard Abu Nasr al-Sarraj al-Tusi say, "A Sufi once visited a shaykh who presented him food and then asked him, 'For how many days have you not eaten?' 'For five days,' the man replied. 'Your hunger is the hunger of a miser,' the shaykh told him. 'You are wearing [decent] clothing while you go hungry? This is not the hunger of dervishes!'"

I heard Muhammad ibn al-Husayn say . . . that Abu Sulayman al-Darani said, "To give up one bite of my supper is dearer to me than to stand in prayer until the end of the night." And I heard him say that he heard Abu 'l-Qasim Jafar ibn Ahmad al-Razi say, "For years Abu 'l

Khayr al-Asqalani had a craving for fish. Then one day it appeared to him in a lawful context. When he stretched out his hand in order to eat it, the point of a fishbone caught his finger and entered that hand. He cried, "O Lord, this is what happens to someone who reaches for a desire that is lawful—what will happen to someone who reaches for an unlawful desire?"

I heard Abu Bakr ibn Furak say, "The result of following lawful desire is preoccupation with one's family. What do you suppose is the outcome of unlawful desire?"

I heard Rustam al-Shirazi say, "Abu Abd Allah ibn Khafif was at a banquet when one of his companions, because of the need he was in, reached for food before the shaykh did. Some of the shaykh's other companions wanted to reproach him for the fault thus displayed in his behavior, so one of them set just a bit of something to eat in front of that dervish. The dervish knew that he had been reproached for his bad conduct, so he resolved not to eat for fifteen days as a punishment and discipline for his lower self and a manifestation of his repentance for his fault—and he had already been in need before that." I heard Muhammad ibn Abd Allah al-Sufi say . . . Malik ibn Dinar says, "When someone conquers the desires of this world, satan is afraid of his shadow!" And I heard him say . . . that Abu Ali al-Rudhbari said, "When a Sufi said, after five days without food, 'I am hungry'—they would send him to the marketplace and command him to earn a living!"

I heard Abu Ali al-Daqqaq tell of a shaykh who said that the lust of the people of the fire had overcome their honor and manifested itself in their being assigned to the fire. And I heard him say, "Someone asked a dervish, 'Do you desire nothing?' He said, 'I desire, but I abstain.'"

A Sufi was asked, "Aren't you hungry?" He replied, "I hunger not to hunger." And it is just so. I heard Abu Abd al-Rahman al-Sulami say . . . that Abu Nasr al-Tammar said, "One night Bishr [al-Hafi] came to see me. I said, 'Praise be to God Who has brought you to me! Cotton reached us from Khurasan, so I gave it to my daughter, and she sold it and bought us meat. So break your fast with us.' He said, 'Were I to eat with anyone, I would eat with you.' Then he said, 'For years I have wished for eggplant and it has never fallen to me to eat it!' 'Surely in all that time there must have been eggplant that was lawful,' I objected. 'Not until the love of eggplant becomes pure for me,' he replied."

I heard Abd Allah ibn Bakawiya al-Sufi say that he heard Abu Ahmad al-Saghir say, "Every night Abu Abd Allah ibn Khafif ordered me to set before him ten raisins with which he would break his fast. One night I worried for him and put out fifteen raisins. He looked at them and said, 'Who ordered you to do this?' He ate ten of them and left the rest."

I heard Muhammad ibn Abd Allah ibn Ubaydullah say . . . that Abu Turab al-Nakhshabi said, "Only once did I grant my lower self its desires. It wanted bread and eggs. I was traveling. I turned off toward a village. Someone stood up and grabbed me and said, 'This one was with the thieves!' So they beat me seventy blows. Then one of them recognized me and cried, 'This is Abu Turab al-Nakhshabi!' They apologized. A man took me to his house out of hospitality and sympathy and laid before me bread and eggs. So I said to my lower self, 'Eat, after seventy blows!'"

12

ON HUMILITY AND SUBMISSIVENESS (*KHUSHU* AND *TAWADU*)

God Most High has said, "*The believers, who are humble in their prayers, have prospered*" [23:1-2].

Abu 'l- Hasan Abd al-Rahim ibn Ibrahim ibn Muhammad ibn Yahya al-Mazaki informed us . . . through Abd Allah ibn Masud that the Prophet said, "No one in whose heart is a grain of pride will enter the garden and no one in whose heart is a grain of faith will enter the fire."

A man asked, "O Messenger of God, what of a man who likes his clothes to be fine?" He said, "God Most High is beautiful and loves beauty. Pride is refusing the truth and showing disdain to people."

Ali ibn Ahmad al-Ahwazi informed us . . . that Anas ibn Malik said, "The Messenger of God used to visit the sick, attend funerals, ride a donkey, and respond to the invitations of slaves. The day of the conquest of Qurayzah and al-Nadir he rode upon a donkey whose halter and saddle were of common rope."

Kushu, humility, is to yield to the truth. *Tawadu*, lowliness, modesty in submission, is to abandon oneself to the truth and give up opposition to God's decrees. Hudhayfah said, "The first thing you will lose out of your religion will be humility."

Asked about humility, a Sufi replied, "Humility is the heart's standing before the Truth with total attention." Sahl ibn Abd Allah said, "Satan will not come near someone whose heart is humble." One of the signs of the presence of humility in the servant is that when he is angered, opposed or rejected, he takes it upon himself to meet that with acceptance.

A Sufi said, "Humility is to restrain the eyes from looking." Muhammad ibn Ali al-Tirmidhi said, "The man of humility is he in whom the fires of lust (attraction to pleasure) have been extinguished and the smoke of his breast abated, while the light of glorification has dawned in his heart. Since his lust has died and his heart has come to life, his limbs are humble."

Hasan al-Basri said, "Humility is perpetual fear attached to the heart." Junayd was asked about humility and said, "It is the abasement of hearts before the signs of the unknowable."

God Most High has said, *"The servants of the Beneficent are those who walk upon the earth with humility"* [25:63]. I heard Abu Ali al-Daqqaq say that the meaning of that was [to act] submissively and humbly. And I heard him say that these servants are people who, when they walk, do not reckon the soles of their shoes to be good.

The shaykhs have agreed that the place of humility is the heart. One of them saw a man of depressed and dejected appearance whose shoulders were knit and tense. "O so-and-so!" he said. "The place of humbleness is here"—pointing to his heart—"not here!"—pointing to his shoulders. And it is related that the Messenger of God saw a man who was absent-mindedly playing with his beard during his prayers. "If his heart possessed

humility," he said, "then his limbs would manifest it."
It is said that the defining condition of humility in
the prescribed prayer is that one does not know who is
on one's right or one's left. This implies, as it is said, that
humility is bowing one's head to attend to one's inner
state in accordance with the proper conduct for bearing
witness to the Truth.

It is said that humility is a fading that comes over
the heart when it becomes aware of the Lord, or else that
it is the heart's melting and drawing back before the
power of reality. Or, it is said, humility is the conquering
vanguard of awe or a shudder that comes upon the heart
suddenly with the shock of the unveiling of reality.

Fudayl ibn Iyad said that he used to hate to see a
man behaving as if he had a humility greater than what
was actually in his heart. Abu Sulayman al-Darani said,
"If all the people were to gather to humble me as I am
humbled when I am alone, they would not be able to do
it." It is said that someone who has no humbleness when
he is alone does not have it with others either. Umar ibn
Abdul-Aziz [one time ruler of the entire Islamic world]
never made a prostration of prayer except upon the dust
of the earth.

Ali ibn Ahmad al-Ahwazi informed us . . . from Ibn
Abbas that the Messenger of God said, "No one in whose
heart there is pride to the extent of a grain of mustard
seed will enter the garden." Mujahid said, "When God,
glory to Him, drowned the people of Noah, all the mountains loomed up, while Mount Judi was lowly, so God
made it the resting-place for Noah's ship."

Umar ibn al-Khattab used to hurry as he walked. He
used to say that he hurried to his work to take himself
far away from haughtiness.

Umar ibn Abd al-Aziz was writing something one
night while he had a guest with him. The lamp had
almost gone out. The guest said, "I will climb up to the

lamp and put it right." "No," said Umar. "It is not hospitality that a guest should be put to work!" "Then I will rouse the slave," he proposed. "No, he is sleeping the best part of his sleep," said Umar. He climbed up to the oil-flask and put oil in the lamp. "You yourself climb up there, Commander of the Faithful?" the guest exclaimed. "I went as Umar and I have come back as Umar," Umar said to him.

Abu Said al-Khudri has related that the Messenger of God used to feed his donkey, sweep the house, mend his sandals, patch his clothes, and milk the ewe. He would eat with his servant and labor along with him when he grew tired. He was not ashamed to carry merchandise home from the market for his family. He would shake hands with rich and poor and was the first to offer a greeting. He did not scorn anything that was offered to him to eat, even unripe dates. He made things easy. He was of a gentle disposition and possessed a natural generosity. It was wonderful to keep company with him. He had an open, cheerful face. He smiled without laughing loudly, was sad without becoming gloomy, humble without abasing himself, and liberal without being extravagant. He was soft-hearted and compassionate to every Muslim. He never belched from satiation or stretched his hand toward an object of selfish interest.

I heard Abu Abd al-Rahman al-Sulami say . . . that Fudayl ibn Iyad said, "The Koran-reciters of God are humble and lowly. The Koran-reciters of the magistrates are haughty and proud." He also said, "He who sees any value in himself has no share in the modesty of submission (*tawadu*)." Asked about lowliness, Fudayl said, "It is humbleness before the truth, yielding to it, and accepting it from whoever speaks it." He said, "God Glorious and Exalted revealed to the mountains, 'I will speak to a prophet upon one of you [mountains]!' So the mountains towered up. But Mount Sinai made itself low, so upon it

God, glory to Him, spoke to Moses."

I heard Muhammad ibn al-Husayn say . . . Junayd was asked of lowliness and said, "It is taking others under one's wing and behaving graciously towards them." Wahb said, "It is written in one of the books revealed by God Most High, 'I brought out the atoms [of future generations] from the loins of Adam and found no heart with fiercer modesty than the heart of Moses, so for that reason I chose him and spoke to him.'"

Ibn al-Mubarak said, "Haughtiness toward the rich and humility toward the poor is part of the modesty of submission." Abu Yazid al-Bistami was asked, "When is a man a possessor of lowliness?" He replied, "When he does not feel himself to possess either station or state and does not see among other people anyone worse than he."

It is said that humility is a blessing no one envies, while pride is a misfortune no one pities. Grandeur is in humility, and anyone who searches for it in pride will not find it. I heard Abu Abd al-Rahman al-Sulami say . . . Ibrahim ibn Shayban said, "Nobility is in humility, grandeur in awe of God, and freedom in contentment." And I also heard him say . . . that Ibn al-Arabi said, "I have been told that Sufyan al-Thawri said that the greatest men are of five kinds: a reenunciate scholar, a Sufi jurist, a humble rich man, a contented poor man, and a descendant of the Prophet who follows his practice and claims no special prestige."

Yahya ibn Muadh said, "Humility beautifies everyone, but it is more beautiful in the rich, pride makes everyone repulsive, but it is more repulsive in the poor!" Ibn Ata said, "Lowliness is to accept the truth from anyone."

It is told that Zayd ibn Thabit was riding. Ibn Abbas descended and took hold of his stirrup. "Uncle of God's Messenger, stop that!" Zayd cried. "This is the way we have been ordered to treat the learned ones among us," was the reply. So Zayd ibn Thabit grabbed the hand of Ibn Abbas and kissed it. "This is the way we have been ordered to treat the family of the Messenger of God!" said he.

Urwah ibn al-Zubayr said, "I saw Umar ibn al-Khattab with a full waterskin upon his shoulder. 'Commander of the Faithful! That is not suitable for you!' I exclaimed. 'Delegations of obedient subjects approached me. A feeling of superiority came into my ego. I wish to break it,' he answered. He went with the waterskin to the rooms of a woman who was one of the early Muslims of Medina and emptied it into her cistern."

I heard Abu Hatim al-Sijistani say that Abu Nasr al-Sarraj al-Tusi said that Abu Hurayra, while he was commander of Medina, was seen with a bundle of firewood on his back, saying "Make way for the prince!" Abd Allah ibn al-Razi said, "Lowliness is to give up making distinction in service."

I heard Muhammad ibn al-Husayn say . . . that Abu Sulayman al-Darani said, "Whoever sees any value in himself has not tasted the sweetness of service." But Yahya ibn Muadh said, "To show haughtiness to one who, on account of what he possesses, shows haughtiness to you is lowliness."

Shibli said, "My humiliation makes idle the humiliation of the Jews." A man came to Shibli, who asked, "What are you?" "Master, I am the dot under the letter '*b*'," he replied. "May you be my example," said Shibli, "since you do not assign yourself any station!" Ibn Abbas said, "It is part of lowliness that a man drink from the dregs of his brother." Bishr said, "Give greetings to the sons of this world by giving up greeting them."

Shuayb ibn al-Harb said, "I was circumambulating the Kabah when suddenly a man shoved me with his elbow. I turned to face him. It was Fudayl ibn Iyad. 'If you thought that someone worse than we two would attend the holy season, Abu Salih,' he said, 'how evil is what you thought!'"

A Sufi said, "During the circumambulation of the Kabah I saw a man preceded by people thanking and praising him so that because of him people were prevented from making the circumambulation. Some time later I saw him on the embankment in Baghdad begging. I was amazed. He said to me, "I made much of myself in a place where people humble themselves, so God, glory to Him, has tried me by humiliating me in a place where people give themselves airs."

Umar ibn Abd al-Aziz heard that one of his sons had bought a ring-stone for a thousand dirhams. Umar wrote to him, "I have been told that you bought a ring-stone for a thousand dirhams." When this letter of mine reaches you, sell the ring and fill a thousand stomachs. Get a ring for two dirhams and make its bezel of Chinese iron, and write there, 'God has mercy upon a man who knows his own worth.'"

A slave was offered to a prince for a thousand dirhams. When the price was named, the prince thought it more than seemed right for the purchase and put the money back in its coffer. The slave said, "O my master, buy me. In me is a trait worth a thousand dirhams for each of those dirhams there!" "What is it?" the buyer asked. "The smallest and least of it is that were you to buy me and set me over all of your slaves, it would not coarsen me. I would know that I am your servant." So the man bought him.

Raja ibn Haya has related that the clothes worn by Umar ibn Abd al-Aziz while delivering a public address were valued at twelve dirhams, including robe, turban, shirt, trousers, shoes, and cap.

It is said that Abd Allah ibn Muhammad ibn Wasi

paraded himself [in a way] that invited disapproval. His father said to him, "You are aware that I bought your mother for three hundred dirhams and your father— may God not make many more fathers like yours among the Muslims! Yet you walk like that?" I heard Muhammad ibn al-Husayn say . . . that Hamdun al-Qassar said, "Lowliness is that you see no one in need of you either in this world or the next." Ibrahim ibn Adham said, "I only rejoiced in my submission to God on three occasions. One time I was on a ship where there was a man given to laughter and ridicule. He used to say, 'We seized the infidels in the land of the Turks like this: we took hold of the hair of their head and shook them. That pleased me because there was no one on the ship more contemptible in his eyes than myself. On another occasion I was in a mosque, sick. The muezzin entered and said, 'Get out!' I was not able, so he grabbed my feet and dragged me outside of the mosque. On the third occasion I was in Syria. I was wearing skins and when I looked at them I could not tell whether there were more hairs or more lice upon them, and that made me happy."

In another account Ibrahim ibn Adham said, "Nothing has ever delighted me as I was delighted one day when I was sitting down and a man came and urinated on me." It is said that Abu Dharr and Bilal quarreled. Abu Dharr insulted Bilal about being black. Bilal complained to the Messenger of God who said, "Abu Dharr, something of the pride of the days of ignorance remains in your heart." Abu Dharr threw himself on the ground and swore that he would not raise his head until Bilal trod on his cheek with his foot. And he did not get up until Bilal had done that.

Hasan ibn Ali passed by two boys who had a few crusts of bread. They invited him to be their guest. He stopped and ate with them. Then he took them to his house and fed and clothed them. He said, "They are the ones who were generous, because they had nothing but what they fed me, and I had more than that."

It is said that Umar ibn al-Khattab was distributing clothing, taken as spoils of war, among the Companions. He sent a Yemeni garment to Muadh. Muadh sold it and bought six slaves whom he set free. Umar heard of this while he was dividing the clothes that remained, so he sent him a lesser garment beside the first. Muadh scolded him. Umar said, "Don't scold me! It is because you sold the first one." "Who cares?" said Muadh. "Give me my share—I swear I will hit you over the head with it!" "This head of mine is in front of you," replied Umar. "Perhaps an old man will treat an old man gently."

13

ON OPPOSING THE EGO AND REMEMBERING ONE'S FAULTS (*MUKHALAFAT AL-NAFS* AND *DHIKR UYUBIHA*)

God Most High has said, "*As for him who fears to stand before his Lord and restrains the ego [ani - mal soul] its desires, the garden is shelter*" [79:40].

Ali ibn Ahmad ibn Abdan informed us . . . through Jabir that the Messenger of God said, "The worst of what I fear for my community is the pursuit of passion and ambition for the future, for the passions leads away from the truth, while ambition makes one forget the next world." So know that opposing the ego [*nafs ammarah*, the animal soul, the passions throughout the chapter] is the beginning of worship.

The shaykhs, asked about submission to God— Islam—have said that it means to slaughter the ego with the swords of opposition to it. You should know that when the disasters of the ego rise in a person, the glories of intimacy with God set.

Dhu 'l-Nun al-Misri said, "The key to worship is reflection. The sign of attaining the mark is to oppose the ego and its desires. To oppose the ego is to abandon what it craves." Ibn Ata said, "The ego is disposed to bad conduct while the servant is commanded to observe the rule of behavior, so the ego falls by its nature into the arena of things to be actively resisted, and the servant with effort can turn it back from the evil of its wishes. He who gives it free rein is partner to its corruption."

I heard Abu Abd al-Rahman al-Sulami say . . . Junayd said, "The ego [animal soul] summons to dangers, assists enemies, pursues whims, and is to be suspected of every sort of wickedness." Abu Hafs said, "Whoever does not suspect his ego at every moment, oppose it in all circumstances, and drag it toward what it hates for all his days, has been fooled. Whoever looks at it expecting any good from it has caused his ruin."

How can an intelligent person be satisfied with himself while the noble, son of the noble, son of the noble, son of the noble—Joseph the son of Jacob, the son of Isaac, the son of Abraham the Friend of God—says, "*I do not absolve myself, for the ego [animal soul] commands to wrongdoing*" [12:53]!

I heard Muhammad ibn al-Husayn say . . . that Junayd said, "One night I could not sleep. I got up to make my private devotions but was unable to find the sweetness and delight I usually find in conversations with my Lord. I was troubled and amazed. I wanted to sleep but was not able. I sat but could not endure the sitting. So I opened the door and went outside. There in the street lay a man wrapped in a cloak. When he felt my presence he raised his head and said, 'O Abu 'l-Qasim, finally!' 'Sir,' I said, 'no appointment was made.' 'Rather I asked the Mover of Hearts to move your heart towards me,' he replied. 'He has done that,' I told him. 'What is your need?' 'When does the disease of the ego [animal soul] become its cure?' he asked. 'When the ego [animal soul] opposes its desire, its disease becomes it cure,' I answered. Directing himself to his ego, he said, 'Listen!

I have given you this answer seven times and you refused to hear it except from Junayd. So now you have heard it!' He turned away from me. I did not know him, and I have never come across him again.

Abu Bakr al-Tamastani said, "The greatest blessing is to escape from the ego, because the ego is the greatest veil between you and God Almighty and Glorious." Sahl ibn Abd Allah said, "There is no way to worship God equal to opposing the ego and its caprice."

I heard Muhammad ibn al-Husayn say . . . that Ibn Ata was asked what thing most quickly brings on God's wrath. He said, "Looking upon the ego and its states, the worst of which is the expectation of compensation for its acts." And I heard him say . . . that Ibrahim al-Khawwas said, "I was on the mountain of al-Lukam [in Damascus] when I saw some pomegranates and wanted them. I came up, took one, and broke it open, but finding it sour I went away and left them. Then I saw a man lying on the ground. He was covered with hornets. Peace be upon you,' I greeted him. 'And upon you be peace, Ibrahim!' he replied. 'How do you know me?' I asked. 'Nothing is hidden from one who knows God Most High,' said he. 'I see that your state is with God Most High,' I said. 'If only you would ask Him to shelter and protect you from the torment of those hornets!' 'And I see that your state is with God Most High,' he returned. 'If only you would ask him to protect you from the desire for pomegranates! For a man but finds the pain of the sting of hornets in this world, while he finds the pain of the sting of pomegranates in the next!' So I left him and went away.

It is told that Ibrahim ibn Shayban said, "I did not sleep under my own roof or in any place that had a lock upon it for forty years. Many times I desired to eat a meal of lentils, but it did not come about. Then one time when I was in Damascus, an earthen vessel full of lentils was presented to me. I ate out of it and was leaving when I saw glasses to which were clinging what seemed to be drops of liquid. I had thought the vessel clean, but somebody said to me, 'What are you looking at? Those are wine dregs, and that jug is a wine jug!' 'I must carry out a duty,' I said to myself. So I went into the wine-seller's shop and kept pouring out that jug. He supposed I was emptying it by order of the Sultan. When he knew that it was not so, he dragged me to the judge Ibn Tulun who ordered that I be flogged with 200 lashes and thrown me into prison. There I stayed for awhile, until my teacher, Abu Abd Allah al-Maghribi, came to that city. He interceded for me. When his eyes fell upon me, he asked, 'What have you done?' 'A meal of lentils and two hundred lashes,' I said. 'You have been protected by shields against the true punishment,' he told me.'"

I heard Abu Abd al-Rahman al-Sulami say . . . that Sari al-Saqati said, "My ego has been pleading with me for thirty or forty years to dip a carrot into date syrup, and I have not fed it!" And I heard him say that he heard my grandfather say, "The bane of the servant is his satisfaction with himself as he is." I also heard him say . . . that Husayn ibn Ali al-Qirmisini said, "I am ibn Yusuf, the Amir of Balkh, who sent a gift to Hatim al-Asamm, who received it from him." Asked why he did so, he said, "In accepting it I found humiliation for me and honor for him, while in returning it was honor for me and humiliation for him, so I chose his honor over mine and my humiliation over his."

Someone told a Sufi, "I want to go on the pilgrimage free of material support." He answered, "First free your heart from distraction, your ego from frivolity, and your tongue from nonsense—then travel however you wish!" Abu Sulayman al-Darani said, "Whoever does good at night is rewarded during the day and whoever does good during the day is rewarded at night. Whoever is sincere in abandoning a desire is saved from catering to it. God is too noble to punish a heart that has abandoned a desire for His sake."

God, glory to Him, revealed to David, "O David, beware! Warn your companions about devouring the objects of desire. When people's hearts are tied to the desires of this world, their intelligence is veiled from Me."

A man was seen seated in mid-air. Someone asked him, "Why were you granted this?" "I gave up idle desire (*hawa*)," he said, "and the air (*hawa;* a play on words because *hawa* means both) became subject to me."

It is said that if a thousand desires were presented to a believer he would drive them away through fear of God, while if a single desire were presented to a libertine, it would drive fear of God away from him. It is said, "Do not give your bridle into the hand of caprice, for it will lead you into darkness."

Yusuf ibn Asbat said, "Nothing will extinguish desires from the heart except an unsettling fear or a troubled yearning." Al-Khawwas said, "Whoever gives up a desire and does not find the recompense for it in his heart is lying about having given it up."

Jafar Ibn Nisar said, "Junayd gave me a dirham and said, 'Go and buy me Wasiti figs.' I bought them, and when he broke fast he took one and put it in his mouth. Then he spit it out, wept, and said, 'Take them away!' I asked him about this. He said, 'A voice spoke in my heart saying, "Aren't you ashamed? A desire you gave up for My sake—now you are returning to it!"'"

They recite:

The last letter of disgrace has been stolen from
    desire.
The victim of every desire is a victim of disgrace.

Know that the ego possesses contemptible characteristics, and one of them is envy.

14
ENVY (*HASAD*)

God Most High said, "*Say: I seek refuge with the Lord of Daybreak from the evil of what He has cre - ated.*" *After this, He said, "and from the evil of the envious one when he envies.*" [113:1, 5] So He ended the *surah* that He made a protection with the mention of envy.

Abu 'l-Husayn al-Ahwazi informed us. . . through Ibn Masud, that the Prophet said, "Three things are the origin of every error so shield yourself from them and beware of them. Beware of pride, for pride made satan not prostrate himself to Adam. Beware of ambition, for ambition made Adam eat from the tree. Beware of envy, for one of the sons of Adam killed his brother out of envy." A Sufi said, "The envious person is an infidel for he is not satisfied with the judgments of the unique One." And it is said, "The envious man will not prevail."

It is stated in the Word of the Most High, "*Say: My Lord has only forbidden indecencies, outer and inner*" [7:33]. "Inner" indecency is said to be envy. According to another holy book, "The envious person is the enemy of My blessing."

It is said that the effect of envy becomes visible in you before it becomes visible in your enemy. Al-Asmai said, "I saw a Bedouin who had lived 120 years. 'How long your life has been!' I marveled. 'I gave up envy and endured,' he replied." Ibn Mubarak said, "Praise be to God Who has not put into the heart of the man who commands me what He has put into the heart of the man who envies me."

According to the ancient traditions, in the fifth heaven is a certain angel. A deed shining like the sun passes before him, and the angel says to it, "Stop! For I am the angel who deals with envy. I will strike the one whose work this is in the face with it, for he was an envier!"

Muawiyah said, "It is possible to please everyone except an envier, for he is not pleased except by the disappearance of good fortune." And it is said, "The envious is a tyrannical oppressor: he will not let you be or leave you alone." Umar ibn Abd al-Aziz said, "I never saw a tyrant who more resembled a victim of tyranny than does an envier: Constant trouble with each successive breath!" One of the marks of the envier is that he will flatter someone when he is present, slander him when he is absent and gloat over misfortune when it befalls. Muawiyah said, "No bad characteristic is more just than envy—it destroys the envier before it destroys the object of his envy."

It is said that God, glory to Him, revealed to Prophet Solomon son of Prophet David, "I will counsel you about seven things. Do not criticize one of My righteous servants and do not envy any of My servants." Solomon said, "O Lord, that is enough for me!"

It is said that Prophet Moses saw a man by the Throne of God and wished for his state. He asked what the man's characteristic had been that he had been granted such a state and was told that he would never envy people for the graces God bestowed upon them.

The envier, it is said, when he sees a blessing criticizes, and when he sees an error, gloats. It is said, "If you wish to be safe from the envier, conceal your affairs from him. The envier is enraged at people who do not sin and miserly about what he does not possess. Beware of exhausting yourself seeking the affection of one who envies you, for he will never accept your gift. When God Most High wishes to give power over a servant to an enemy who will show him no mercy, He gives that power to the one who envies him.

The Sufis have recited:

It is enough for you to say of a man
That you see his enviers merciful to him.

And they have recited:

You may hope for the end of all enmity
But that of the hater from envy.

Ibn Mutazz said:

When you see the envier pant with envy;
Say: 'O tyrant who appears tyrannized
May your lungs burst!'

They recited:

When God wants an open virtue hidden
He assigns it an envier's tongue.

Another contemptible characteristic of the ego is habitual backbiting.

15
ON BACKBITING (*GHIBA*)

God, glory to Him, said, *"Let not some of you criti -cize others. Would one of you like to eat the dead flesh of his brother? You would abhor that. Fear God for God is mot forgiving, merciful"* [49:12]. Abu Said Muhammad ibn Ibrahim al-Ismaili informed us . . . from Abu Hurayra, "A man who had earlier been seated with the Messenger of God stood up and left. Some people said, 'How weak and helpless is so-and-so!' The Prophet said, 'You have devoured and backbitten your brother.'"

God, glory to Him, revealed to Prophet Moses, "He who dies having repented from backbiting will be the last to enter paradise, and he who dies persistent in it will be the first to enter hell."

Awf said, "I went to see Ibn Sirin,and talked against the tyrant Hajjaj. Ibn Sirin said, 'God Most High arranges things justly. As God will ask the rights of others from Hajjaj, He will ask the rights of Hajjaj from others. If you were to meet God Almighty and Glorious tomorrow, the smallest sin you have committed would be worse for you than the greatest sin committed by Hajjaj.'"

It is said that Ibrahim ibn Adham was invited to a banquet and attended. The other guests mentioned someone who was not among them. "What a disagreeable man!" they said. "This ego of mine has only worked upon me so that I would be present in a place where people are criticized!" Ibrahim declared. He left, and would not eat for three days.

A person who maligns other people is like someone who sets up a catapult with which he throws his good deeds East and West. He criticizes one person from Khurasan, another from Damascus, another from the Hijaz, another from Turkistan—he scatters his good deeds, gets up, and has nothing left!

It is said that the servant may be given his book on the resurrection day and not see a good deed in it. He will ask, "Where is my prayer, my fasting, my obedience?" and will be told, "All of your work disappeared through your maligning of people." It is said that God will forgive half the sins of anyone who is attacked with slander.

Sufyan ibn al-Husayn said, "I was sitting with Iyas ibn Muawiya and talking about somebody. He said to me, 'Have you made any forays against the Turks or the Byzantines this year?' 'No,' I said. 'The Turks and the Byzantines are safe from you,' he exclaimed, 'but not your Muslim brother!'"

It is also said that a man may be given his book and see in it good deeds that he did not perform. He will be told, "This is through people's criticism of you of which you were unaware." Sufyan al-Thawri was asked about the saying of the Prophet, "God hates the carnivorous household." He said, "They are those who malign people and eat their flesh."

Backbiting was mentioned to Abd Allah ibn al-Mubarak. He said, "If I were to criticize anybody, I would criticize my parents—they have the greatest right to my good deeds!" Yahya ibn Muadh said, "Let the believer's share from you be three traits, 'If you cannot help him, then do not harm him. If you cannot make him happy, then do not make him unhappy. If you cannot praise him, then do not blame him."

Hasan al-Basri was told, "So-and-so has talked against you." He sent that person a tray of sweets, and said, "It has come to my attention that you have directed your good deeds to me, so I thank you!"

Ali ibn Ahmad al-Ahwazi informed us . . . through Anas ibn Malik that the Messenger of God said, "To criticize someone who casts the veil of shame from his face is not unlawful." I heard Hamzah ibn Yusuf al-Sahmi say . . . that Junayd said, "I was sitting in the Shuniziyyah mosque waiting for the arrival of a coffin I was to pray over, along with citizens of Baghdad of all ranks who were sitting waiting for the funeral, when I saw a dervish upon whom were the marks of piety. He was begging from people. 'Were he to do some work that would sustain him, it would be more becoming,' I said to myself. When I returned to my house I had some of my night's devotions to do—weeping and prayer and so forth—but all of them weighed heavily upon me. I sat awake, but sleep overcame me and I saw that dervish. They were bringing him spread out upon a table, and they said to me, 'Eat his flesh! You have slandered him!' 'What slander?' I objected. 'I only said something to myself!' 'You are not a person from whom that sort of thing is acceptable,' I was told. 'Go and resolve it.' So in the morning I went out and did not come back until I had seen him. He was in a place where, through the pooling of water, leaves that had been discarded in the washing of vegetables were collected. I offered him a greeting. 'Will you return to what you have done, Abu 'l-Qasim?' he asked. 'No,' I replied. 'May God forgive us and you,' said he."

I heard Abu Abd al-Rahman al-Sulami say . . . that Abu Jafar al-Balkhi said, "There used to be a young man from Balkh with us who would make great efforts and devote himself to worship. But he was always criticizing people, saying this person is like this, that person is like that, someone else is some other way. I saw him one day among the homosexuals in the baths. He came out from among them and I asked him, "What is happening to you?" "That which I brought down upon people has brought this down upon me," he said. "I have been afflicted with passion for one of these — so now, because of him, I am the one who serves them. All my old states have vanished so ask God to forgive him."

16
ON CONTENTMENT (QANAA)

God Most High said, "*Whoever does good works, whether man or woman, and is a believer, We will certainly cause to live a good life*" [16:97]. Many commentators have said that the "good life" in this world is contentment with one's lot.

Abu Abd al-Rahman al-Sulami related . . . through Jabir ibn Abd Allah that the Messenger of God said, "Contentment is an inexhaustible treasure." Abu 'l-Hasan al-Ahwazi related . . . through Abu Hurayra that the Messenger of God said, "Be one who abstains and you will be the most thankful of men. Wish for others what you wish for yourself, and you will be a believer. Treat your neighbors well, and you will be a Muslim. Laugh little, for much laughter kills the heart."

It is said, "The poor are as dead, except those whom God Most High gives life with the honor of contentment." Bishr al-Hafi said, "Contentment is a king who dwells only in a believing heart." Muhammad ibn al Husayn said . . . that Abu Sulayman al-Darani said, "Contentment is to satisfaction as the station of abstinence is to renunciation. Contentment is the beginning of satisfaction, while abstinence is the beginning of renunciation." It is said, "Contentment is to remain calm when facing that to which one is not accustomed." Abu

Bakr al-Maraghi said, "The intelligent person is the one who treats the affairs of this world with acceptance and deferment, the affairs of the next with ambition and hurry, and the affairs of religion with knowledge and effort." Abu Abd Allah ibn Khafif said, "Contentment is not to wish for what you lack and not to need what you have."

It is said that the meaning of His saying, *"God will provide them with a beautiful sustenance"* [22:58] is contentment. Muhammad ibn Ali al-Tirmidhi said, "Acceptance is one's satisfaction with one's allotted sustenance." And it is said, "Acceptance means to find what exists sufficient and to stop hoping for what is not obtainable." Wahb said, "Honor and riches went out wandering in search of a friend. They ran into contentment and settled down with it." It is said, "He whose contentment is fat finds every broth good." He who turns to God in every circumstance, God provides with contentment. Abu Hazim passed by a butcher who had good fat meat. He said, "Take some, Abu Hazim, it is fat." "I don't have a dirham with me," he replied. "I will wait for it," said the butcher. "It seems better to me that my ego should wait than that you should," said he.

A Sufi was asked, "Who is the most contented of men?" He answered, "The one who gives people the most help and who asks the least." In the Psalms of David it says, "The contented person is rich even if he goes hungry." It is said that God Most High put five things in five places: honor in obedience, humiliation in disobedience, awe in standing in prayer at night, wisdom in an empty belly, and wealth in contentment.

I heard Abu Abd al-Rahman al-Sulami say . . . that Ibrahim al-Maristani said, "Take revenge on your ambition with contentment as you take revenge on your enemy with retaliation." Dhu 'l-Nun al-Misri said, "He who is contented is at rest from his contemporaries and towers over his fellows." And it is said, "He who is contented is at rest from preoccupation and towers over everything." Al-Kattani said, "Whoever sells ambition for contentment has triumphed in honor and moral goodness (*murawwa*)." And it is said, "For the one whose eyes follow what is in people's hands, sorrow and care grow long." They recite:

Generosity and hunger — better for a true person
Than a day of disgrace that brings cash!

Someone saw a wise man eating discarded vegetables from a gutter. He said, "If you were to wait on the sultan, you would not need to eat this!" "And were you content with this, you would not need to wait on the sultan!" the wise man replied.

It is said that the flying eagle is mighty. Neither the hunter's eye nor the attraction of his bait can rise to it. It is only when the eagle has an appetite for carrion that it becomes entangled in the snare. It descends from its flight and is trapped in a net. When Prophet Moses spoke mentioning appetite—*"If you wished, you could get a reward for that"*—Khidr said to him, *"This is the parting between you and me"* [18:77-78]. And it is told that when Prophet Moses had said that, a gazelle stopped in front of he and Khidr. They were both hungry. The side which faced Prophet Moses was not roasted, while the side which faced Khidr was roasted.

His saying, *"The righteous are in bliss"* [82:13] refers to contentment in this world, while *"and the corrupt are in hellfire"* [82:14] refers to avidity in this world. His saying, *". . . the emancipation of a slave . . ."* [90:13] is said to mean freeing him from the humiliation of greed. His saying *"God only wishes to remove impurity from you, People of the Household,"* [33:33] means miserliness and appetite. *"And to cleanse you in purification"* [33:33] means with generosity and selflessness. And it is said that His saying, ". . . *give me a kingdom which is not appropriate for anyone after me . . .*" (the prayer of Prophet Solomon) [38:35] means, "a station in contentment by which I would be singled out from those like me. In it I would be satisfied with Your judgment." And it is said that His saying, "*We will certainly punish him with a severe punishment*" [27:21] means "We will strip him of contentment and try him with ego desires"—that is, he would ask God to inflict such punishment.

Abu Yazid was asked, "Through what did you reach what you have reached?" He answered, "I gathered together all the ways and means of this world, bound them with the rope of contentment, set them in the catapult of truthfulness, and cast them into the sea of resignation—and I was at rest." I heard Muhammad ibn Abd Allah al-Sufi say . . .that Abd al-Wahhab, the uncle of Farhan of Samarrah, said, "I was sitting with Junayd during the pilgrimage season while all around us was a gathering of many foreigners and strangers. A man came with five hundred dinars, placed them before him, and said, 'Distribute these among your dervishes.' 'Do you have more than this?' Junayd asked. 'Yes, I have many dinars,' he said. 'Do you desire more than what you possess?' 'Yes,' he said. 'Take these,' Junayd said to him. 'You have greater need of them than we do.' And he would not accept them."

17
ON TRUST IN GOD (*TAWAKKUL*)

God Almighty and Glorious said, "*Whoever trusts in God, He suffices him*" [65:3], and "*In God let the believers place their trust*" [5:23].

Abu Bakr Muhammad ibn al-Hasan ibn Furak related to us . . . through Abd Allah ibn Masud, "The Messenger of God said, 'I was made to see the religious communities at the time of pilgrimage. I saw that my community filled the plain and the mountain. I marveled at their number and appearance. I was asked, "Are you pleased?" And I said, 'Yes.'"

He said, "Together with these were seventy thousand who will enter paradise without any reckoning. They do not cure by cauterization (surgery) nor practice divination nor cure by spells. They trust in their Lord."

Ukashah ibn Muhsin al-Asadi got up and said, "O Messenger of God, pray to God that He place me among them." The Messenger of God said, "O God, place him among them." Someone else got up and said, "Pray to God that he place me among them!" "Ukashah has preceded you in this," the Prophet replied.

I heard Abd Allah ibn Yusuf al-Ispahani say . . . that Abu Ali al-Rudhbari said, "I asked Amr ibn Sinan, 'Tell me something about Sahl ibn Abd Allah al-Tustari." Amr answered, "He said, 'Three signs show someone who trusts in God: not begging from anyone, not rejecting anything that is given, and not accumulating whatever comes to hand.'"

I heard Abu Abd al-Rahman al-Sulami say . . . that Abu Musa al-Dabili said that Abu Yazid was asked, "What is trust?" "What do you say?" he inquired of me. I answered, "Our companions say that if there were lions and poisonous snakes on your right and your left, your inner being would not be disturbed by it." Abu Yazid said, "Yes, that is close. But if you were to see the people of the garden in bliss in the garden and the people of the fire in torture in the fire and it then occurred to you to have a preference, you would have left the category of trust."

Sahl ibn Abd Allah said, "The first station of trust is when the servant in the hands of God Almighty and Glorious be like a corpse in the hands of the washer who turns him however he wishes, while he has neither motion nor self-will." Hamdun al-Qassar said, "Trust is clinging to God Most High."

I heard Muhammad ibn al-Husayn say . . . that Ahmad ibn Khadruyah said that a man asked Hatim al-Asamm, "From whence do you eat?" He replied, "*To God belong the treasures of the heaven and the earth, but the hypocrites do not understand*' [63:7]."

Know that the place of trust is in the heart. Outward action does not contradict trust in the heart. Once the servant has become sure that the ordering of things is from God Most High, he knows that if something is difficult, He has ordained it, and if it is agreeable, He had made it easy.

I heard Ali ibn Ahmad ibn Abdan related . . . from Anas ibn Malik that a man came to the Prophet on his camel, and said, "O Messenger of God, I will leave her loose and trust in God." He said, "Tie up [the camel]— and trust in God."

Ibrahim al-Khawwas said, "He who properly trusts God with his own self will also entrust everything else to Him." Bishr al-Hafi said, "Some dervishes say, 'I trust in God Most High,' while they are lying to God Most High. If they really trusted, they would be satisfied with what God does with them." Yahya ibn Muadh was asked, "When is a man one of those who trust?" He replied, "When he is satisfied with God Most High as a trustee."

I heard Abd al-Rahman al-Sulami say . . . that Ibrahim al-Khawwas said that while he was journeying in the desert, suddenly a voice called out from he knew not where. He turned and there was a traveling bedouin! The bedouin said to him, "Ibrahim, we possess trust. Stay with us until your trust is sound. Don't you know that you are being sustained by looking forward to entering a town where there is food? Cut off your hope of towns, and trust!" And I heard him say that when Ibn Ata was asked the meaning of trust, he said, "Though you are in great need, you feel no anxiety about means of subsistence. Though you find means, you do not lose the peace there is in reliance upon the Truth." I heard Abu Hatim al-Sijistani say that he heard Abu Nasr al-Sarraj say, "The condition for trust is what Abu Turab al-Nakhshabi has said—abandoning the flesh in servanthood, attaching the heart to the divine lordship, and serenity through feeling the all-sufficiency of God. So if He gives, one is thankful, and if He forbids, one is patient."

As Dhu 'l-Nun said, "Trust in God is to give up directing oneself, to divest oneself of ability and power. The servant will only have the strength for trust when he knows that God, glory to Him, knows and sees his situation."

I heard Muhammad ibn al-Husayn say . . . that Abu Jafar ibn Abu 'l-Faraj said he saw a man known as "Ayisha's camel" among outcasts being beaten with whips. He asked him, "When will the pain of the beating be eased for you?" He said, "When He for Whose sake we are beaten has looked upon us." And I heard him say that he heard Abd Allah ibn Muhammad say "Husayn ibn Mansur al-Hallaj asked Ibrahim al-Khawwas, 'What have you accomplished with these journeys, the crossing of these deserts?' 'I maintained the condition of trust and confirmed myself in it,' he said. 'You have made your life vanish in the culture of your inner self,' said Husayn. 'Where is vanishing into unity (*tawhid*)?'"

I heard Abu Hatim al-Sijistani say that he heard Abu Nasr al-Sarraj say, "Trust is what Abu Bakr al-Daqqaq said, 'Reducing livelihood to one day's worth and dropping concern about tomorrow'—and what Sahl ibn Abd Allah al-Tustari said, 'Trust is to be at ease with God Most High about what He wishes.'"

I heard Abu Abd al-Rahman al-Sulami say . . . that Abu Yaqub al-Nahrajuri said, "Trust in God, in the true meaning of the word, is what occurred in Prophet Abraham at the moment when he was about to be thrown into the fire. Gabriel came and asked, 'Do you need anything' and he said to Gabriel, 'Not from you!' For Abraham's ego [animal soul] was absent with God Most High and he could not see anything other than God along with Him.' And I heard him say . . . that Said ibn Uthman al-Khayyat said that a man asked Dhu 'l-Nun al-Misri, 'What is trust in God?' I heard him reply, 'Deposing lords and cutting off means.' 'Tell me more,' the questioner said. 'Casting the ego into servanthood and driving it out of lordship,' said he.'

And I heard him say . . . when asked about trust, Hamdun al-Qassar said, "If you had ten thousand dirhams and owed one penny of debt, you would not feel that it was safe for you to die while it remained in your pocket. But if you owed ten thousand dirhams of debt, the payment of which you could not leave to another, you would not despair of God Most High's discharging it for you."

Abu Abd Allah al-Qarshi was asked about trust. He said, "Clinging to God Most High in every state." "Say more," the inquirer asked. He said, "It is to give up relying on any means leading to livelihood until the Truth becomes your guide."

Sahl ibn Abd Allah said, "Trust is the state of the Prophet while earning is his practice. Who can remain in his state and not establish his practice?" Abu Said al-Kharraz said, "Trust is uncertainty without rest and rest without uncertainty." And it is said, "Trust means that having much and having little are the same to you." Ibn Masruq said, "Trust is to give oneself up to the course of God's judgments and decisions."

I heard Muhammad ibn al-Husayn say . . . that Abu Uthman al-Hiri said, "Trust is contentment with God Most High together with confidence in Him." And I heard him say . . . that Husayn ibn Mansur al-Hallaj said, "The true man of trust will not eat a thing while there is anyone around who has a greater right to it than he does." And I heard him say . . . Umar ibn Sinan said, "Ibrahim al-Khawwas stopped with us. We asked him, 'Tell us the strangest thing you have seen in your travels.' 'Khidr met with me and asked for my companionship,' he said, 'but I was afraid my trust would be spoiled by staying with him, so I left him.'"

Sahl ibn Abd Allah was asked of trust. He said, "It is a heart that lives with God Most High without attachment to anything else." I heard Abu Ali al-Daqqaq say, "Those who trust possess three degrees: trust (*tawakkul*), surrender (*taslim*), and self-abandonment (*tafwid*). The man of trust relies upon His promise. The man of surrender finds His knowledge sufficient. The man of self-abandonment is well-satisfied with His judgment." And I heard him say, "Trust is a beginning, sur-

render a middle, and self-abandonment an end."
Al-Daqqaq was asked about trust and said, "Eating without greed." Yahya ibn Muadh said, "To wear wool like a dervish is a shop to keep, to speak of asceticism is a trade, and to seek the company of caravans is a venture. All of these are worldly attachments."
A man came to Shibli and complained to him that his family was too numerous. He said, "Go back to your house. Anyone there whose sustenance does not come from God—chase him away!
I heard Abu Abd al-Rahman al-Sulami say . . . that Sahl ibn Abd Allah said that he recited over Muhammad ibn al-Husayn, "Whoever talks against working for a living is talking against prophetic practice. Whoever talks against trust in God is talking against faith." And I heard him say . . . that Ibrahim al-Khawwas said, "I was on the road to Mecca when I saw a wild-looking person. 'Jinn or human being?' I wondered. 'Jinn!' said he. 'Where are you going?' 'To Mecca.' 'Without provisions?' 'Yes. Among us also are those who travel in the way of trust.' 'What is trust?' I asked. 'To receive from God Most High,' he said." And I heard him say . . . that al-Farghani said, "Ibrahim al-Khawwas lived detached from the world in a condition of trust. He was meticulous about this. Yet he was never without a needle and thread, a water flask, and a scissors. Someone asked, 'Abu Ishaq al-Fazari, why do you carry these, while you abstain from everything else?' 'This sort of thing does not contradict trust,' he said. 'There are obligations that we owe to God. A poor dervish has no more than one garment and sometimes his garment tears. If he does not have a needle and thread with him, the parts of his body that should be covered will show and his prayer will not be accepted. If he has no water flask with him, he cannot perform his ritual ablution when he needs it. If you see a dervish without flask or needle or thread, suspect the perfection of his prayers.'"

I heard Abu Ali al-Daqqaq say, "Trust is the attribute of believers, surrender the attribute of the friends of God, and self-abandonment the attribute of those who know unity [*tawhid*]. Thus trust is the attribute of the majority, surrender is that of the elite, and self-abandonment is that of the elite of the elite." And I heard him say, "Trust is the attribute of the prophets, surrender the attribute of Prophet Abraham and self-abandonment the attribute of our Prophet Muhammad."

I heard Muhammad ibn al-Husayn say . . . that Abu Jafar al-Haddad said, "I lived some dozen years tied to trust in God. I was employed in the market. Every day I would receive my pay. I did not use it for a drink of water or to enter a public bath, but would bring it to the dervishes in Shuniziyyah mosque. I continued uninterrupted in my state." And I heard him say . . . that Husayn, the brother of Sinan, said, "I made fourteen pilgrimages barefoot in the way of trust. When a thorn would enter my foot, I would remember that I had bound my lower self to trust, so I would scratch it out in the earth and walk on." And I heard him say . . . that Abu Hamzah said, "I am ashamed before God Most High to enter the desert with a full belly when I have bound myself to trust, lest my effort be dependent upon the provision of satiety with which I have equipped myself."

Hamdun al-Qassar was asked of trust and said, "I have not yet reached that degree. How is someone whose state of faith has not become sound supposed to speak about trust?" It is said that the one who trusts is like an infant. He knows nothing to resort to but his mother's breast. Just so, the one who trusts is guided to nothing but his Lord."

A Sufi said, "I was in the desert at the head of a caravan when I saw someone in front of me. I hurried to catch up. It was a woman! She had a staff in her hand and was walking slowly and deliberately. I supposed her to be exhausted, so I put my hand in my pocket, took out twenty dirhams, and said, 'Take this, and wait until the caravan joins you. You can engage it, then spend the night, until your situation has improved.' She reached her hand—thus!—in the air. Suddenly there were dinars in her palm. 'You take dirhams from your pocket,' she said, 'while I take dinars from the unseen!'"

Abu Sulayman al-Darani saw a man in Mecca who would not accept any food whatsoever except a sip of Zamzam water. Day after day he passed by him. One day Abu Sulayman said to him, "If Zamzam were to dry up, what would you drink?" The man stood up and kissed him upon the head. "May God reward you, for you have guided me well!" he exclaimed. "I have been worshipping Zamzam for days!" And he went away.

Ibrahim al-Khawwas said, "On the road to Damascus I saw a young man of beautiful appearance. He asked, 'Will you keep company with me?' 'I am going hungry,' I said. 'If you go hungry, I will go hungry with you,' he replied. We continued that way for four days. Then something came our way. 'Have some!' I urged. He answered, 'I have committed myself not to receive anything from an intermediary.' 'Young man, you are fastidious!' I complained. 'Ibrahim, don't make yourself out to be something you're not!' said he. 'If you are a critic of patience, what trust can you possess?' Then he added, 'The least degree of trust is that when times of need come upon you, your ego aspires to nothing but the One Who is All-Sufficient. Trust is negation of doubts, and giving oneself up to the King of Kings.'"

It is told that a group of people went to Junayd and asked, "Where shall we seek our sustenance?" "If you know the place where He is," he said, "go and seek it there." "Request this of God Most High for us," they asked. "If you know Him to have forgotten you, then you remind Him!" he returned. "We have entered the House and trusted," they said. "To make trial of God is doubt," he replied. "Then what is the means?" "To abandon means."

Abu Sulayman al-Darani said to Ahmad ibn Abu 'l-Hawari, "Ahmad, the roads to the next world are many. Your shaykh is familiar with many of them, but not with this blessed trust. I have not smelled the fragrance of it." It is said that trust is confidence in what is in the hands of God and giving up hope of what is in the hands of men. And it is called removing from your inner being any thought of seeking sustenance by laying claim to it. Harith al-Muhasibi was asked whether appetite afflicts the one who trusts in God. "Dangers reach him by way of his natural disposition," he answered, "but they do him no harm. Giving up hope of what is in the hands of men empowers him to let go of his ego and its desires."

It is told that Nuri was hungry in the desert when a voice called out to him, "Which is dearer to you, the normal means of receiving your sustenance or to find what is sufficient?" "Sufficiency has no goal above it," he said. So he continued seventeen days without eating.

Abu Ali al-Rudhbari remarked, "If a dervish says, after five days, 'I am hungry,' let him go to the market and busy himself with work and earning a living.'" It is said that Abu Turab al-Nakhshabi looked at a Sufi who, after three days, stretched his hand toward a watermelon rind in order to eat it and told him, "Sufism is not suitable for you! Go to the marketplace!"

Abu Yaqub al-Aqta al-Basri said, "One time at the Kabah I went hungry for ten days and became weak. My ego spoke to me, so I went out to the valley in order to find something that might quiet my weakness. I saw a discarded turnip and picked it up. I found a kind of wildness in my heart from this, as if someone were saying to me, 'You have gone hungry ten days and after all that your portion is some old turnip?' So I threw it away, and went back to the mosque and sat down. All of a sudden a stranger came up to me. He sat in front of me, put down a satchel, and said, 'This is for you.' 'Why have you singled me out?' I asked. He said, 'For ten days we were at sea and the ship was on the verge of foundering. Every one of us vowed that if God Most High were to save us we would give something in charity. I swore that if God rescued me I would give this to the first person my eyes fell upon at the holy place. You are the first whom I have met.' 'Open it,' I said. He opened it and there were Egyptian wheat cakes, shelled almonds, and pearl sugar. I took a handful of each and said, 'Take the rest back to your children. It is a gift from me to you. I have received the charity you intended.' Then I said to my ego, 'Your sustenance has been coming to you for ten days, and you go out looking for it in the valley!'"

I heard Abu Abd al-Rahman al-Sulami say that he heard Abu Bakr al-Razi say, "I was with Mumshad al-Dinawari when there was talk of debt. He said, 'I owe a debt,' and this troubled my heart. Then I dreamed that someone was saying to me, 'O miser, you hold this amount against Us! Take! It is for you to take, and it is for Us to give!' After that I asked neither grocer nor butcher nor anybody else for an accounting."

It is related that Bunnan al-Hammal said, "I was on the road to Mecca going from Egypt, and I had provisions with me. A woman came up to me and said, 'Bunnan, you are a baggage carrier (*hammal*) indeed—you carry provisions on your back and imagine that He will not sustain you!' So I threw my provisions away. Afterward there came upon me three days without food. Then I found an anklet in the road and said to myself, 'I will carry this until its owner appears. Maybe he will give me something for returning it to him.' Suddenly, there was that woman! 'You are a merchant,' she accused. 'You say, "...until its owner appears, so I will get

something from him!'" She threw a few dirhams at me,
and said, 'Spend them!' So I contented myself with these
until I was almost at Mecca."

It is also related that Bunnan had need of a maidservant to wait on him. News of this spread to his
brethren who collected the cost for him, saying, "Here it
is. A caravan is coming, so buy whatever suits you."
When the caravan arrived, the opinions of all agreed on
one woman. They said, "She is the one for him!" They
asked her owner, "How much is this one?" And he said,
"She is not for sale." They insisted, and he said, "But she
is for Bunnan al-Hammal! She has been given to him by
a woman of Samarkand." She was taken to Bunnan, and
the story was recounted to him.

I heard Muhammad ibn al-Husayn say . . . that
Hasan al-Khayyat reported, "I was with Bishr al-Hafi
when a group of travelers came in. They greeted him,
and he asked, 'Where are you from?' 'We are from
Damascus,' they said. 'We have come to greet you and we
wish to make the pilgrimage.' 'May God reward you,' he
said. 'Will you come out with us?' they asked. 'On three
conditions: if we do not carry anything with us, if we do
not ask anything from anyone, and if, should anyone
offer us anything, we decline to accept it.' 'As for not carrying anything, yes,' they said. 'As for not asking anything, yes. But as for not accepting anything given to us,
that we cannot do.' 'You have gone forth placing your
trust in the provisions of the pilgrims!' he said. He spoke
again. 'Hasan, there are three kinds of dervishes: there
is a dervish who will not ask and, if he is given something, will not accept it. This sort has real spiritual substance. There is a dervish who will not ask, but if he is
given something accepts because of what has been
appointed for him. These are protected within the enclo-
sures of paradise. And there is a dervish who will ask,
and, if he is given something, he will take to the point of

repletion. The penance of this sort is charity.'"
Habib al-Ajami was asked, "Why did you give up
trade?" He said, "I found that giving surety was placing
trust in creatures."
Long ago a man went on a journey carrying a loaf of
bread. "If I eat this up, I will die of hunger!" he said. So
God Most High assigned an angel to him, saying, "If he
eats it, give him sustenance, but if he does not eat it,
give him nothing!" The loaf stayed with him until he
died. He did not eat. They laid his bread next to him in
his grave. It is said, "He who falls into the arena of self-
abandonment is conducted to the object of his desire as
a bride is conducted to her husband."
The difference between neglect and self-abandonment is that neglect means neglecting the rights of God
Most High. That is blameworthy. Abandonment means
abandoning your own rights. That is praiseworthy. Abd
Allah ibn al-Mubarak said, "He who takes a penny that
is unlawful has no trust in God."
I heard Muhammad ibn Abd Allah al-Sufi say . . .
that Abu Said al-Kharraz said, "Once I went into the
desert without provisions, and need beset me. I saw an
oasis at a distance. I rejoiced that I had reached it. Then
I thought to myself, 'I have been reassured by and
dependent upon other than He!' so I swore that I would
not enter the oasis unless I was carried in. I dug a hole
for myself in the sand and concealed my body in it up to
the chest. In the middle of the night the villagers heard
a voice from on high saying, 'People of the oasis! God
Most High has a friend who has confined himself in this
sand—go and fetch him!' So they all came to me together, brought me out, and carried me to the town."
I heard Abu Abd al-Rahman al-Sulami say . . . that
Abu Hamzah al-Khurasani said, "One year I went on the
pilgrimage. While walking on the road, I fell into a hole.
I fought with my ego over whether to try and get help.
'No, by God,' I said, 'I will not look for human assistance!'

Scarcely was this thought completed when two men passed by the mouth of the hole. One of them said to the other, 'Come on, let's block off the mouth of this pit so that no one will fall into it.' They came with cane and matting and covered over the opening. I was about to call out when I said to myself, 'Call out to the One who is closer!' So I remained silent. After about an hour, suddenly something was there with me. It uncovered the mouth of the pit, let its foot hang down, and seemed to say, 'Grab hold of me!'—in its muttering I understood that much. So I took hold of it, and it drew me out. It was a lion! Then it went away. A voice from nowhere said to me, 'O Abu Hamzah, isn't this better? We have saved you from destruction by means of a destruction!' So I walked on, all the while saying:

> I was afraid to show my need to You Who are Most
>   Hidden,
> But my soul shows forth what my sight says to it.
> My shame before You forbade me; I restrained my
>   desire
> And through understanding from You, discovery
> became needless.
> You dealt subtly with my case. You showed my state
> To be not plain, but hidden—the fire is grasped by
>   the fire —
> You revealed Yourself in a hidden way; it was as if
> You gave word in that hidden place—You were in the
> lion's paw!
> I saw You, and in me from awe of You was wildness.
> You turned me with Your loving sympathy
> You gave life to a lover when You were his death in
>   love.
> Life together with death—a marvelous thing!

I heard Muhammad ibn al-Husayn say . . . that Hudhayfah al-Murashi, who was the servant and companion of Ibrahim ibn Adham, when asked, "What was

the most amazing thing you saw around him?"' said, "We
endured on the road to Mecca for days without finding
anything to eat. Then we came to Kufa and took shelter
in a ruined mosque. Ibrahim ibn Adham looked at me
and said, 'Hudhayfah, I see a sign of hunger in you!' 'It
is as the Shaykh has seen,' I said. 'I have an inkwell and
pen with me,' he said. So I brought them, and he wrote:
'In the Name of God, the the Merciful, the
Compassionate. You are that which is sought in every
state, and that which is indicated by every idea.'"

> I am the praiser, the thanker, the rememberer.
> I am the hungry, the thirsty, the naked. These are
>   six qualities: I am responsible for half.
> Be You responsible for the other half, O Maker!
> My lauds for other than You are a flame of fire
>   into which I have rushed.
> Hold back Your worshipper from entering the fire!
> The fire, to me, is begging.
> Do not compel me to enter the fire.

Then he handed the scrap of paper to me and said, 'Go
out not attaching your heart to anything other than God
Most High and hand this paper to the first person whom
you meet.' So I went out, and the first person I met was
a man riding a mule. I gave it to him and he took it, and
he wept. He asked, 'What is the owner of this paper
doing?' 'He is in such-and-such a mosque,' I said. He gave
me a purse in which were six hundred dinars. Then I
met another man and asked him, 'Who was the man on
that mule?' 'He is a Christian,' he told me. I went back to
Ibrahim ibn Adham and told him the story. 'Don't touch
that purse,' he said. 'He will come within the hour.' When
an hour had passed the Christian appeared, prostrated
himself before Ibrahim ibn Adham, and accepted Islam.

18
ON THANKFULNESS (*SHUKR*)

God Almighty and Glorious said, "*If you are grate-ful, I will give you more*" [14:7].

Abu 'l- Hasan Ali ibn Ahmad ibn Abdan reported . . . from Ata that he went to see Ayisha together with Ubayd ibn Umayr and asked, "Tell us the most wonderful thing you ever saw from the Messenger of God." She wept and said, "What affair of his was not wonderful? One night he came to me and came in under the bedclothes with me (or perhaps she said 'under the blanket') until his skin touched mine. Then he said, 'O daughter of Abu Bakr, let me worship my Lord.' 'I love your being close,' said I, and I gave him permission. He arose and went over to a waterskin and made ablution, pouring a great deal of water. Then he stood and prayed and wept until his tears flowed upon his chest. Then he bowed and wept, then made prostration and wept, then raised his head and wept. He continued like this until Bilal came to give him the announcement of morning prayer. I said to him, 'O Messenger of God, what has made you weep? God has forgiven you your sins, whether they came before or might come later.' 'Shall I not be a grateful servant?' he said. 'And why should I not do this, when God has sent down upon me the verse, "*In the creation of the*

121

heavens and the earth . . . are signs for people who reflect' [2:164]."

The true meaning of *shukr*, thankfulness, according to the ones who know, is acknowledging the benefactor's gift with humility. Thus the Truth, glory to Him, is described as Thankful (*shakur*) by extension, not in reality. The sense of this is that He rewards His servants for thankfulness. The recompense of thankfulness is called thankfulness, just as in the saying of the Most High, *"The recompense of an evil is an evil like it"* [42:40]. It is said that the gratitude of the Most High is His giving much as a reward for just a few good deeds. This sort of usage is found in the expression, a "grateful" mount, which means that the animal shows itself to be fatter than the amount of fodder it is given.

It is also possible to say that the proper meaning of gratitude is to praise the one who does good by mentioning the good he does in his presence. In that case the servants' gratitude toward God Most High is their praising Him by recollecting His goodness before Him, and the gratitude of the Truth, glory to Him, towards His servants is His praising them by recollecting their goodness before them. The goodness of the servant, then, is his obedience to God Most High, and the goodness of the Truth is His grace towards the servant in enabling him to offer Him thanks.

The thankfulness of the servant, in reality, is only to tell with the tongue and confirm in the heart the blessings of the Lord. Thankfulness is subdivided into thanksgiving of the tongue, which is recognition of the blessing together with humility; thanksgiving of the body and the limbs, which is characterized by loyalty and service; and thanksgiving of the heart, which is to withdraw oneself into contemplation of God's attributes with a continual preservation of reverence.

The thankfulness common to everybody pertains to

what one says; the thankfulness proper to devoted worshippers pertains to what one does; the thankfulness proper to gnostics pertains to perseverance throughout one's states. Abu Bakr al-Warraq said, "Thankfulness for a blessing is to see it as grace and maintain respect." Hamdun al-Qassar said, "Thankfulness for a blessing is to see yourself, in relation to it, in the position of an uninvited guest." Junayd said, "In thankfulness there is an ill: someone who cultivates gratitude seeks increase for himself and clings to the portion of his ego as well as to God, glory to Him."

Abu Uthman said, "Thankfulness is the realization of the inability to give thanks." It is said that thankfulness for thankfulness is more perfect than thankfulness itself—that is, you see your gratitude as being through His enabling, and that enabling becomes the most profound blessing to you so that you give thanks to Him for your thanksgiving, then for your thankfulness for your thanksgiving, and so on without end.

It is said that thankfulness is to connect the blessing to its Bestower and feel your lowliness. Junayd said, "Thankfulness is that you not see yourself as deserving of the blessing." Ruwaym said, "Thankfulness is to expend every effort to demonstrate your gratitude."

The ordinary thankful person, it is said, is he who gives thanks for that which exists. The deeply grateful person is he who gives thanks for that which is lacking. The ordinary thankful one gives thanks for God's permission, while the deeply grateful one gives thanks for His refusal. Or, the ordinary thankful one gives thanks for benefit, while the deeply grateful one gives thanks for prohibition. Or, the one gives thanks for the gift while the other gives thanks for the trial. Or the one gives thanks for free generosity while the other gives thanks for the postponement of his hopes.

I heard Abu Abd al-Rahman al-Sulami say . . . that Junayd said, "Once I was playing in front of Sari al-Saqati. I was seven years old. Before him was a congregation engaged in the discussion of thankfulness. He asked me, 'My boy, what is thankfulness?' I said, 'It means that you do not disobey God with what He has given you.' He said, 'It seems that your portion from God will be your tongue!' Junayd said, 'I have never stopped crying over that saying of Sari's.'"

Shibli said, "Thankfulness is seeing the Giver, not seeing the gift." It is said that thankfulness securely ties up that which is and then goes hunting for that which is lacking. Abu Uthman said, "The gratitude of the majority is for the stuff of food and clothing. The gratitude of the elite is for the insights that have reached their hearts."

It is told that the Prophet David said, "My God, how can I thank You, while my gratitude to You is a gift from You?" God revealed to him, "Now you have truly thanked Me." Prophet Moses is said to have asked in his intimate prayers, "My God, You created Adam by Your own hand, and did this and did that—how can one thank You?" He replied, "Know that all that is from Me. Your realization of that is your thanks to Me."

A dervish had a close friend who was imprisoned by a sultan. He sent word of this to the dervish who answered his companion, "Give thanks to God Most High." Then the man was beaten. He wrote to the dervish who said, "Give thanks to God Most High." Then they brought a Zoroastrian who had a intestinal ailment and chained him up. One shackle was linked to that man's foot and the other to the foot of the Zoroastrian. The Zoroastrian had to get up many times at night. The man was obliged to stand in front of him until he was finished. He wrote this to his friend, who answered, "Give thanks to God Most High." "How long are you going to be saying this?" he asked. "What trial is worse than this one?" His friend replied, "Suppose the belt, the sign of dualism, which is around his waist, was placed around yours, as the shackle which is on his foot has been placed upon yours? Then what would you do?"

It is said that a man came in to Sahl ibn Abd Allah al-Tustari and told him, "A thief came into my house and took my possessions!" "Give thanks to God Most High," he said. "What if the thief—satan—had come into your heart and spoiled your knowledge of unity (*tawhid*)? What would you do?"

The gratitude of the eyes, it is said, is that they cover over the shame they see in your companion and the gratitude of the ears is that they cover over the shame they hear from him. It is said that thankfulness is to take delight in praising Him for those gifts that He was not obliged to give.

I heard al-Sulami say . . . that Junayd said that when Sari wanted to give him a benefit, he used to ask him a question. One day he said to him, "Abu 'l- Qasim, what is thankfulness?" He replied, "It is not to make use of any blessing of God Most High in order to disobey Him." "Where did you get this from?" he asked. "From your sessions," he told him.

It is told that the grandson of the Prophet, Hasan ibn Ali, clung to the corner of the Kabah and said, "My God, You have done good to me and have not found me grateful. You have tested me and have not found me patient. Yet You have not taken Your blessings away from me for all my lack of gratitude, nor made difficulty continue, for all my lack of patience! My God, nothing comes from the Generous except generosity."

It is said that if you cannot stretch your hand to give recompense, you should stretch your tongue to give thanks. And it is said that there are four whose labors are fruitless: anyone who whispers to a deaf man, sets a benefit before the unthankful, sows in a salt marsh, or lights lamps in the sunshine. When Prophet Idris was given the good news of God's forgiveness, he requested a long life. Asked why, he said, "In order to thank Him, for before this I was working for forgiveness." The angel unfurled his wings and carried him off to heaven. One of the prophets passed by a little rock from which was issuing great amounts of water. He wondered at that, so God caused it to speak to him. "Since I heard God Most High say, '*A fire whose fuel is men and stones*' [66:6] it said, 'I have wept.'" So that prophet prayed to God to protect that rock. God Most High revealed to him that He had indeed protected it from the fire. The prophet went on. When he came by again he found the water gushing from it as before. He wondered, and God caused the rock to converse with him. "Why are you crying," he asked it, "When God has forgiven you?" "Those were tears of grief and fear," it said. "These are tears of gratitude and joy."

It is said that the grateful person is present with God's bounty, because what he sees is the blessing. God Most High said, "*If you are thankful, I will give you more*" [14:7]. The patient person, though, is present with God Most High, because what he sees is the One who is putting him to the test. God, glory to Him, said, "*Certainly God is with the patient*" [2:153; 8:46; 8:66].

It is said that a delegation came before caliph Umar ibn Abd al-Aziz. There was a young man among them who began to speak, but Umar cried, "Seniority, seniority! [Let the elders speak!]" "O Commander of the Faithful," the youth said to him, "If command were a matter of age, there are those among the Muslims who are older than you!" "Speak on," he said. "We are not a delegation of desire," he said, "nor are we a delegation of fear. Our desire has been conveyed to us by your gra-

ciousness, just as we have been made secure against our
fear by your justice." "Who are you, then?" "We are a delegation of gratitude. We have come to you to thank you
and go away." He recited:

> It would be a disaster if my gratitude were silent
> About what you have done, while your goodness is
>   eloquent.
> To see the benefit from you and keep it secret—
> That would make me a thief from the hand of the
>   Generous.

It is said that God Most High revealed to Prophet
Moses, "Be compassionate to My servants, both those
who are in tribulation and those who are protected from
it." "What troubles have the protected?" Prophet Moses
asked. "The smallness of their gratitude for My protection of them!" God Most High replied.

And it is said, "Praise is due for the breaths you
draw, gratitude for the capacities of your body." It is also
said, "Words of praise are a beginning and come to you
from Him, while thankfulness is an imitation that comes
to Him from you." According to a sound tradition, "The
first who will be summoned to paradise are those who
have praised God in every circumstance." And it is said,
"Praise is due for what He has prevented, but thankfulness is due for what He has done."

It is related that a Sufi said, "In one of my journeys
I saw a reverend man who had grown very old. I asked
him about his state. He said, 'Early in my life I fell in
love with the daughter of my uncle, and she likewise
with me, so it was arranged that she be wed to me. The
night of the wedding we said, "Come, let us enliven this
night with thanks to God Most High that He has
brought us together." So we prayed that night, and neither of us turned our attention to the other. When the

second night came we said the same thing. It is now seventy or eighty years that we have been this way every night. Is it not so, my dear?' 'It is just as the shaykh says,' the old lady replied."

19

ON CERTAINTY (YAQIN)

God Most High said, "Those who believe in what has been sent down to you and what has been sent down before you, and about the afterlife they are sure" [2:2-4].

Abu Bakr Muhammad ibn al-Hasan ibn Furak related to us . . . from Abd Allah ibn Masud that the Prophet said, "Do not try to satisfy any person by risking the displeasure of God Most High. Do not praise any person for the grace that comes from God Almighty and Glorious. Do not blame any person for what God has not given you—the greed of the greedy will not drive God's sustenance to you, nor will the hater's hatred turn it away from you. God, with His justice and equity, has set rest and joy in being satisfied with Him and in certainty. He has set worry and grief in doubt and discontent."

Abu Abd al-Rahman al-Sulami reported . . . that Abu Abd Allah al-Antaki said, "The smallest amount of certainty on reaching the heart fills it with light and denies it all doubt. Through it the heart is filled with gratitude and fear of God Most High."

Abu Jafar al-Haddad said, "Abu Turab al-Nakhshabi saw me while I was in the desert sitting by a spring. I had gone sixteen days without eating or drinking. He asked me, 'Why are you sitting here?' 'I am poised between religious knowledge and spiritual certainty, waiting to see which one will dominate so that I can bring myself together with it. For if knowledge gains control over me, I will drink, and if certainty gains control over me, I will go away.' 'A great undertaking will be yours,' he said to me."

Abu Uthman al-Hiri said, "Certainty means to care little about tomorrow." Sahl ibn Abd Allah al-Tustari said, "Certainty comes from increase of faith and its actualization." Sahl also said, "Certainty is a branch of faith and comes before attestation to truth." A Sufi said, "Certainty is knowledge deposited in hearts." This speaker is pointing out that it is not to be acquired by human effort but is given by the Truth.

Sahl said, "The beginning of certainty is discovery of the hidden—thus one of our ancestors said, 'If the veil were lifted, my certainty would not increase.' Next comes direct vision, and then contemplation."

Abu Abd Allah ibn Khafif said, "Certainty is the confirmation of the secrets pertaining to the order of the hidden mysteries." Abu Bakr ibn Tahir said, "Knowledge is the opposite of doubt, but in certainty there is no doubt." He was hinting at acquired and intuitive knowledge: the Sufi sciences are acquired in the beginning, but at the end become intuitive.

I heard Muhammad ibn al-Husayn say, "A Sufi declared that the first stage is knowledge of God. Then comes certainty, then confirmation, then sincerity, then bearing witness, then obedience in action, and the name of all of these together is faith."

The Sufi who said this was pointing out that the first thing one requires is the knowledge of God. Knowledge does not come about except by the prior fulfillment of its conditions—that is, one must examine things in a pertinent and relevant way. Then when hints of the divine have become continuous and clear demonstrative evidence has been obtained, the perceiver, through this succession of lights and his deep reflection upon them, becomes seemingly independent of the consideration of proof. This is the state of certainty. After this comes the power of confirming things about the future actions of God that one has heard reported from the divine messages brought by the Prophet—for confirmation can only relate to transmitted information. Next comes sincerity in all that follows from fulfilling God's commandments. After that, the divine response manifests by creating within one a beautiful witness to faith. Then comes carrying out the acts of obedience He has ordered and stripping oneself of what He has banished—but all within the unity.

Abu Bakr Muhammad ibn Furak hinted at the same idea when I heard him say, "Verbal remembrance of God is the surging up of the grace in the heart to the tongue." Sahl ibn Abd Allah said, "It is unlawful for a heart to smell the fragrance of certainty while relying upon what is other than God Most High." Dhu 'l-Nun al-Misri said, "Certainty calls one to drop ambitions. Dropping ambitions calls one to renunciation. Renunciation bequeaths wisdom. Wisdom bequeaths seeing the consequences of acts."

I heard Muhammad ibn al-Husayn say . . . that Dhu 'l-Nun al-Misri said, "Three signs of certainty are: mixing little with people; not praising them when they give something; not blaming them when they withhold something. Three signs of the supreme degree of certainty are: looking toward God Most High in everything, returning to Him in every matter; seeking His help in every state."

Junayd said, "Certainty is the establishment in the heart of knowledge that does not reverse itself, transform, or alter." Ibn Ata said, "Whatever certainty people obtain corresponds to the measure of their closeness to real fear of God. The foundation of this real fear is to stand opposed to what is prohibited. To oppose the prohibited is to oppose the ego. To the extent to which they separate themselves from the ego, they arrive at certainty."

A Sufi said, "Certainty is discovery, and discovery has three aspects: discovery of the meaning of transmitted information, of the manifestation of divine power, and of the realities of faith."

Know that discovery, *mukashafa*, when used in Sufi discourse, means the appearance of a thing to the heart with the force of something remembered, so that no doubt can remain. Sometimes the Sufis mean by the term 'discovery' an event resembling a dream between wakefulness and sleep, but usually they use the term *thibat*, 'sureness,' for this condition.

I heard Abu Bakr ibn Furak say that he asked a question of Abu Uthman al-Maghribi. "What is this thing you are saying?" he inquired. "I saw such-and-such people, and they said it," he told me. "Did you see them by ocular vision or by inward discovery?" I asked. "By discovery," he replied.

Amir ibn Abd Qays said, "Were the veil to be lifted, my certainty would not increase." Certainty, it is said, is looking at evident things with the force of faith. It is called "the disappearance of resistance." Junayd said, "Certainty is the elimination of doubt by witnessing of the unseen."

I heard Abu Ali al-Daqqaq say about the saying of the Prophet about Jesus the son of Mary, "Had his certainty increased, he would have walked on the air, as I did." The Prophet thus indicated his own state on the night of his Nocturnal Journey because it was regarding the subtleties of the Nocturnal Journey that he said, "I saw that the celestial steed al-Buraq would stay, so I walked on."

I heard Muhammad ibn al-Husayn say . . . that Sari asked about certainty, saying, "Certainty is your still-ness in the face of the wandering among expedients that takes place in your breast because you are sure that your own action will neither benefit you nor turn aside from you anything appointed." And I heard him say . . . Ali ibn Sahl said, "The peace in being present with the Truth is superior to certainty because presence is a place to settle, while certainty is a place of danger."

He seems to make of certainty the beginning of pres-ence with the Truth and presence with the Truth, the continuity of certainty. Thus he holds it possible to acquire certainty while devoid of presence, but holds it absurd to conceive of presence without any certainty. Regarding this, Nuri said, "Certainty is contemplation." That is, in contemplation is certainty without doubt, because no one can contemplate God without placing reliance in what comes from Him.

Abu Bakr al-Warraq said, "Certainty is the founda-tion of the heart and through it comes the perfection of faith. By certainty one knows God Most High, while by intellect one understands things from God Most High." Junayd said, "By certainty some men have walked on water, while those of greater certainty have died of thirst."

I heard Abu Abd al-Rahman al-Sulami say . . . that Ibrahim al-Khawwas said that he met a youth like a sil-ver ingot in the desert waste. "Where are you going, young man?" he asked. "To Mecca." "Without provisions, or a caravan, or any money for your support?" "O you whose certainty is weak!" he said to me. "Is not the One Who is able to preserve the heavens and the earth able to bring me to Mecca without attachment?" When I entered Mecca, while circumambulating the Kabah, I suddenly found myself with him. He was saying:

O eye that is tearful always, O ego dead and dark
Do not love anyone except the Sublime, the Absolute!

When he saw me, he asked, "O Shaykh, is your certainty still so weak?" And I heard him say . . . that al-Nahrajuri said that when the servant has perfected the inner dimensions of certainty, trouble becomes a blessing for him and ease becomes a misfortune.

Abu Bakr al-Warraq said, "Certainty has three faces: the certainty of a received report, the certainty of a piece of evidence and the certainty of seeing for oneself." Abu Turab al-Nakhshabi said, "I saw a youth walking in the desert without provisions. 'If he has no certainty with him, he is destroyed,' I said to myself. So I called, 'Young man! To be in a place like this without any supplies . . . .' 'O Shaykh,' he said, 'raise your head! Do you see anything but God Almighty and Glorious?' 'Now go howsoever you will,' said I."

I heard Muhammad ibn al-Husayn say . . . that Abu Said al-Kharraz said, "Knowledge is what urges you to work. Certainty is what carries you." And I heard him say . . . that Ibrahim al-Khawwas said, "I worked for a living in order to eat lawfully. I was a fisherman. One day a fish fell into the net, so I drew it out and cast the net into the water. Another fell in. I threw it out too, and then went back home. An unseen voice said to me, 'You only find your living in catching those who remember Us, so kill you them!' He said, I tore the net and gave up fishing."

20
ON PATIENCE (SABR)

God Glorified and Exalted said, *"Be patient; and you cannot be patient except through God"* [16:127].

Ali ibn Ahmad al-Ahwazi reported . . . from Abu Hurayra from Ayisha that the Messenger of God said, "Patience is the forbearance shown at the initial shock." (The same Tradition is reported by Ali ibn Ahmad. . . from Anas ibn Malik).

Thereafter patience is of different sorts. There is patience with what the servant has brought on himself and patience with what has come to him independently of his will. Patience with things for which he is responsible is itself in two parts: patience in what God Most High has commanded him to do and patience in what He has forbidden him from doing. As for patience in what the servant has not earned, it consists of enduring whatever hardship attaches itself to him by the decree of God.

I heard Abu Abd al-Rahman al-Sulami say . . . that Junayd said, "The journey from this world to the next is smooth and simple for the believer, but leaving ordinary life for the sake of God is difficult. The journey from the ego to God Most High is extremely difficult, and patience in God is more difficult still." Junayd was asked about

135

patience. He said, "It means swallowing gall without a frown."

Ali ibn Abi Talib said, "Patience in relation to faith is like head in relation to the body." Abu 'l- Qasim al-Hakim said, "The saying of the Most High, 'Be patient' is a command relating to worship, while His saying, '*You cannot be patient except through God*' [16:127] relates to servanthood itself. Whoever progresses from the degree of 'for You' to the degree of 'through You' has been transported from the level of worship to the level of servanthood. The Prophet said, 'Through You I live and through You I die.'"

I heard Abu Abd al-Rahman al-Sulami say . . . that Ahmad ibn Abil-Hawari said he asked Abu Sulayman al-Darani about patience. "By God, we are not patient with what we love!" he told him. "How shall we be patient with what we hate?"

Dhu 'l-Nun said, "Patience is to keep your distance from acts of opposition to God, to keep silent while swallowing choking lumps of distress, and to show independence although poverty afflicts you in the fields of daily life." Ibn Ata said, "Patience is to dwell in tribulation with the finest of conduct." And it is described as vanishing into trouble without manifesting complaint.

Abu Uthman said, "The continuously patient one is he whose ego has been accustomed to unpleasant things by the surprises of life. It is said that patience is to settle down with tribulation in good fellowship, as one settles down with well-being." He also said, "The best reward granted for any act of worship is that which is given for patience. There is no reward higher. God Almighty and Glorious has said, '*We shall grant those who are patient their recompense according to the best of what they have done*' [16:96]."

Amr ibn Uthman al-Makki said, "Patience means standing firm with God Glorified and Exalted, meeting trials with equanimity and welcome." Al-Khawwas said,

"Patience is to persevere in the principles of the Book and the *Sunnah*." Yahya ibn Muadh said, "The patience of lovers is harder than the patience of ascetics. I am amazed that they keep patient!" And he recited:

Patience is to be praised in every realm
Except in wanting You.
That is not to be praised!

Ruwaym said, "Patience is to stop complaining." Dhu 'l-Nun said, "Patience is to seek help through God Most High." I heard Abu Ali al-Daqqaq say, "Patience is like its name. [*Sabr* also means aloes, an important medicine that is very bitter].

Abu Abd al-Rahman al-Sulami recited to me . . . what Ibn Ata recited to himself:

I will be patient, if it pleases You, and be ruined by sorrow.
It is enough for me that You are satisfied,
though my patience destroy me.

Abu Abd Allah ibn Khafif said, "Patience has three phases: there is the person who attempts patience (*mutasabbir*), the patient person (*sabir*), and the continuously patient or steadfast person (*sabbar*)." Ali ibn Abi Talib said, "Patience is a mount that does not stumble." Muhammad ibn al-Husayn said he heard Ali ibn Abd Allah al-Basri say that a man stopped before Shibli and asked, "What sort of patience is hardest on the one who is patient?" "Patience for God's sake," he replied. "No," said the man. "Then patience toward God." "No." "Then patience in God." "No!" "Then what thing is it?" "Patience away from God," the man said. And Shibli screamed such a scream that his spirit might have departed! And he heard him say . . . that Abu Muhammad al-Jurayri said, "Real patience means making no distinction between hardship and ease, together with peace of mind in both states. The effort of patience is to be tranquil despite tribulation, despite the agony of the weight of trouble.

One of them recited:

> I was patient, and the desire of You
> did not break upon my patience.
> I concealed what I felt toward You
> from the place of patience,
> Out of fear that my soul
> would complain of my longing
> To my tears, in secret,
> and they flow without my knowing.

I heard Abu Ali al-Daqqaq say, "The patient win the glory of both worlds because they obtain from God His company. God Most High has said, *'God is with the patient'* [2:153].

It is said that the meaning of His saying, *"Be patient, and strive in patience, and take a fighting position"* [3:200] is that patience is less than striving in patience (*musabira*), which is less than taking a fighting position (*murabita*). It is said *"Be patient"*—with your ego in maintaining obedience to God Most High; *"strive in patience"*—with your heart, in troubles for God's sake; *"and take a fighting position"*—with your innermost being, in yearning for God. And it is also said, *"Be patient"* for God, *"strive in patience"* through God, *"and take a fighting position"* in God.

God Most High revealed to Prophet David, "Qualify yourself with My qualities. One of My qualities is that I am the Most Patient." And we are told, "Drink patience! For if He kills you, He will kill you as a martyr and if He allows you to live, He will make you live honorably."

Patience toward God is a form of hardship, while patience through God is a form of abiding in Him.

Patience for God's sake is a trial, while patience together with God is loyalty. Patience away from Him is alienation!

They recited:

> Patience away from You—its results are
> blameworthy,
> While patience in everything else is deserving of
> praise.

And they recited:

> How patience, away from one who is as free of me
> as the place of the right hand is free from that of
> the left?
> While men have amused themselves with everything,
> I have seen that Love amuses itself with men!

"Patience in quest," it is said, "is the token of victory, patience in trouble the sign of release."

I heard Mansur ibn Khalaf al Maghribi say, "Once a dervish was beaten with whips. When he was returned to prison, he called over one of his companions and spit into his hand. Some bits of silver fell from his mouth into the man's hand. Asked about this, he said, 'I had two dirhams in my mouth. I did not want to cry out while in the sight of a certain person who is on the fringes of my circle, so I bit on the dirhams. They broke in my mouth.'"

It is said that your state is your fortress, and all things below God Most High are your enemies so take up a good fighting position in the fortress of your state! And it is said that "striving in patience" is patience upon patience, patience drowned in patience, and patience overpowered by patience. As it is said:

> He who is patient with patience, patience seeks help
> from him.
> Patiently the lover gives patience its due.

It is told that Shibli was once held in an insane asylum. A group of people went to see him. "Who are you?" he asked. "Your friends who have come to visit you," said they. So he started to throw stones at them, and they ran away. "O liars!" he called. "If you were my friends, you would have been patient with my trial!"

According to some reports God Most High has said, "By My Essence, what the sufferers endure is for My sake." God Most High said, *Be patient with the decision of your Lord; you are in Our sight* [52:48]."

A Sufi said, "In Mecca I saw a dervish circumambulating the House of God. He took a scrap of paper out of his pocket, looked at it and went away. The next day he did the same thing. I observed him for many days, and he always performed the same action. One day he made the circumambulation, looked at the scrap, then moved away a little and fell down dead! I took the scrap from his pocket. It said, *"Be patient with the decision of your Lord; you are in Our sight* [52:48]."

A young man was seen striking an old man in the face with his sandal. "Aren't you ashamed? Hitting an old gentleman in the face like that!" people asked. "His crime is great," the youth replied. "And what is that?" "This old man claims that he longs for me, but for three days he hasn't been to see me!"

A dervish said, "I went to India, and saw there a man with one eye who was called 'The Patient One'. I asked about his condition. They told me that in the prime of his youth a dear friend of his left on a journey. As he returned from saying farewell, tears flowed from one of his eyes, but the other did not weep. He said to his dry eye, 'Why are you not crying over my separation from my friend? I will forbid you to look on this world!' He shut his eye, and for sixty years he has not opened it."

It is said that the expression "beautiful patience" in

the saying of the Most High, *"So be patient with a beau -
tiful patience"* [70:5] refers to a person who suffers trouble and distress, yet cannot be told apart from other people. Umar ibn al-Khattab said, "If patience and thankfulness were two camels, I would not care which one of
them I rode."

When trials came upon him, Ibn Shubrumah used to
say, "It is only a cloud—soon it will scatter." In a hadith,
the Prophet, when asked about faith, replied, "Patience
and generosity of action." (Abu Abd al-Rahman al-
Sulami reported this hadith . . . from the great-grandfa-
ther of Umayr).

Sari al-Saqati was asked about patience. He had
begun to speak of it when a scorpion stung him in the
foot, striking him with its tail many times. He kept
quiet. When asked, "Why didn't you brush it away?" he
replied, "I would have been ashamed before God to speak
of patience and not be patient."

According to one hadith, the patient poor will sit
with God Most High on the day of judgment. God Most
High revealed to one of the prophets, "I sent My trials
upon My servant, so he prayed to Me and I was long in
answering him. Then he complained to Me, and I said, 'O
My servant, how shall I deliver you from something
which is in itself the means of delivering you?'"

Ibn Uyaynah commented on the meaning of the
Koranic verse, *"When they were patient, We made them
leaders guided by Our command"* [32:24], saying,
"Because they took hold of the chief thing, We made
them chiefs."

I heard Abu Ali al-Daqqaq say, "The definition of
patience is that one not resist the ordainment of destiny.
To talk about trouble without complaining about it does
not invalidate patience. God Most High said in the story
of Job, *"We found him patient. How excellent a servant!
Surely he turned to Us,"* [38:44] although He also report-

ed that Job had said, "*Trouble has touched me*" [21:83].
And I heard him say, "God drew this statement out of
him (that is, his saying, '*Trouble has touched me*,') in
order that it might be a relief for the weak ones of this
community.

A dervish said, "'*We found him patient*'—He did not
say 'totally patient'! For not all of his states were
patience. In some conditions he used to seek pleasure
from trials and find sweetness in them, and in this state
of finding delight he was not enduring with patience.
Therefore he was not called 'totally patient'."

I heard Abu Ali say that the essence of patience is
that one leave trouble as one entered into it. The example is Prophet Job. At the end of his trials he said,
"*Trouble has touched me, and You are the most merciful
of the merciful*" [21:83]. Thus he maintained the best
conduct in addressing God, for in saying "You are the
most merciful of the merciful" he only hinted, rather
that making a plain declaration and saying "Have mercy
upon me."

Know that patience is of two sorts: the patience of
servants and the patience of lovers. The best thing is for
the patience of servants to be preserved and for the
patience of lovers to be abandoned.

With this meaning they have recited:

It was clear, on the day of separation:
His promise of patience was a lie from the start!

And with this meaning I heard Abu Ali al-Daqqaq
say that when Prophet Jacob had sworn himself to
patience, he began by saying, "*And so a beautiful
patience*" [12:83]. That means, "So my business is a
beautiful patience." After that, he could not be moved
until he cried, "*O my grief for Joseph!*" [12:84].

21

ON VIGILANCE (*MURAQABA*)

God Most High has said, *"God over everything is Vigilant"* [33:52].

Abu Naim Abdul-Malik ibn al-Hasan ibn Muhammad ibn Ishaq reported . . . from Jurayr ibn Abd Allah al-Bajli that Gabriel appeared to the Prophet in the form of a man. "O Muhammad," he said, "What is faith (*iman*)?" The Prophet replied: "To believe in God, His angels, His books, His messengers, and destiny—its good and bad, its sweet and bitter, come from God." "You have spoken the truth," said the visitor. We were surprised that someone would corroborate the Prophet, both questioning him and confirming what he said. "And inform me: What is *islam* (submission to God's will)?" he continued. "Islam is to establish prayer, give the poor-rate, fast during the month of Ramadan and make the pilgrimage to the House of God." "You have spoken the truth," he said again. "So tell me about doing what is beautiful (*ihsan*)?" "Doing what is beautiful is to worship God as if you see Him, and if you do not see Him, certainly He sees you." "You have spoken the truth," he said.

What the Prophet has here spoken—"And if you do not see Him, certainly He sees you"—points to the state

143

of vigilance, for vigilance is the servant's knowledge that the Lord is aware of him. Perseverance in this knowledge is vigilant awareness of the Lord which is the foundation of every good for the servant. One can hardly attain to this degree until one has emptied oneself through *muhasaba*, self-observation and inner accounting. The person who has taken account of what he has done in the past and improved his state in the present has attached himself to the path of the Truth. In his relationship with God Most High, he has learned how to keep a heedful heart. He has guarded his breaths for God and turned his attention to God in all his states. So he knows that God is watchful over him— close to his heart, knowing his states, seeing his acts, hearing his words. Whoever is neglectful of all of this is far from the beginning of contact—how far, then, from the realities of nearness to Him?

I heard Abu Abd al-Rahman al-Sulami say . . . that al-Jurayri said that whoever does not establish awe of duty and vigilance in his relationship to God will not arrive at disclosure of the unseen or contemplation of the divine. I heard Abu Ali al-Daqqaq say, "A prince had a vizier who, while attending upon his sovereign one day, turned his regard to some serving youths who were standing there, not because of any misgiving, but because some motion or sound from them had caught his attention. It so happened that the prince looked at his vizier at that moment. The vizier feared the prince would suppose that he had looked at the youths with suspicion and begin to look at him in the same way. After that day that vizier would always come into the prince's presence looking to the side until the prince supposed that his physical disposition had changed. Such was the attentiveness of a creature toward a creature—what then should be the vigilance of the servant towards his Lord?

I heard a dervish tell the following story. A prince possessed a serving youth whom he admitted to his presence more often than his other slaves. This youth was not more valuable than they, nor was he fairer of form. The others therefore were curious about it. The prince wanted to demonstrate to them the young man's superiority in service. One day he was out riding together with his entourage. In the distance was a snow-capped mountain. The prince looked toward the snow and bowed his head. At this, the youth raced off on his horse and nobody knew why! After awhile he returned, bringing some snow with him. "What made you know that I wanted the snow?" asked the prince. "You looked at it," said the youth, "and the sultan's looking at anything can only arise from a clear intention." "I have selected him for my hospitality and acceptance," said the prince "because while everyone has some occupation, his occupation is to consider my glances and attend upon my states."

A Sufi said, "Whoever is vigilant towards God Most High in his thoughts will be made blameless by God in his acts." Abu 'l-Husayn ibn Hind was asked, "When does the shepherd use his staff to drive the flock away from dangerous pastures?" "When he knows that someone is watching," he replied.

It is said that while traveling, Ibn Umar saw a young man keeping watch over a flock. He asked him, "Would you sell me one of these sheep?" "They do not belong to me," the youth replied. "Tell their owner that the wolf took one of them!" he suggested. "And where is God during all of this?" the servant asked. For a long time afterward Ibn Umar would repeat, "That servant said, 'And where is God during all of this?'"

Junayd said, "If someone has made vigilance to God a reality, he will fear how far his worldly fortune is from his Lord—nothing else."

Once a shaykh chose to keep company with one of his

students more often than he received the others. They complained to him about this and he said, "I will make it clear to you." He handed a bird to each of them and said, "Go and kill this where no one can see." He gave one to his favorite as well. They went away and each one of them came back having slaughtered his bird. Then the favorite came back with his bird still alive. "Did you not kill it, then?" the shaykh asked. "You ordered me to kill it where no one could see," explained the student, "but I didn't find any place where Someone could not see!" "This is why I have singled him out for my company," announced the shaykh.

Dhu 'l-Nun al-Misri said, "The sign of vigilant awareness is to prefer what God Most High prefers, to hold to be important that which He holds to be important, and to see as trivial that which He sees as trivial." Al-Nasrabadhi said, "Hope moves you to acts of obedience. Fear removes you from acts of disobedience, and vigilance directs you to the paths of the realities."

I heard Muhammad ibn al-Husayn say he heard Abu 'l-Abbas al-Baghdadi say that Jafar ibn Nisar was asked what vigilance was. He said, "Watchfulness over your inner being because of awareness of God's gaze with every thought." And I heard him say . . . al-Jurayri said, "This business of ours is constructed in two parts: that you oblige yourself to devote your attention to God Most High and that your outer aspect be in conformity with religious knowledge." And I heard him say . . . al-Murtaish said, "Vigilance means watchfulness over the innermost because of attentiveness to the unseen with every glance and expression."

Ibn Ata was asked, "What is the best act of obedience?" He replied, "Vigilance of God at all times." Ibrahim al-Khawwas said, "Attentiveness bequeaths vigilance. Vigilance bequeaths purity of being and openness to God Most High."

I heard Abu Abd al-Rahman al-Sulami say that he heard Abu Uthman al-Maghribi say, "The best thing to which a person can attach himself in this Way is self-observation, attentiveness, and governance of his works by knowledge." And he heard him say . . . that Abu Uthman said that Abu Hafs said to him, "When you sit with people, be a warner of your heart and your ego, and their company will never lead you astray. Remember that they are looking at your exterior, but God is looking at your interior." And he heard him say . . . that Abu Said al-Kharraz said, "One of my shaykhs told me, 'Your duty is reverence of soul and vigilance towards God.' Afterwards, as I was traveling one day in the desert, I was terrified by a noise behind me. I wanted to turn around but did not. Then I saw something over my shoulder so I turned, and was appalled. I turned full around and there I was with a tremendous lion!"

Al-Wasiti said, "The best act of obedience is to guard your every moment—that is, the servant should not study beyond his limit, attend to anything but his Lord, or keep company with anything but the present moment."

22
ON SATISFACTION (RIDA)

God Most High has said, *"God is pleased with them and they with Him"* [98:8].

Ali ibn Ahmad al-Ahwazi reported . . . that Jabir said that the Messenger of God said, "While the people of paradise are sitting together, a light will shine upon them from the gate of paradise. They will raise their heads and lo! the Lord Most High will be looking down upon them. He will say, 'O people of paradise, ask of Me!' They will say, 'We ask that You be pleased with us.' The Most High will say, 'You have entered My House because I am pleased with you. This is the time when I will honor you with My gifts, so ask of Me.' They will say, 'We ask You for increase.' So they will be given camels of red ruby with halters of red ruby and green emerald. They will travel upon them, and each step that they set their hoofs will be as far as the eye can see. God, glory to Him, will command trees with fruit upon them. The maidens of paradise will come to them and say, 'We are tender virgins who do not fade. We are eternal and we do not die— mates for a noble believing people!' And God, glory to Him, will order a sand dune of fragrant white musk, and the wind called 'The Arouser' will rouse them to excitement, until ultimately they come to the garden of Eden,

which is the citadel of paradise. Then the angels will say,
'O Our Lord, the people have come!' And God will say,
'Welcome, O truthful ones! Welcome, O obedient ones!'
The veils will be lifted for them, and they will look upon
God Almighty and Glorious. They will be provided with
the light of the Beneficent, so much so that one of them
will not see another. Afterwards He will say, 'Return
them to the palaces with rare gifts.' So they will be
returned and will recognize each other again. And the
Messenger of God said, 'That is the meaning of the say-
ing of the Most High, *"A provision from a Forgiving and
Merciful One'* [41:32].'"

The Iraqis and the Khurasanis disagree over
whether full satisfaction in God should be counted
among the spontaneously granted spiritual states
(*ahwal*) or the earned stations of development (*maqa -
mat*). The people of Khurasan say that full satisfaction
belongs to the stages and that it is the highest evolution
of trust. This means that it is one of those things that
the servant may reach as a result of his own efforts. The
Iraqis, however, say that such satisfaction belongs to the
states, that the servant cannot acquire it, but that it is
an event that befalls the heart like the rest of the states.
Agreement is possible between these two positions, for it
is said that the beginning of pleasure in God's will can be
obtained by the servant and is one of the stages, while
its end belongs to the states and cannot be acquired.

Many people have talked of full satisfaction in God,
each one expressing his own state and his own experience of it. Their statements vary since their experiences
and portions of it are dissimilar. According to religious
knowledge, the necessary definition of the condition of
full satisfaction is: someone who is satisfied with God
Most High and does not oppose what He has destined.

I heard Abu Ali al-Daqqaq say, "Satisfaction does not
mean that you do not feel difficulties. Satisfaction only
means that you do not oppose God's decision and judgment."

Know that the thing with which the servant must be pleased is destiny itself. He has been commanded to be satisfied with this. It is neither necessary nor possible for the servant to be pleased with much of what destiny contains, such as acts of disobedience or the various sorts of trials that Muslims undergo. The shaykhs have said, "Satisfaction with the divine will is the greatest gate of God."

They mean that whoever is ennobled by satisfaction has been fully welcomed by God and been honored by the the most exalted proximity. I heard Muhammad ibn al-Husayn say . . . that Abd al-Wahid ibn Zayd said, "Satisfaction with the divine will is the greatest gate of God and the paradise of this world."

Know that the servant can hardly be satisfied with the Truth, glory to Him, until the Truth is satisfied with him because God Almighty and Glorious has said, "*God is pleased with them and [then] they with Him*" [98:8]. I heard Abu Ali al-Daqqaq say that a student asked his master, "Is the servant aware when God Most High is pleased with him?" "No. How should he know that," his master said, "while His pleasure belongs to the unseen?" "But indeed, he does know that!" the student rejoined. "How?" inquired the master. "When I find my heart to be satisfied with God Most High," the student said, "I know that He is satisfied with me." "Well done, my boy!" said the master.

It is said that Prophet Moses prayed, "My God, show me a work such that if I performed it, You would be pleased with me on account of it." God replied, "You are not capable of that." Moses fell to the ground, prostrating himself in entreaty and God Most High revealed to him, 'O son of Imran, My satisfaction is in your satisfaction with My judgment!'"

Abu Abd al-Rahman al-Sulami reported . . . that Abu Sulayman al-Darani said, "When the servant thinks no more about desires, he is satisfied." And I heard him say that al-Nasrabadhi said, "Whoever wishes to reach the

place of full satisfaction should cling to that in which
God has set His satisfaction." Muhammad ibn Khafif
said, "Satisfaction has two parts: satisfaction in Him and
satisfaction with Him. Satisfaction in Him is to be
pleased with Him as Orderer of affairs. Satisfaction with
Him pertains to what He has decided."
I heard Abu Ali al-Daqqaq say, "The seeker's road is
long. It is the road of training the ego. The road of the
elite of God's servants is shorter but also harder. On that
road one's acts must correspond to satisfaction in God,
and one's satisfaction must correspond to one's destiny."
Ruwaym said, "Full satisfaction means that if God were
to place hell at someone's right hand [in the direction of
paradise], he would not ask Him to move it to his left."
Abu Bakr ibn Tahir said, "Full satisfaction means that
negativity leaves your heart until there is nothing in it
but happiness and delight." Al-Wasiti said, "The state of
satisfaction in God has a use for your effort. Do not stop
its making use of you, or you will become veiled by its
delight and vision from the reality of what it reveals."
Know that this saying of al-Wasiti is a thing of great
importance. It contains a warning against a hidden trap
for Sufis. For them, settling into states is a veil over the
transformer of states. If you seek the pleasure of satisfaction and find in your heart the ease and rest of satisfaction, you will be veiled by your state from witnessing
the Truth. Therefore al-Wasiti has also said, "Beware of
seeking the sweetness of devotions—it is deadly poison!"
Ibn Khafif said, "Full satisfaction is the heart's peace in
relying upon His judgments and the heart's agreement
with and preference for that which pleases God." Rabia
al-Adawiyyah was asked, "When is the servant truly satisfied?" She replied, "When bad fortune pleases him as
well as does good."
In front of Junayd, Shibli spoke the formula used
when something disturbs one, "There is no power nor
strength save in God!" Junayd said, "Your saying that

comes from distress of the heart, and distress of the heart comes from abandoning satisfaction with the decision of God!" Shibli was silent.

Abu Sulayman al-Darani said, "Taking pleasure in God's will means that you neither ask God Most High for the garden nor seek refuge with Him from the fire!" I heard Muhammad ibn al-Husayn say . . . that Dhu 'l-Nun al-Misri said, "Three of the signs of satisfaction are: having no preference towards God's decision, feeling no bitterness after His decision, and the passion of love in the midst of trials." And I heard him say that . . . Muhammad ibn Yazid al-Mubarrid said that Husayn ibn Ali ibn Abi Talib heard that Abu Dharr said, "Poverty is dearer to me than wealth, and sickness is dearer to me than health." He said, "May God have mercy upon Abu Dharr! As for me, I say that whoever trusts in the goodness of God's choice for him has no wish for anything but what God Almighty and Glorious has chosen for him."

Fudayl ibn Iyad said to Bishr al-Hafi, "Satisfaction is better than asceticism in this world because the satisfied person does not wish for what is above his station." Abu Uthman al-Hiri was asked about the prayer of the Prophet, "I ask You for satisfaction after the decision." He said, "To be satisfied before a trial takes place is the intention to be satisfied, whereas satisfaction after it takes place is really satisfaction."

I heard Abu Abd al-Rahman al-Sulami say . . . that Abu Sulayman al-Darani said, "I hope I know a little bit about being pleased with God. If He sent me into the fire, I would be satisfied with that." Abu Umar al-Dimashqi said, "Full satisfaction is the disappearance of anxiety, whatever the judgment may be." Junayd said, "Full satisfaction is the suspension of preference." Ibn Ata said, "Full satisfaction means the heart looks at the eternal dimension of God Most High's choice for the servant. It is abandoning resentment." Ruwaym said, "Full satisfaction is meeting the judgments of God with joy."

Al-Muhasibi said, "Satisfaction is quietness of heart in the midst of troubles." Nuri said, "Full satisfaction is happiness of heart in the bitterness of destiny."

I heard Muhammad ibn al-Husayn say that . . . that al-Jurayri said, "If someone is satisfied with less than his due, God will raise him beyond his utmost goal." And I heard him say . . . that Abu Turab al-Nakhshabi said, "Satisfaction in God is not granted to anyone in whose heart the world finds scope."

Abu Abd al-Rahman al-Sulami reported . . . from Abbas ibn Abd al-Muttalib that the Messenger of God said, "Whoever is satisfied with God as Lord has tasted the sweetness of faith." It is told that Umar ibn al-Khattab wrote to Abu Musa al-Ashari, "In satisfaction is the whole of good. If you are able, be satisfied—if not, be patient."

It is said that Utbah al-Ghulam spent a whole night until morning saying, "If You punish me, know that I love You, and if You have mercy upon me, know that I love You!" I heard Abu Ali al-Daqqaq say, "The human being is earthenware. Earthenware does not have enough value that it should resist the judgment of the Truth, may He be exalted.

Abu Uthman al-Hiri said, "For forty years God Almighty and Glorious has not established me in a state that I hated or transported me to another that I resented." I heard Abu Ali al-Daqqaq say, "A man was angry with his slave. The slave asked someone to intercede with his master. He forgave him, and the slave began to cry. The one who had interceded asked, 'Why are you crying when your master has forgiven you?' "He seeks my pleasure alone, and he cannot reach that," the master told him. "It is only because of this that he cries."

23
ON SERVANTHOOD (*UBUDIYAH*)

God Almighty and Glorious has said, "*So serve your Lord until that which is certain [death] comes to you*" [15:99].

Abu 'l-Hasan al-Ahwazi reported . . . from Abu Hurayra, that the Messenger of God said, "Seven are they whom God will shade with His shade on the day when there will be no shade but His shade: a just leader; a youth raised in the service of God Most High; a man whose heart clings to the mosque from the time he leaves it until he returns to it; two men who love each other in God, coming together and parting from each other for the sake of God; a man who remembers God in solitude so that his eyes stream with tears; a man who is invited by a charming and beautiful woman but says, 'I fear God, the Lord of the Worlds'; a man who gives charity and conceals it so that his left hand does not know what his right hand has spent."

I heard Abu Ali al-Daqqaq say, "Servanthood is more perfect than worship (*ibada*). First comes worship, then servanthood, then total adoration (*ubuda*)." Thus worship is for ordinary believers, servanthood for the elite, and total adoration for the elite of the elite. I heard him say, "Worship is for the one who has received true information about God. Servanthood is for the one who has seen the truth. Total adoration is for the one who has truth of being." And I heard him say, "Worship belongs to people engaged in the struggle against the lower self, servanthood belongs to the masters of endurance in that fight, while total adoration is an attribute of those who have reached the contemplation of God. Whoever does not spare his own ego is involved in worship. Whoever does not withhold his heart is involved in servanthood. Whoever is not miserly with his soul is involved in adoration."

It is said that servanthood means to fulfill the duties of obedience unstintingly, to look at what proceeds from you as insufficient, and to view what is produced by your virtues as ordained by God. And it is said that servanthood means to give up your own will for the sake of the manifest orders of God. Servitude or servanthood is to free yourself from pretensions to strength and power and to affirm that prosperity and favor have but been entrusted to you. Servanthood is to embrace that to which you have been commanded and to leave that against which you have been warned.

Muhammad ibn Khafif was asked, "When is servanthood sound and whole?" He replied, "When one has cast one's weight upon one's Master, and is patient with Him under His trial." I heard Abu Abd al-Rahman al-Sulami say . . . that Sahl ibn Abd Allah al-Tustari said, "Concentrated devotion is not right for anyone until four things cease to worry him: hunger, wearing rags, poverty, and humiliation."

Servanthood means that you surrender all of yourself to Him and let Him carry your burden. One of its signs is that you abandon planning and precaution and bear witness to destiny. Dhu 'l-Nun al-Misri said, "Servanthood is that you are His servant at all times, as He is your Lord at all times."

Al-Jurayri said, "The servants of benefit are many,

but the servants of the Benefactor are precious." I heard Abu Ali al-Daqqaq say, "You are the slave of the one who holds you in bondage and captivity. If you are in bondage to your ego, you are the slave of your ego, and if you are in bondage to your worldly life, you are the slave of your worldly life."

The Messenger of God said, "How wretched is the servant of the dirham! How wretched is the servant of the dinar! How wretched is the servant of the fine garment!"

Abu Zayn saw a man and asked him, "What is your trade?" "Donkey server," the man replied. "May God Most High kill your donkey so that you may be the servant of God, not the servant of the donkey!" said he.

I heard Abu Abd al-Rahman say that his grandfather Abu Amr ibn Nujayd said, "You are not truly ready for the first step in servanthood until you can testify that as far as you are concerned, your works are all show and your states pretension."

I heard him say . . . that Abd Allah ibn Munazil said, "Only the servant who does not seek others to serve him is a real servant. If he has looked for a servant for himself, he has fallen outside the bounds of servanthood and abandoned its behavior." And I heard him say . . . Sahl ibn Abd Allah al-Tustari said, "It is not appropriate for the servant to pursue a life of exclusive devotion until he is such that no trace of wretchedness is visible upon him in a time of poverty nor any trace of luxury in a time of wealth."

It is said that servanthood is the witnessing of the divine lordship. I heard Abu Ali al-Daqqaq say that al-Nasrabadhi said, "The value of a worshipper is determined by what he worships, just as a knower is ennobled by what it is that he knows." Abu Hafs said, "Servanthood is the ornament of the servant. Whoever abandons it lacks all adornment."

I heard Muhammad ibn al-Husayn say . . . that al-Nibaji said, "The foundation of worship is three things: refusing none of His decisions, withholding nothing from Him, and not letting Him hear you ask what you need from anyone else." I heard him say . . . that Ibn Ata said, "Servanthood is in four traits: keeping your promise; staying within the bounds of the divine law; being pleased with what you have; being patient with what you lack." And I heard him say . . . Amr ibn Uthman al-Makki said, "I never saw anyone, among all those I met in Mecca or elsewhere or those who reached us at the pilgrimage season, who made a fiercer effort in God's service or worshiped more continuously than al-Muzani [student of the great codifier of the divine law, al-Shafii]. Neither have I seen anyone who took more seriously the grandeur of God's commands nor anyone harder on himself and more liberal towards other people than he was."

I heard Abu Ali al-Daqqaq say, "There is nothing nobler than servanthood nor any name more perfect for a believer than having a name for servanthood. Thus God Most High, describing the Prophet on the night of the nocturnal journey, which was the moment of his highest honor in this world, said, *"Exalted is He Who transported His servant by night from the Sacred Mosque,"* [17:1] and *"And revealed to His servant that which He revealed"* [53:10]. If there had been a name more glorious than that of servanthood, He would have called him by it.

With this meaning they recite:

O Amr, to avenge my blood is Zahra's right
As anyone who hears and sees will know.
Call me by no name but, "O her servant!"
It is my noblest title.

One of the Sufis said, "There are only two obstacles:

Finding peace in one's own pleasure and relying upon one's own actions. When these two things fall away from you, you truly become a servant." On this subject Al-Wasiti said, "Beware of the bliss that comes with God's gifts. It is a veil for the pure."

Abu Ali al-Juzjani said, "Satisfaction with God's will is the house of servanthood. Patience is its door. Self-abandonment is its inner room. One knocks at the door, is free of labor in the house and finds comfort in the inner room."

I heard Abu Ali al-Daqqaq say, "Just as Lordship is an eternal attribute of the Truth, so servanthood is a continuous attribute of the servant, which can never leave him.

The Sufis recite:

If you ask me, I say I am His slave.
If He is asked, He says He is my master.

I heard Abu Abd al-Rahman al-Sulami say, "Worship performed in search of pardon and forgiveness for one's shortcomings is closer to being real service than is worship performed in hopes of compensation and reward." And I heard him say that al-Nasrabadhi said, "Servanthood is losing sight of one's attempts at service in the vision of the One served." And I heard him say . . . that Junayd said, "Servanthood is to give up every sort of occupation and employment for the sake of a work which is the root of freedom from your own work."

24
WILL POWER (*IRADA*)

God Almighty and Glorious said, "*Do not drive away those who call upon their Lord in the morning and evening, wishing for His Face*" [6:52].

Ali ibn Ahmad ibn Abdan related . . . through Anas that the Prophet said, "When God Most High wishes good to a servant, He makes use of him." He was asked, "How does He make use of him, O Messenger of God?" He replied, "By making him successful in a righteous work before death."

Irada, the will to find God, is the beginning of the path of spiritual travelers, the first title given to those who are determined to reach God Most High. This attribute is only called *irada* because will is the preface to every undertaking. What the servant does not will, he does not carry out. Since this is the start of the enterprise of one who travels the path of God Almighty and Glorious, it is called 'will' by analogy to the resolution involved at the beginning of everything else.

According to etymology, the disciple is 'he who possesses will', just as the knower is 'he who possesses knowledge' because the word belongs to the class of derived nouns. But in Sufi usage, the disciple is he who possesses no will at all! Here, one who does not abandon will cannot be called a disciple, just as, linguistically, one who does not possess will cannot be called a disciple. Many people talked about the meaning of will, each expressing the extent it has manifested to his heart. Most shaykhs say that will means the abandonment of what has become habitual. What is habitual for people, in the vast majority of cases, is dwelling in the realms of unconsciousness, basing one's life upon he pursuit of appetite and inclining toward whatever one's desires call for. The spiritual aspirant is someone who has cast off all of this. His emergence becomes a token and a guide to the soundness of his wish. This condition is called spiritual wish: it means the emergence from the habitual.

While the abandonment of what is habitual is the mark of spiritual wish, its inner reality is the activation of the heart in searching for the Truth. Thus is is called a pain of love which sets at nought every object of fear. I heard Abu Ali al-Daqqaq give an account that Mumshad al-Dinawari said, "Since I learned that the states of the dervishes are entirely serious, I have never joked with them."

Once a dervish presented himself to me. He said, "O shaykh, I wish you would get me some candy." "Wish," I said involuntarily, "together with candy?" The dervish disappeared without my noticing it. I ordered candy to be fetched and went to search for him, but I could not find him. On seeking news of him, I was told that his mind had become disordered, so that he would say to himself, "Wish—and candy? Wish—and candy?" He wandered about aimlessly and finally went into the desert and never stopped saying those words until he died.

One of the shaykhs said, "I was alone in the desert. My heart was so distressed that I was saying, 'O human beings, talk to me! O jinns, talk to me!' A voice from the unseen addressed me. 'What do you wish?' 'I wish for God Most High,' I said. 'When are you wishing for God?' it said. 'Somebody who says to people and spirits, "Talk to me!"—when is he a seeker of God Almighty and Glorious?'"

Through the whole night and day the aspirant does not slacken his endeavors. Outwardly he has the characteristics of struggle, inwardly the attributes of endurance. He has separated himself from his bed and bound himself to concentration. He bears difficulties and defies pains. He treats the ills of his character and applies himself to problems. He embraces terrors and leaves outward appearances. As it is said,

> Then I passed the night in a desert,
> Fearing neither wolf nor lion.
> Overcome by desire, I travel the night quickly.
> The one who desires continues overwhelmed.

I heard Abu Ali al-Daqqaq say, "Spiritual wish is a pain of love in the soul, a burning in the heart, a passion in the mind, an agitation of inward being. Fires that blaze in hearts!" I heard Muhammad ibn al-Husayn say . . . that Yusuf ibn al-Husayn said, "'There was a pact between Abu Sulayman al-Darani and his dervish, Ahmad ibn Abu 'l-Hawari, that Ahmad would not oppose Abu Sulayman in anything that he might order him to do. One day Ahmad went to the shaykh while he was giving a discourse to his circle and said, "The baking oven is hot. What do you command?" Abu Sulayman did not answer him. He repeated it two or three times. Finally Abu Sulayman said, "Go and sit in it!" Abu Sulayman was distracted, and he forgot about Ahmad for an hour. Then he remembered and said, "Go and find out if Ahmad is in the oven, because he promised himself that he would never disobey me!" So they looked, and he was indeed in the oven and not a hair of him was singed.

I heard Abu Ali say, "In my early youth I was on fire with spiritual wish. I used to say to myself, 'If only I knew what the real meaning of spiritual wish might be!' It is said that among the qualities of the aspirant is such love of extra devotions as: sincerity in offering counsel to the community; intimacy with God in retreat; patience with the difficulties of the divine judgments; preferring His command to everything; shyness in the face of His vision; lavishing what he has struggled for on what he loves and risking every means that might bring him to it; contentment with obscurity; and restlessness of heart until he attains to his Lord.

Abu Bakr al-Warraq said, "Three things are the bane of the student: marriage, writing down hadiths, and journeying." He was asked, "Why have you given up collecting hadiths?" He said, "Spiritual wish has prevented me from it."

Hatim al-Asamm said, "If you see a Sufi aspirant wishing for something other than his goal, know that this has manifested from his baseness." I heard Muhammad ibn al-Husayn say . . . that al-Kattani said, "Among the principles of the spiritual student are three rules: to sleep only when overwhelmed, to eat only at need, and to speak only when obliged to it."

And I heard him say . . . that Junayd said, "When God Most High wishes the aspirant well, He throws him among the Sufis and prevents him from the company of professional reciters of the Quran." And I heard him say . . . that al-Raqqi said that he heard al-Daqqaq say, "The object of spiritual wish is that you point toward God Most High, so that you may find Him with the pointing." He asked, "So what thing is large enough to comprehend spiritual wish?" He said, "Your finding God Most High without any pointing."

I heard Muhammad ibn Abd Allah al-Sufi say . . . that Abu Bakr al-Daqqaq said, "The spiritual aspirant is not truly an aspirant until the angel on his left [who records transgressions] has not written anything against him for twenty years. Abu Uthman al-Hiri said, "If someone does not have a firm wish in the beginning, the passing days will only advance him in falling back." Abu Uthman said, "When an aspirant hears some Sufi knowledge and acts upon it, it becomes wisdom in his heart until the end of his life. He benefits from it, and if he talks about it, it benefits whoever hears him. But if someone hears some of their knowledge and does not act upon it, it becomes a story that he remembers for a few days, and then forgets."

Al-Wasiti said, "The first stage for the spiritual aspirant is to wish for the Truth by abandoning his own will." Yahya ibn Muadh said, "The hardest thing for Sufi students is the company of people who oppose the Sufi way." I heard Abu Abd al-Rahman al-Sulami say . . . that Yusuf ibn al-Husayn said, "If you see a spiritual student occupying himself with indulgences and the earning of benefit, nothing will come of him."

And I heard him say . . . that Jafar al-Khuldi said Junayd was asked, "What can students find in the telling of anecdotes and stories with which Sufi discourse is often concerned?" He said, "Such stories are one of the armies of God Most High with which he strengthens aspirants' hearts." "Have you an authoritative proof of this?" he was asked. "Yes," he said. "It is the saying of the Almighty and Glorious, 'We have related to you from the stories of the Messengers things through which We have made firm your heart' [11:120]." And I heard him say . . . that Junayd said, "The true spiritual student has no need of the learning of the learned."

The difference between the disciple (*murid*) [is that he is] the one who wishes for God, while the shaykh (*murad*) is the one for whom God wishes. In reality, everyone who wishes is wished-for. If it were not the object of God's wish that someone should wish for Him, that person could not be an aspirant, since nothing exists but what God Most High has willed. And every wished-for one is likewise one who wishes because when the Truth wanted him among the elite, He suited him for spiritual wish.

However, the Sufis do make a difference between the *murid* and the *murad*. According to them, the *murid*, the wisher, is the beginning; the *murad*, the wished-for one, is the end. It is the *murid* who is exhausted by toil and plunged into the endurance of hardships. It is the *murad* who is saved by command from further difficulty. The *murid* is a laborer. The *murad* is soothed and gently treated.

God's treatment of those who aspire to Him is of different kinds. Most of them He prepares for struggles. Then after the endurance of all sorts of things they attain to the splendor of the realm of meaning. But many of them have the sublimity of the spiritual realm revealed to them in the beginning and attain to that which the majority of those engaged in self-training and discipline have not reached. However, most of these are returned to effort after this kindness in order that He may give them a full share of the principles of the people of discipline, which would otherwise have escaped them.

I heard Abu Ali al-Daqqaq say, "The *murid* bears. The *murad* is borne." And I heard him say, "Prophet Moses was a *murid*, one who wished for God, for he said, '*My Lord, expand my breast for me*' [20:25]. Our Prophet was a *murad*, one for whom God wished, so that God Most High said, '*Have I not expanded your breast for you and lifted from you the burden that galled your back, and exalted for you your recollection?*' [94:1-4]. Thus Moses prayed, "*My Lord, show Yourself to me so that I may look upon You.*" God replied, "*You shall not see Me*" [7:143]. But to our Prophet He said, "*Have you not seen your Lord, how He extends the shadow?*" [25:45].

Abu Ali used to say that what God intended by saying "Have you not seen your Lord?" and "How He extends the shadow" was a veil and a barricade to protect the inner and outer meaning from those who would not be able to understand it.

Junayd was questioned about the *murid* and the *murad*. He said, "The *murid* is governed by the policy of knowledge. The *murad* is governed by the guardianship of the Truth. So the *murid* journeys, while the *murad* flies. When has a wayfarer ever overtaken a bird?"

It is said that Dhu 'l-Nun sent a man to Abu Yazid with the instruction, "Ask him, 'How long will he sleep and rest, while the caravan passes on?'" Abu Yazid replied, "Tell my brother Dhu 'l-Nun, 'A true man sleeps the whole night, yet the morning finds him in the oasis before the caravan arrives!'" Dhu 'l-Nun said, "Very good. In our present state we cannot answer this."

25
ON STEADFASTNESS
(*ISTIQAMA*)

God Most High has said, *"Those who say, 'Our Lord is God,' and then be steadfast, the angels descend upon them'"* [41:30]. Abu Bakr Muhammad ibn al-Husayn ibn Furak reported . . . from Thawban, the client of the Prophet, that the Prophet said, "Even if you cannot do it perfectly, be steadfast on the straight path. Know that the best of your religion is prescribed prayer and that no one but a believer will ever maintain a constant state of ablution."

Steadfastness, continuing straight ahead without deviation, is a level that contains the perfection and completion of everything. By its existence the good things are attained and their balance and harmony kept. If someone lacks the quality of steadfastness, his effort is weak and his exertion fails. God Most High has said, *"Do not be like the woman who unravels the thread she has spun"* [16:92]. If someone does not possess this directness as his attribute, he will not progress from the stage he is occupying to another, for his undertaking has not been firmly founded. One of the conditions for the future development of the beginner is that he remains steadfast in the conduct that pertains to the goal.

One of the marks of steadfastness in beginners is that their ordinary daily conduct is not adulterated by apathy. One of its marks in those of the middle stages is that they do not indulge themselves in the stages they reach. And one of its marks in the advanced is that no veil interrupts their transactions with God.

I heard Abu Ali al-Daqqaq say, "Steadfastness on the path has three steps: first, preparation (*taqwim*), then performance (*iqama*) and then steadfastness (*istiqama*). Preparation is the disciple of the ego, performance is the refinement of the heart; and steadfastness is the drawing near to God."

Abu Bakr commented that His saying, "Those who say, '. . . *and then be steadfast . . .* [41:30],'" means that they do not attribute partners to Him." Umar said that it meant that they do not swindle as foxes do. Abu Bakr al-Siddiq refers to the observance of the fundamental principles of unity (*tawhid*). The statement of Umar refers to the search for interpretations that obscure the clear sense of the Koran and commitment to the terms of one's responsibilities. Ibn Ata said, "They '*then continue steadfast*' in singleness of heart with God Most High."

Abu Ali al-Juzjani said, "Be content with the state of steadfastness; do not be a seeker of miracles. It is your ego that is excited by the search for miracles, while your Lord Almighty and Glorious calls for you through steadfastness."

I heard Abu Abd al-Rahman al-Sulami say that Abu Ali al-Shabbuwi said, "I saw the Prophet in a dream and asked him, 'It is related, O Messenger of God, that you said, "Sura Hud has turned my hair white." Which part of it affected you like that? The stories of the prophets and the destruction of nations?' 'No, none of these,' he said to me. "It was the saying of the Most High, '*Continue steadfast as you have been ordered.*'" [11:112]

It is said that only the great have the capacity for

undeviating travel because it means leaving familiar things and separation from outward forms and customs and standing before God Most High in true candidness and integrity. It was thus that the Prophet said, "Even if you cannot do it perfectly, be steadfast on the straight path."

Al-Wasiti said, "Direction is the trait through which good qualities are perfected and through lack of which they are corrupted." The story is told that Shibli said, "Steadfastness on the path is to see the day of judgment now."

It is said that steadfastness in speech is to abandon backbiting; in actions, to prohibit deviation; in spiritual works, to forbid apathy; and in states, getting rid of the veil." I heard Abu Bakr Muhammad ibn al-Husayn ibn Furak say, "The letter *sin* in *istiqama* is grammatically the *sin* of asking for something. People with *istiqama* request that the Truth establish them first in unity (*tawhid*), then in constancy in fulfilling their promise to Him and adhering to the guidelines of the divine law."

Know that steadfastness on the straight path necessarily produces continuous miracles and acts of grace. God Most High said, "If they had continued steadfast on the path, We would have brought them to the drinking of abundant water." He did not say, "We would have given them a drink," but rather, "we would have brought them to the drinking." The form, "I brought him to the drinking," implies "I gave him that which provides water." This indicates it to be perpetual.

I heard Muhammad ibn al-Husayn say . . . that Junayd said, "I met a young seeker in the desert under an acacia tree. 'What has brought you to sit here,' I asked. He said, 'A treasure I have lost.' I continued on and left him. When I returned after the pilgrimage, I found myself again with this young seeker. He had moved off to a place nearby the bush. 'What is the meaning of your sitting here?' I asked. 'I found what I had been searching for in this place,' he said, 'so I will remain here.' Junayd said, 'I don't know which was the more noble, his attachment to the search for his state or his attachment to the place in which he was granted his desire.'"

26
ON SINCERITY (*IKHLAS*)

God Most High has said, "*Does not sincere religion belong to God?*" [39:3].

Ali ibn Ahmad al-Ahwazi reported . . . from Anas ibn Malik that the Messenger of God said, "Three things prevent the heart of a Muslim from betrayal: sincerity of effort for God's sake; giving good counsel to leaders; attachment to the community of Muslims."

Sincerity, *ikhlas*, is to give one's obedience, with firm intention, exclusively to the Truth—that is, above all one wishes one's good works to bring one closer to God. One does not engage in them to impress someone, to acquire a good reputation in society, out of the love of people's praise, or for any other reason than to come closer to God Most High. It is truly said that sincerity is the purification of action from the consideration of created beings. And it is also well-said that sincerity means to guard against giving attention to the opinions of others.

There is an authenticated tradition that the Prophet reported from Gabriel that God Glorified and Exalted said, "Sincerity is a secret from My secret. I have bestowed it upon the hearts of the ones I love among My servants." When I asked him "What is sincerity?" I heard Abu Abd al-Rahman al-Sulami say . . . that the

173

Lord of Power said this. I heard Abu Ali al-Daqqaq say, "Sincerity is to guard against paying attention to the opinions of other people, while true integrity, *sidq*, is to be cleansed from looking at one's own ego. Thus the man of sincerity has no hypocrisy, while the man of integrity has no spiritual pride."

Dhu 'l-Nun al-Misri said, "Sincerity is only perfected by truthfulness in it and patience with it, while truthfulness is only perfected by sincerity in it and continuous perseverance with it." Abu Yaqub al-Susi said, "When people see sincerity in their sincerity, their sincerity is in need of sincerity!"

Dhu 'l-Nun said, "Three of the signs of sincerity are that praise and blame from ordinary people become equal to you; that you forget to watch yourself performing good deeds while you are performing them; and that you forget the necessary reward for good works in the next world."

I heard Abu Abd al-Rahman al-Sulami say that Abu Uthman al-Maghribi said, "Sincerity is that in which the ego takes no pleasure whatever. Such is the sincerity of ordinary people. The sincerity of the elite is something that comes upon them, not from them, so that they manifest acts of obedience to God while remaining detached, without seeing or relying upon these acts. Such is the sincerity of the elite."

Abu Bakr al-Daqqaq said, "The flaw in the sincerity of every sincere person is that he sees his own sincerity. When God Most High wants to purify someone's sincerity, He will cause that person's sight of his sincerity to fall away from the sincerity itself. Thus he becomes a 'purified one' (*mukhlas*) rather than a 'possessor of purity' (*mukhlis*)." Sahl al-Tustari said, "Only a sincere person knows what hypocrisy is."

I heard Abu Hatim al-Sijistani say . . . that Abu Said al-Kharraz said, "The hypocrisy of gnostics is superior to the sincerity of students." Dhu 'l-Nun said, "Sincerity is that which is preserved from the corruption of the enemy." Abu Uthman said, "Sincerity is to forget to see the creation while continually looking at the goodness of the Creator." Hudhayfah al-Marashi said, "Sincerity means that the actions of the servant are inwardly and outwardly the same." Sincerity is called, "that which is intended for the Truth and aims at truthfulness," and it is called "blindness to one's own good deeds."

I heard Muhammad ibn al-Husayn say . . . that Sari al-Saqati said, "Whoever decks himself out before people with what he does not possess has fallen from God's grace." And I heard him say . . . that Fudayl said, "To give up working for people's sake is pretension, while to work for people's sake is to set up partners to God. Sincerity is when God release you from both of these."

Junayd said, "Sincerity is a secret between God Most High and His servant. Even the recording angel knows nothing of it to write it in the recording of one's deeds. Satan does not know it to corrupt it, nor is passion [ani mal soul] aware of it that it might influence it." Ruwaym said, "Sincerity in the performance of good deeds means that a person wishes no compensation for his deeds in this world or the next, nor any favors from his recording angels." Sahl ibn Abd Allah was asked, "What thing is hardest on the ego?" He said, "Sincerity—because the ego has no share in it." Questioned about sincerity, a Sufi said, "It means not showing your deeds to anyone but God."

Another Sufi said, "I came to see Sahl ibn Abd Allah at his house one Friday before the time of congregational prayer. I saw a snake in his house. I started forward on one foot but pulled back the other. 'Come in!' he said. 'No one attains the reality of faith while he is afraid of anything on the face of the earth.' Then he added, 'Do you want to make the congregational prayer [at the

Prophet's Mosque]?' 'There is a day's and night's journey
between us and the mosque!' I said. But he took my hand
and in a short while I saw the mosque. So we entered it,
prayed with the congregation and left. He stopped to
look at the people as they went out and remarked, 'The
people of "There is no god but God!" are many, but the
sincere among them are few.'"

Hamzah ibn Yusuf al-Jurjani reported . . . that
Makhul said, "If a servant be sincere for forty days, the
springs of wisdom will well up from his heart to his
tongue." I heard Abu Abd al-Rahman al-Sulami say . . .
that Yusuf ibn al-Husayn said, "The most powerful thing
in the world is sincerity; yet how often have I striven to
drive hypocrisy from my heart, while it has sprouted up
again in another form?"

And I heard him say . . . that Abu Sulayman al-
Darani said, "When the servant acts with sincerity, it
cuts off most of imagination and pretense from him."

27

ON TRUTHFULNESS (*SIDQ*)

God Most High has said, "*O you who believe, fear God and be together with the truthful*" [9:119].

Abu Bakr Muhammad ibn Furak reported . . . from Abd Allah ibn Masud that the Prophet said, "If the servant is unceasingly truthful and strives for truthfulness, it will be written down that he is a truthful person. If he lies unceasingly and strives for the lie, it will be recorded that he is a liar.

Sidq, truthfulness, is the supporting pillar of Sufism. In truthfulness this Way finds its perfection and balance. It is a degree next to prophethood. God Most High said, "*Such are together with those whom God has blessed—the prophets and the truthful . . .* " as the verse runs [4:69].

Sadiq, a person who tells the truth, is the noun derived from *sidq*, and *siddiq*, a person of total integrity, in its intensive form. *Siddiq* means someone who has a great deal of truthfulness, in whom truthfulness is the dominant characteristic, just as *sikkir* [of the same intensive form] means a drunkard, or *khimmir,* one who is overcome by wine, and so forth. The minimum of truthfulness requires that what one is in private and and in public be the same. The *sadiq* shows this truth-

177

fulness in his words, while the *siddiq* is truthful in all of his words, his actions, and his states.

Ahmad ibn Khadruyah said, "Whoever wants God to be with him should attach himself to truthfulness. For God Most High has said, '*Certainly God is with the truth - ful ones*' [2:153]. I heard Abu Abd al-Rahman al-Sulami say . . . that Junayd said, "The truthful person is transformed forty times in a single day, while the hypocrite is stuck in a single state for forty years." Abu Sulayman al-Darani said, "Even if the speaker of truth wanted to describe what is in his heart, his tongue could not articulate it."

It is said that real truthfulness means to speak the truth in times of peril. It is also called the agreement of inner being and outer expression. Qannad said, "Truthfulness forbids the jaw unlawful things," while Abd al-Wahid ibn Zayd said, "Truthfulness is loyalty to God in action." I heard Muhammad ibn al-Husayn say . . . that Sahl ibn Abd Allah said, "A servant who flatters himself or others will never smell the fragrance of truthfulness." Abu Said al-Qurashi said, "The truthful person is prepared to die and would not be ashamed of his secret if it were revealed. God Most High said, '*So long for death, if you are truthful*' [2:94]."

I heard Abu Ali al-Daqqaq say that Abu Ali al-Thaqafi was giving a talk one day when Abd Allah ibn Munazil said to him, "Abu Ali, get ready for death! It is inevitable!" Abu Ali said, "You too, Abd Allah! Get ready for death, it is inevitable!" Abd Allah laid his head down on his arm and said, "I have died." And he died. Abu Ali stopped short because he was not able to do what Abd Allah had done. For Abu Ali had worldly attachments, while Abd Allah was unattached, without any worldly concern.

I heard Abu Abd al-Rahman al-Sulami say that Abu 'l- Abbas al-Dinawari was giving a talk when an old woman in the assembly let out a shout. Abu 'l- Abbas al-Dinawari said to her, "Die!" She got up, took a few steps, then turned to him and said, "I have died!" And she fell dead.

Al-Wasiti said, "Truthfulness is sound belief in the unity along with conscious intention." It is told that Abd al-Wahid ibn Zayd looked at a youth among his companions whose body had become emaciated and asked, "Young man, are you constantly fasting?" "I am not constantly breaking my fast," he replied. "Do you always stay up at night to pray?" "I do not always sleep," said he. "What is it that drives you?" "A continual love and a continual secrecy about it." Abd al-Wahid said, "Be silent! What boldness is this?" The youth stood up, took a few steps, and said, "My God, if I am truthful, take me!" And he fell down dead.

It is related that Abu Amr al-Zujjaji said, "My mother died and left me a house, so I sold it for fifty dinars and went on the pilgrimage. When I reached Babel I was met by one of those rough men who works as a professional guide and water-finder. 'What do you have with you?' he asked. "I said to myself, 'Truthfulness is best.'" 'Fifty dinars,' I replied. 'Give it to me,' he said. So I gave him the purse, and he counted it, and indeed it was fifty dinars. 'Take it!' he said. 'Your truthfulness has captured me.' Then he got off his mount and said, 'Ride!' 'I don't want to,' I said.'You must!' said he. And he insisted until I rode. 'I am following in your track,' he said. For the next year he kept close by me and attached himself to me until he died."

I heard Muhammad ibn al-Husayn say . . . that Ibrahim al-Khawwas said, "You will not see the truthful person engaged in anything but a religious duty that he is fulfilling or an act of excellence upon which he is working."

And I heard him say . . . that Junayd said, "Real

truthfulness is to tell the truth in a situation from which only lying can save you." It is said that three things are never missing from a truthful person: gentleness, reverence, and inward beauty.

It is told that God revealed to the Prophet David, "O David, if someone confirms Me as truthful in his interior life, I will confirm him as truthful before the people in his exterior life."

Ibrahim ibn Dawhah and Ibrahim ibn Sitanba went into the desert together. Ibrahim ibn Sitanba said, "Cast off whatever attachments you have with you." Ibrahim ibn Dawhah tells, "So I threw away everything except one dinar. Then he said to me, 'Ibrahim, don't distract my awareness. Cast off whatever attachments you have with you!' So I threw away the dinar. And he said again, 'Ibrahim, cast off whatever attachments you have with you!!' Then I remembered that I had some thongs for my sandals and threw them away. And on the road I never had need of a shoelace without finding one in front of me. Ibrahim ibn Sitanba said, 'That is the way of one who deals with God Most High with integrity.'"

Dhu 'l- Nun al-Misri said, "Truthfulness is the sword of God. It never falls upon anything without cutting through it." Sahl ibn Abd Allah said, "The beginning of disloyalty in the truthful is their discussing things with their egos." Fath al-Mawsili was questioned about integrity. He thrust his hand into the blacksmith's forge, brought out the hot iron, and placed it on his palm. "That is integrity," he said. Yusuf ibn Asbat said, "One night spent working for God Most High in truthfulness is dearer to me than wielding my sword for God's sake."

I heard Abu Ali al-Daqqaq say, "Truthfulness means to be with others as you are by yourself or to be by yourself as you are with others. Harith al-Muhasibi was asked about the signs of truthfulness. He said, "Because of the integrity of his own heart, the truthful person does not care if all sense of his value leaves the hearts of others. He does not want people to find out an atom's worth of the goodness of his actions nor does he hate people finding out what is bad in them. To object to this would indicate his wanting something more from people, and that is not one of the characteristics of the truthful."

A Sufi said, "If someone does not fulfill a religious obligation that is always due, obligations due at particular times will not be accepted from him." He was asked, "What obligation is always due?" and replied, "Integrity."

It is said that if you seek God with integrity, He will give you a mirror in which you will see all the wonders of this world and the next. And it is said, "Keep to the truth, though you fear that it will harm you, for you will benefit from it. Do not lie, though you believe that it will benefit you, for it will do you harm."

"Everything is something," it is told, "but the friendship of a liar is nothing at all." And, "The mark of a liar is that he offers many oaths without anyone asking him to swear." Ibn Sirin said, "Speech has too much range for an eloquent man to have to lie." And it is said, "An honest merchant is never bankrupt."

28
ON SHAME (*HAYYA*)

God Most High has said, "*Does he not know that God sees?*" [96:14].

Abu Bakr Muhammad Abd al-Hiri al-Mazaki related . . . from Ibn Umar that the Messenger of God said, "Shame is part of faith."

And Abu Said Muhammad Ibrahim al-Ismaili related . . . from Ibn Masud that the Prophet of God one day said to his companions, "Be ashamed before God with shame that is real." They said, "We are ashamed, O Prophet of God, and praise be to God!" He said, "It is not that. If someone is ashamed before God with shame that is real, he should guard his head and what it holds and his belly and what it craves and remember death and tribulation. Whoever wants the next life, abandons the adornment of the life of this world. Someone who has done this has been ashamed before God with shame that is real."

I heard Abu Abd al-Rahman al-Sulami say . . . that a wise man said, "People keep their sense of shame alive by seeking the company of those before whom they feel ashamed." And I heard him say . . . that Ibn Ata said, "The greatest knowledge is awe and shame, for if awe and shame leave, no good remains in one." And I heard him say . . . that Dhu 'l- Nun al-Misri said, "Shame is the existence of reverence in the heart together with the feeling of desolation caused by how badly you have dealt with your Lord." Dhu 'l- Nun al-Misri said, "Love makes one speak, while shame makes one remain silent and fear makes one agitated."

Abu Uthman al-Hiri said, "Whoever discourses on shame without being ashamed before God Almighty and Glorious because of what he is talking about is being drawn to destruction by seemingly acceptable acts." I heard Abu Bakr ibn Ishkib say that Hasan ibn al-Haddad went to see Abd Allah ibn Munazil, who asked, "Where have you come from?" "From Abu 'l- Qasim the preacher's meeting," he replied. "What was he speaking about?" "About shame." "Amazing!" Abd Allah said. "Someone who is not ashamed before God Most High— how can he talk about shame?"

I heard Muhammad ibn al-Husayn say . . . that Sari al-Saqati said, "Shame and intimacy with God knock upon the door of the heart. If they find renunciation of the world and careful action to be at home, they camp there. If not, they pass by." And I heard him say . . . that al-Jurayri said, "The first generation of Muslims dealt with each other on the basis of religion, until religion grew thin. Then the second generation dealt with loyalty, until loyalty departed. The third generation dealt with spiritual chivalry, until spiritual chivalry departed. The fourth generation dealt with shame, until shame departed. Then people came to deal with each other on the basis of desire for reward and fear of punishment."

It is told about the saying of the Most High, "*She desired him, and he [Joseph] would have desired her, were it not that he saw the evidence of his Lord*" [12:24], that the "evidence" was this: Zulaykha [the wife of Pharaoh's minister who was attempting to seduce Joseph] cast a garment over the face of the idol that was in a corner of the house. Prophet Joseph asked, "What are you doing?" "I am ashamed before it," she told him. "I have more right than you to be ashamed before God Most High!" said Prophet Joseph.

And it is told concerning His saying *"One of the two [maidens] came to him [Moses] walking with shyness"* [28:25] that she was shy before him because she was inviting him to hospitality and was afraid that Prophet Moses might not respond. Shyness is a characteristic of the hospitable. It is the bashfulness of generosity.

I heard Muhammad ibn al-Husayn say . . . that Abu Sulayman al-Darani said, "God Most High said, 'O My servant, as long as you are ashamed before Me, I will make the people forget your shameful acts and the places of the earth forget your sins. I will erase your errors from the original Book and will not examine your account on the day of judgment.'"

It is told that a man was seen praying outside of a mosque. He was asked, "Why don't you go into the mosque to pray?" "I am ashamed to go into His house while I have disobeyed him!" said he.

It is said that one of the signs of the possessor of shame is that he is not to be seen in a place that would make him ashamed. A Sufi said, "We went out one night and, passing through a forest, found a man lying asleep, his horse grazing by his head. So we woke him up and asked him, 'Aren't you afraid to sleep in a fearful place like this full of wild beasts?' "He raised his head and said, 'I am ashamed before the Most High to fear anything but Him.' He put his head back down and went back to sleep."

God, glory to Him, revealed to Jesus, "Warn yourself, and if you take warning, then warn others—otherwise be ashamed before Me while you are warning others."

It is said that shame has different aspects. There is shame for the commission of a fault, like that of Adam when it was said to him, "In flight from Us!" and he replied, "Rather, ashamed before You!" There is the shame of one's shortcomings, as when the angels said, "Glory to You, we have not worshiped You with the worship of which You are worthy!" There is the shame of reverence as with Israfil's wrapping himself in his wings out of shame before God Almighty and Glorious. There is the shame of generosity, like that of Prophet Muhammad who used to be ashamed to say, "Go home!" to his community, so that God said, *"[Leave his house after the meal to which you have been invited]* . . . *do not seek to listen to talk"* [33:53]. There is the shame of bashfulness, like that of Ali ibn Abi Talib when he asked al-Miqdad ibn al-Aswad to ask the Messenger about what ablution was necessary in the case of the emission of seminal fluid, rather than asking himself because of the position of Fatima. There is the shame of distaste, as when Prophet Moses said, "If some need of this world were to befall me, I would be ashamed to ask it of you, Lord!" and God Almighty and Glorious replied, "Ask of Me even the salt for your bread and the fodder for your donkey!" And there is also the shame of beneficence, which is the shame of the Lord, glory to Him. After the servant has crossed the the narrow bridge into paradise, God will present him with a sealed book, saying, "You did what you did, and I would be ashamed to manifest it to you. So go! I have forgiven you."

I heard Abu Ali al-Daqqaq say about this hadith that Yahya ibn Muadh commented, "Glory to Him against whom the servant sins—and He is ashamed of it!" I heard Muhammad ibn al-Husayn say . . . that Fudayl ibn Iyad said, "Five signs of spiritual failure are: cruelty of heart, an eye incapable of tears, small conscience, love of the world, and elaborate ambition." And in a certain holy book, "My servant does not treat Me well. When he calls upon Me I am ashamed to turn him away, but when he disobeys Me, he is not ashamed of it!"

Yahya ibn Muadh said, "If someone is ashamed before God when he is obedient, God will be ashamed before him when he is a sinner." Know that shame requires melting [to "die of shame"]. It is said, "Shame is one's insides dissolving because of the awareness of the Lord." And it is said, "Shame is the heart's shrinking because of feeling the Lord's grandeur."

When a man sits down to preach and give admonition to people, two angels call out to him, "Preach to yourself that which you would preach to your brother! And if not, be ashamed before your Master! He sees you!" Junayd, questioned about shame, said, "There is the vision of His gifts and there is the vision of your shortcomings. Between the two of them a state is generated which is called *hayya*, shame."

Al-Wasiti said, "Someone who is close to transgressing a guideline or violating a promise will not taste the burnings of conscience." He also said, "Sweat pours from the man of conscience, which is the excellence in him. As long as there is any substance to the ego, one is distracted from conscience."

I heard Abu Ali al-Daqqaq say, "Shame means to abandon pretensions before God Almighty and Glorious." I heard Muhammad ibn al-Husayn say . . . that Abu Bakr al-Warraq said, "Sometimes I pray two cycles of ritual prayer to God and leave them feeling such shame that I might have just returned from robbing a house."

29

ON FREEDOM (*HURRIYA*)

God Almighty and Glorious has said, "*And they pre -
fer others over themselves even when they are des -
titute*" [59:9].

They only prefer others to themselves in order to
strip themselves of what they have abandoned anyway
and preferred to leave to others. Ali ibn Ahmad al-
Ahwazi reported . . . from Ibn Abbas, that the Messenger
of God said, "That which minimally satisfies the needs of
your flesh is sufficient for any one of you. Finally it
comes down to four cubits and a span [the size of a
grave]. The whole business returns to its end."

Freedom means that the servant is not a slave to created beings and that things and events do not exercise
control over him. The sign that it is sound and whole is
that preferring one thing to another drops from a person's heart so that it makes no difference whatever may
chance to occur.

Harithah said to the Messenger of God, "I have
turned myself away from this world and its stones and
its gold are all the same to me." I heard Abu Ali al-
Daqqaq say, "If someone comes into this world and is
independent of it, he will be transported to the next and
be independent of it." I heard Muhammad ibn al-Husayn
say . . . from al-Daqqaq, "Whoever is free of this world in

this world will be free of the next world in the next world.

Know that the reality of freedom is the perfection of servanthood. When you are sincere in being a servant to God Most High, your independence will save you from bondage to anything other than Him. If anyone imagines that the servant surrenders to God in order to throw off the restraints of servanthood at some other time and turns his attention away from the guidelines of what is commanded and what is forbidden—which are proper to this realm of responsibility—he is casting off the religion. God, glory to Him, said to His Prophet, "*Serve your Lord until that which is certain comes to you*" [15:99]. That means the end of life, and upon this all the commentators are agreed.

What the Sufis have indicated by *hurriyah*, freedom, is that the servant is not under the domination of any created thing, whether it pertains to this world or the next. He belongs solely to the One. He is not enslaved by any pressure of this world, by the occurrence of any desire, by any future fate—not by a want nor by an intention nor by a need nor by a worldly fortune.

Shibli was asked, "Do you not know that He is the unconditionally Merciful?" He said, "Indeed, but since I have realized His mercy I have not asked Him to have mercy upon me!"

The station of freedom is one of great power and dignity. I heard Abu Ali say that Abu 'l- Abbas al-Sayyari used to say that if there were anything but recitation of the Koran that would make a prayer complete, it would be this verse:

I always desire an impossible thing—
That my eyes should see as the eyes of a free man.

Here are the sayings of the shaykhs about freedom.

Husayn ibn Mansur al-Hallaj said, "If someone wishes for freedom, let him attain servanthood." Junayd was asked about the case of someone who had no more of this world than could be sucked off a date pit. He replied, "When a servant contracts to buy his freedom from his master, as long as he owes one dirham, he is still a slave." Abu Abd al-Rahman al-Sulami said . . . that Junayd said, "You will not attain to pure freedom while any remnant of the reality of servanthood remains for you to achieve."

Bishr al-Hafi said, "Whoever wants to taste the food of freedom and find rest from being a slave, let him purify the secret understanding that exists between him and God Most High." Al-Husayn ibn Mansur said, "When the servant has fulfilled all the stations of servanthood he becomes free of all the toil of being a slave and pursues servanthood without care or ceremony. That is the station of the prophets and the truthful. It means that they are borne rather than having to bear. Such a one encounters no difficulty in his heart, even if he is made to appear to be in difficulty."

Abu Abd al-Rahman recited to us . . . what Mansur al-Faqih recited of his own composition:

In all humanity no free man remains.
None. And none is free among the *jinn*
The free of these two groups have passed away.
The savor of life has passed.
Know that the greater part of freedom is found in
    service to the dervishes.

I heard Abu Ali al-Daqqaq say, "God Most High revealed to Prophet David, 'If you see anyone who seeks Me, be his servant.' The Prophet said, 'The master of a people is their servant.'"

I heard Muhammad ibn al-Husayn say . . . that

Yahya ibn Muadh said, "The sons of this world are served by slaves and slavegirls, while the sons of the next are served by the righteous and the free." And I heard him say . . . that Ibrahim ibn Adham said, "The generous free man gets out of this world before he is taken out of it." Ibrahim ibn Adham also said, "Keep company with no one except a generous free man: he listens and does not lecture."

30

ON REMEMBRANCE (*DHIKR*)

God Most High has said, "*O you who believe, remember God with much remembrance*" [33:41].

Abu 'l- Husayn Ali ibn Muhammad ibn Abd Allah ibn Bushran in Baghdad reported . . . from Abu Darda that the Messenger of God said, "'Have I not told you about the best of your works and attested to it before your King and exalted it in your ranks? It is better than the gift of gold and silver or encountering your enemies and beheading them while they are beheading you.' 'What is that, O Messenger of God?' they asked. 'The remembrance of God,' he replied."

Abu Naim Abdul-Malik ibn al-Hasan reported . . . from Anas that the Messenger of God said, "The hour [of the end of the world] will not come while there is one person saying, 'God, God!'" And Ali ibn Ahmad ibn Abdan reported from Anas ibn Malik that the Messenger of God said, "The hour will not come until 'God, God!' is no longer said upon the earth."

Dhikr, the practice of remembering God, is a strong pillar in the way of the Truth. Indeed, it is the mainstay of this Way. No one attains to God except through continuous remembrance.

There are two kinds of remembrance: that of the

tongue and that of the heart. By means of the tongue's remembrance, the servant reaches constant remembrance of the heart. Its object and result is the remembrance of the heart. If the servant becomes one who remembers both with his tongue and with his heart, the state of his spiritual search is described as perfect.

I heard Abu Ali al-Daqqaq say, "The practice of remembering God is a proclamation of office. Whoever has been made successful in remembrance has been granted the proclamation and whoever has been denied remembrance has been dismissed from office."

It is told that in the beginning of his practice Shibli lived each day upon the road. He would carry with him a bundle of sticks, and if some unconsciousness entered his heart, he would beat himself with a stick until he broke it upon himself. Sometimes the bundle would be gone before evening came, so he would strike his hands and feet against a wall.

Remembering God with the heart is called the sword of seekers. With it the seeker slays his enemies and drives off troubles that are headed for him. Even if difficulty should overshadow the servant, his fleeing to God Most High in his heart immediately turns away from him the thing he hates.

Al-Wasiti was asked about the practice of remembrance and said, "It is leaving the enclosed court of unconsciousness for the vast space of contemplation through the power of fearing Him and the intensity of loving Him."

I heard Abu Abd al-Rahman al-Sulami say . . . that Dhu 'l- Nun al-Misri said, "Whoever really remembers God Most High forgets everything else at the time of his remembrance. God Most High takes care of everything for Him and sets Himself in the place of everything." And I heard him say . . . that Ahmad al-Masjidi said that Abu Uthman was asked the question, "We practice remembering God Most High [with our tongues], but we do not find any sweetness in our hearts." He answered, "Give praise to God that He has adorned one of your limbs with obedience to Him!" There is a famous hadith that the Messenger of God said, "When you see the gardens of paradise, feast in them." He was asked, "What are the gardens of paradise?" and said, "The congregations for remembrance." Abu 'l- Hasan Ali ibn Bushran in Baghdad reported . . . that Jabir ibn Abd Allah said, "The Messenger of God came out among us and said, 'O people, feast in the gardens of paradise!' 'Messenger of God, what are the gardens of paradise?' we asked. 'The congregations for remembrance,' he said."

So go about your business and remember. Whoever would like to know his place with God, let him look at God's place with him! For certainly God, glory to Him, gives rank to a servant according to the rank the servant assigns God himself. I heard Muhammad ibn al-Husayn say . . . that Shibli said, "Hasn't God Most High said 'I am the companion of the one who remembers Me?' What is it that you have profited from the society of the Truth?" And I heard him say . . . that Shibli recited in his gathering:

I spoke Your remembrance—not that I had
    forgotten You for an instant—
But my tongue's recollection eased the remembrance
itself.
Without ecstasy I nearly died of desire;
My heart was frantic with heartbeats within me.
When ecstasy showed me that You were there
I bore witness that You exist in every place.
So I announced something existent without any
    discourse
Perceived something known, without seeing it.

One of the special features of the practice of remembrance is that it has no assigned time. Indeed, there is no moment in which the servant is not commanded to the remembrance of God, whether it be an obligatory duty or a recommended one. The ritual prayer, though it is the noblest of all devotions, is not possible at some times, while the heart's remembrance is continuous in all circumstances.

God Most High has said, *"Those who remember God standing and sitting and lying on their sides . . . "* [3:191]. I heard Abu Bakr ibn Furak say, "Standing is true remembrance, while sitting is pretending to it." I heard Abu Abd al-Rahman ask Abu Ali al-Daqqaq, "Which is more perfect, the practice of remembrance (*dhikr*) or meditation (*fikr*)?" Abu Ali inquired, "What do you say?" Abu Abd al-Rahman said, "It seems to me that *dhikr* is more perfect than *fikr* because remembrance is known to be an attribute of the Truth, whereas meditation is not. Whatever is an attribute of the Truth is more perfect than something that is specific to the creation." Abu Ali was pleased with this.

I heard Abu Abd al-Rahman al-Sulami say . . . that al-Kattani said, "Were my practice of remembrance not an obligation that I owe, I would not do it out of respect for Him. The likes of me, remembering Him! Someone who has not even cleansed his mouth with a thousand acts of accepted repentance!"

I heard Abu Ali recite to a dervish:

> I would not have remembered You, but a care drove
> me—
> Heart and soul and secret—into Your remembrance.
> It was as if Your watcher was whispering to me
> "Beware, O Rememberer! Woe to you! Beware!"

Another special feature of remembrance is that it

produces remembrance in response. God Most High has said, "*Remember Me—I will remember you!*" [2:147]. According to a hadith, Gabriel said to the Messenger of God, "God Most High says, 'I have given to your community what I have not given to any other community.'" "What is that, O Gabriel?" the Prophet asked. "It is the saying of the Most High, 'Remember Me—I will remember you.' He has not said that to anyone outside this community." It is said that the angel of death consults with the one who remembers God before taking his soul.

In one of the holy books it is written that Prophet Moses said, "O Lord, where do You dwell?" God Most High revealed to him, "In the heart of My believing servant." The meaning of this is the indwelling of remembrance in the heart, for the Truth, may He be glorified and exalted, transcends every kind of inhabiting and incarnation. It is only the affirmation and attainment of remembrance that is intended here.

I heard Muhammad ibn al-Husayn say . . . that Thawri said, "I asked Dhu 'l Nun about remembering God. He told me, 'It is the absence of the one who remembers from the act of remembrance.' Then he extemporized:

It's not from forgetting You that I remember You so
     much.
Only, that is what comes off my tongue!

Sahl ibn Abd Allah al-Tustari said, "There is no day when the Sublime One is not calling, 'O My servant, you do not treat Me justly! I remember you and you forget Me. I call you to Me, and you go to something else. I drive trials away from you, while you are addicted to sins! O son of Adam, what will you have to say when you come to Me tomorrow?'" Abu Sulayman al-Darani said, "There are plains in paradise and when anyone starts to practice the remembrance of God, the angels begin to plant trees there. Sometimes an angel stops. When they ask him, 'Why did you stop?' he answers, 'The one for whom I am planting this tree has grown lax.'"

Hasan al-Basri said, "Seek sweetness in three things: in prayer, in the remembrance of God, and in the recitation of the Quran. If you find it, good. If not, know that the door is shut." Hamid al-Aswad said, "I was on a journey with Ibrahim al-Khawwas. We came to a place that was full of snakes. He set down his cooking pot and sat down, so I sat down too. When the night grew cold, with a cold wind, the snakes came out. I cried out to the shaykh, and he said, 'Remember God!' So I began to practice remembrance, and they went back. Then they returned, so I cried out again, and he said the same thing. I carried on until morning in that way. When day broke upon us, he got up and walked and I walked along with him. Out of his bedroll fell an enormous snake! It had wrapped itself all around him. "Didn't you feel that?" I exclaimed. "No," he said. "It is a long time since I spent a night as pleasant as the last!"

Abu Uthman said, "Whoever has not tasted the loneliness of unconsciousness will not find the food of the intimacy of remembrance." I heard Muhammad ibn al-Husayn say . . . that Sari al-Saqati said, "It is written in one of the Books sent down by God, 'If what dominates My servant is My remembrance, then he loves Me and I love him.'" Through the same chain of narrators, God Most High revealed to Prophet David, "In Me rejoice, and in My remembrance take pleasure."

Thawri said, "For everything there is a punishment, and the punishment for the gnostic is to be kept from practicing remembrance." In the Gospel, it says, "Remember Me when you are angry. I will remember you when I am angry. Be satisfied with My aid to you, for My aid to you is better for you than your aid to yourself."

A monk was asked, "Do you fast?" He answered, "I fast by remembering God. When I remember something other than Him, I have broken my fast." It is said that when remembrance of God has taken possession of a heart, if satan comes close to it he falls into a fit—just as a person may fall into a fit when satan comes close to him. All the little satans gather around him asking, "What is this?" And it is said, "A human being has touched him!"

Sahl al-Tustari said, "I know no disobedience uglier than forgetfulness of the Lord." It is said that no angel presents to God the act of interior remembrance because no angel has any awareness of it. It is a secret between the servant and God Almighty and Glorious.

A Sufi said, "People described to me a man who practiced remembrance in the midst of the forest. I went to see him. While he was seated, suddenly a huge beast struck him a blow and tore a piece out of him! He fainted and so did I. When I regained consciousness, I asked, "What was that?" "God's grace has set this beast upon me," he said. "Every time some laxness enters into me it takes a bite out of me, as you have seen."

I heard Abu Abd al-Rahman al-Sulami say . . . that al-Jurayri said, "There was a man among my companions who was always chanting, 'God, God!' One day a tree fell on his head and fractured his skull. Blood flowed, and it wrote upon the earth, 'God, God!'"

31
ON SPIRITUAL CHIVALRY (*FUTUWWA*)

G od Most High has said, *"They were spiritual war -
riors who believed in their Lord and He increased
them in guidance"* [18:13].

The essence of *futuwwa*—noble, generous, and hon-
orable conduct—is that the servant should always be
working for the sake of something other than himself.
The Prophet said, "God Most High never ceases to be
concerned with the need of a servant while the servant
is concerned with the need of his Muslim brother."

Ali ibn Ahmad ibn Abdan related to us . . . from Zayd
ibn Thabit that the Messenger of God said that he heard
Abu Ali ibn al-Daqqaq say, "This characteristic
(*futuwwa*) only reached its perfection in the Messenger
of God. At the resurrection everyone will be saying
'Myself, myself!', but he will be saying, 'My people, my
people!'"

I heard Abu Abd al-Rahman al-Sulami say . . . that
Junayd said, "Spiritual chivalry is in Damascus, eloquence in Iraq and truthfulness in Khorasan." And I
heard him say . . . that Fudayl said, "Spiritual chivalry
is pardoning the slips of brothers."

It is said that spiritual chivalry means not to see in

yourself any superiority over other people. Abu Bakr al-Warraq said, "The spiritual warrior is he who has no enemy." Muhammad ibn Ali al-Tirmidhi said, "Spiritual chivalry is to fight for your Lord against yourself." And it is said, "The spiritual warrior is he who is not the enemy of anyone else."

I heard Abu Ali al-Daqqaq say that al-Nasrabadhi said, "*The Companions of the Cave were called 'spiritual warriors'* [18:13] because they placed their faith in their Lord without intermediary.

The *fata*—the spiritual warrior, the person of honor—is called "he who breaks the idol." God Most High has said, "*We heard a spiritual warrior named Abraham speak of them [the idols Abraham broke]*" [21:20]. And He said, "*And he made them fragments*" [21:60]. The idol of every person is his own ego, so in reality, whoever opposes his own desires is a "spiritual warrior."

Harith al-Muhasibi said, "Spiritual chivalry is to deal fairly with others while not demanding fairness for yourself." Umar ibn Uthman al-Makki said, "Spiritual chivalry is good character." Junayd, when asked about noble conduct, said, "It means not to avoid a poor man nor imitate a rich one." Al-Nasrabadhi said, "Moral goodness (*muruwwa*) is a branch of spiritual chivalry. It means turning away from this world and the next and having disdain for them both."

Muhammad ibn Ali al-Tirmidhi said, "Spiritual chivalry means that native and foreigner are the same to you." I heard Muhammad ibn al-Husayn say . . . that Abd Allah ibn Ahmad ibn Hanbal said, "I asked my father [Ahmad ibn Hanbal, the great jurist and champion of the divine law], 'What is spiritual chivalry?' He told me, 'To give up what you want because of what you fear.'"

A Sufi was asked, "What is spiritual chivalry?" He

said, "That it make no difference whether a saint or an unbeliever is eating with you." I heard a scholar say that a Magian asked hospitality from Prophet Abraham, the Friend of God, who said, "On the condition that you surrender to God (accept *islam*)." So the Magian went his way. Then God Most High revealed to Abraham, "For fifty years I have fed him in his unbelief. Is it too much for you to give him a morsel without requiring that he change his religion?" Abraham followed the Magian's track until he caught up with him and apologized to him. Asked the reason, he told the man. The Magian surrendered to God.

Junayd said, "Spiritual chivalry means to restrain yourself from causing trouble while giving freely." Sahl ibn Abd Allah said, "Spiritual chivalry is to follow the practice of the Prophet."

It is called:

— Loyalty and guarding what is precious.
— A virtue you attain without seeing it in yourself.
— Not running away when a beggar approaches.
— Not hiding yourself from those who come to you in need.
— Not hoarding and not making excuses.
— Manifesting blessing and concealing trouble.
— Inviting ten people and not caring whether nine or eleven come.
— To abandon making distinctions.

I heard Abu Abd al-Rahman al-Sulami say that Ahmad ibn Khidruya said to his wife, Umm Ali, "I want to have a feast and invite so and so (a spiritual warrior who was head of the neighborhood watch)." "Are you worthy to invite the chivalrous to your table?" she asked. "Certainly," said he. "If you would do it," she advised, "slaughter sheep and cattle and donkeys and distribute them to the neighbors from the door of your guest's house to your own door." "Sheep and cattle I understand," he said, "but what is this about donkeys?" "You are inviting a man of honor to your house," she said. "The least one can expect is that there be some good in it for the dogs of the neighborhood!"

It is told that a dervish gave a feast. Among the guests was Shaykh Shirazi. After they had eaten, at the time of the spiritual concert, sleep overcame them all. Shaykh Shirazi asked the host, "What is the reason for this sleep of ours?" "I have no idea," he replied. "I worked hard that all of what I fed you [would be lawful] . . . except the eggplant! About that I did not inquire." When morning came they questioned the seller of the eggplant. "I had nothing," he said, "so I stole the eggplant from the premises of so-and-so and sold it." They took the thief to the owner of the land so that he might make the eggplant lawful. "You are asking of me a thousand eggplants!" said he. "I am giving him this land, two garments, a donkey, and the tools of agriculture so that he will never return to the like of what he has done!"

It is told that a man arranged marriage with a woman and before the time of consummation she contracted smallpox [and became disfigured]. "My eyes have been injured!" the man declared, and then, "I have gone blind." So the woman entered into the marriage. After twenty years she died and the man opened his eyes. Asked about this, he said, "I was not blind but I pretended to be for fear that she would be saddened." "You have surpassed all the chivalrous!" they told him.

Dhu 'l-Nun al-Misri said, "Whoever wants to know elegance, let him look at the water-sellers of Baghdad!" "How is that?" he was asked. He replied, "When I was brought before the caliph because of the heresy attributed to me, I saw a water-carrier wearing a turban wrapped about with Egyptian kerchiefs. In his hands were two jugs of fine porcelain. 'This must be the sultan's cupbearer,' I said. 'No,' they told me, 'It is the public water-bearer.' So I took the jug and drank. Then I said to the one accompanying me, 'Give him a dinar.' But the man would not accept it! 'You are a prisoner,' he insisted, 'and it is not chivalrous that I should take anything from you!'"

It is also not chivalrous to make a profit on a friend. One of our friends said, "There was a spiritual warrior named Ahmad ibn Sahl the Merchant. I bought a white cloak from him. He took as price the amount it had cost him. "Won't you take some profit?" I asked. "I have accepted its price," he told me. "I am not going to make you bear the weight of having received a favor because this is not of sufficient importance that my relations with you should be shaped by it. I am not going to take any profit because it is not according to spiritual chivalry to make a profit from your friend."

A man who lay claim to chivalry left Nishapur for Nisa. There another man, who was accompanied by a number of adherents to the code of honor, invited him to dinner. When they had finished the food, a serving-maid came out and poured water over their hands. The Nishapuri held back from washing his hands. "It is not according to spiritual chivalry that women should pour water over the hands of men!" he said. "I have been coming to this house for two years," one of the company commented, "and I didn't know whether the water was poured by a woman or a man!"

I heard Mansur al-Maghribi say that someone wanted to put the hero, Nuh al-Nishapuri, to a test. He sold him a serving-maid dressed as a boy, stipulating that she was in fact a boy. She had a shining face, so Nuh bought her as a boy, and she remained with him for many months. "Did he know that you were a woman?" she was asked. "No," she said. "He never touched me, for he supposed that I was a youth."

It is told that some villains demanded that Nuh give up to the Sultan a youth who served him. He refused. They flogged him with a thousand lashes, but he did not surrender the lad. That night it was intensely cold, and it so happened that Nuh experienced one of those dreams that requires a total ablution. When he got up he immersed himself in the icy water. "You risked your life!" people told him. "I was ashamed before God to have been patient under a thousand lashes for the sake of a creature," he said, "and not to be patient under the pain of a cold ablution for His sake!"

It is told that a party of men of honor arrived to visit a man who lay claim to spiritual chivalry. "Boy, prepare the table!" ordered the man. But the youth did not prepare it. The man said the same thing to him a second, and then a third time. The guests looked at one another, saying, "It is not according to spiritual chivalry that the man should employ someone who would disobey him like this in the matter of setting the table!" So the man asked, "Why are you so slow about the table?" "There is an ant on it!" the youth answered. "It is not courtesy to set the table for spiritual warriors together with an ant, but it is not according to spiritual chivalry to throw the ant off the table. So I am waiting until it crawls off." "Proceed, young man!" they said. "It is the likes of you that should serve great-hearted men!"

A man who had come to Medina for the pilgrimage fell asleep. He imagined that his purse had been stolen. He went out and saw Jafar al-Sadiq, grabbed hold of him, and said, "You took my purse!" "What was in it?" Jafar asked him. "One thousand dinars!" So Jafar took the man to his house and counted out for him a thousand dinars. The man went back home, entered his house, and saw in his house the purse he had thought stolen. He went back to Jafar to apologize and return him the dinars, but Jafar refused to accept them. "A thing I have sent forth from my hand I shall not take back into it again," he said. The man asked, "Who was that?" and was told it was Jafar al-Sadiq.

Shaqiq al-Balkhi asked Jafar al-Sadiq about greatness of heart. "What do you say?" the other inquired. "When God gives something to us, we are thankful," Shaqiq replied, "and when He withholds something from us, we are patient." "The dogs in our city do that!" exclaimed Jafar. "O son of the Prophet's daughter," Shaqiq asked, "what is spiritual chivalry according to you?" "When God gives something to us, we prefer it for others, and when He withholds something from us we are thankful," Jafar said.

I heard Abu Abd al-Rahman al-Sulami say . . . that al-Jurayri said, "One night Abu 'l- Abbas ibn Masruq invited us to his house. We met with a friend of ours and urged him, "Come back with us! We are accepting the hospitality of the shaykh." "But he hasn't invited me!" he protested. "We will ask permission for you," we told him, "just as the Messenger of God used to for Ayisha." So we brought him with us. When he came to the shaykh's door, we informed the shaykh of what he had said and what we had said. "The place I hold in your heart should bring you here without an invitation," declared the shaykh. "I vow that you shall walk to your seat upon my cheek!" And he insisted, placing his cheek upon the ground! So the man was lifted up and set his foot upon the shaykh's cheek without hurting him, while the shaykh dragged his face along the floor until he reached the man's seat.

Know that it is part of spiritual chivalry to cover over the shames of one's friends, especially when there is something in them that would give malicious pleasure to enemies. I used to hear Abu Abd al-Rahman al-Sulami say to al-Nasrabadhi, "Ali, the Singer, drinks by night and attends your sessions by day!," but al-Nasrabadhi would not listen to what was said. It so happened that one day the shaykh was walking with one of those who used to talk to him that way about Ali, the Singer, when they came across Ali, the Singer, lying on the ground somewhere. He was clearly intoxicated and in need of washing out his mouth. "How many times have we told the shaykh about this, but he would not listen!" the man said. "This Ali, the Singer, is just as we have described him!" Al-Nasrabadhi looked at the critic and said, "Carry him on your shoulders and take him to his house!" And the man could not escape from obeying him in this.

I heard him say . . . that al-Murtaish said that he went with Abu Hafs to see a sick man whom they were tending. There was a whole group of them. Abu Hafs asked the sick man, "Would you like to recover?" "Yes!" said he. So Abu Hafs said to his companions, "Take this away from him and upon yourselves." The invalid stood up and went out with us! The next day all of us were in bed under treatment.

32
ON SPIRITUAL INSIGHT
(*FIRASA*)

God Most High has said, "*In that are signs for those who read the signs*" [15:75]. "By those who read the signs" means "for those who can see the inward state of things" or "those who have insight."

Abu Abd al-Rahman al-Sulami reported . . . from Abu Said al-Khudri that the Messenger of God said, "Fear the spiritual insight of the believer, for he sees by the light of God."

Firasa, the precise insight of people, comes suddenly upon the heart and negates whatever might contradict it. It has a kind of jurisdiction over the heart. The term is derived from "prey (*farisa*) of a lion." The ego cannot oppose the spiritual insight of that which is usually regarded as correct and possible. It exists to the same degree as one's strength of faith: whoever has stronger faith has sharper insight.

Abu Said al-Kharraz said, "One who sees with the light of spiritual insight, sees with the light of the Truth. The very substance of his knowledge comes from God, unmixed with either negligence or forgetfulness. Indeed, it is a judgment of Truth flowing from the tongue of a servant." Abu Said's expression "looking with the light of the Truth" means seeing by a light with which the Truth has favored him. Al-Wasiti said, "Spiritual insight means the rays of light that gleam in hearts and the solid establishment of a spiritual knowledge that conveys secrets of the invisible realm from one hidden place to another. Thus the possessor of insight witnesses things in the way that the Truth brings him to witness them, and he speaks what is in people's minds."

It is related that Abu Hasan al-Daylami said, "I went into Antakya for the sake of a black man whom they told me could speak of secrets. I waited there until he came down the mountain of Likam with some lawful goods to sell. I had gone hungry for two days, having not eaten anything at all. 'How much is this?' I asked him, to lead him to believe that I would buy what he had before him. 'Sit over there,' he said, 'until we have sold it, and we will give you some money to buy something to satisfy your hunger.' I left him and went on to someone else to convince him that I was only a customer. Then I came back to him and said, 'If you are going to sell this, then tell me how much it is!' 'You have gone hungry for two days! Sit over there until we have sold it, and we will give you some of what you would have bought!' he said. So I sat down. When he had sold it, he gave me something and went away. I followed him, and he turned and told me, 'When a need befalls you, take it to God Most High. But if your ego has some share in it, you will be prevented from your need.'"

I heard Muhammad ibn al-Husayn say. . . that al-Kattani said, "Spiritual insight is the disclosure of certainty and the direct witnessing of the unseen. It is one of the stages of faith." Once al-Shafii and Muhammad ibn Hasan al-Shaybani, his teacher, were at the Kabah when a man came in. Muhammad ibn al-Hasan said, "It comes to me that he is a carpenter," and al-Shafii said, "It comes to me that he is a blacksmith!" So they asked him and he said, "I used to be a blacksmith, but now I do carpentry!"

Abu Said al-Kharraz said, "The one who draws out knowledge is one who constantly observes the unseen. It is not invisible to him. Nothing is hidden from him. It is he to whom the saying of the Most High points, '. . . *Those of them who can search out knowledge of it would have known it'* [4:83]." The close examiner is one who knows the sign. He is familiar with what is in the depths of the heart through indications and signs. God Most High has said, *'Indeed in that are signs for those who read the signs'* [15:75]. The person of insight looks with the light of God Most High—that is, with the rays of light that gleam in his heart by which he becomes aware of the meaning of hidden things. This is one of the special characteristics of faith. Those who have a greater share of this are called "those learned in God." God Most High said, *'Be ones learned in God'* [3:79], meaning knowers, wise men, qualified with the attributes of the Truth in perception and character. Such people possess no information concerning what is hidden in other people or any perception of them or any business with them."

Once Abu 'l- Qasim al-Munadi fell ill. He was of great importance among the shaykhs of Nishapur so Abu 'l-Hasan al-Bushanji and Hasan al-Haddad came to see him, having bought an apple on credit for half a dirham. They brought it to him, and when they sat down Abu 'l-Qasim said, "What is this darkness?" They left. "What have we done?" they asked each other. So they thought about it and said, "Perhaps it is that we did not pay for the apple!" They gave the grocer its price and then went back to Abu 'l- Qasim. "This is amazing!" he said, when his eye fell upon them. "Is it possible for a person to get out of the darkness with such speed? Tell me what has been happening with you!" So they related the story to him, and he said, "Yes. Each of you had relied upon his companion to pay and the man was ashamed to call you to account. Yet the responsibility remained, and I was the cause of it. But I saw that in the two of you."

Abu 'l- Qasim al-Munadi, the Crier, used to go into the market every day to cry his wares. When what he needed—from a penny to half a dirham—came into his hands, he would leave, and return to his main occupation and the observation of his heart. Abu 'l- Husayn ibn Mansur al-Hallaj said, "When the Truth takes possession of one's secret, He grants possession of secrets so that one sees them directly and can tell of them."

A Sufi was asked about spiritual insight and said, "There are souls that are at home in the realm of invisible causation, so that they look down over unseen meanings and speak of people's secrets with the speech of direct vision, not that of thinking or approximation."

It is told that before his repentance Zakariya al-Shakhtani had intimate relations with a woman. One day—after he had become one of Abu Uthman al-Hiri's special students—this situation came into the head of the shaykh. Zakariya was thinking about her. Abu Uthman raised his head and asked him, "Aren't you ashamed?"

In the early days when I had found Abu Ali al-Daqqaq, he appointed me to hold a session in the mosque of Mitraz. From time to time I would ask permission of him to travel to Nisa, and he would give it to me. One day I was walking with him on the way to his teaching session. The thought in my mind was, "If only he would take my place in my meetings for the days I am gone!" He turned to me and said, "I will stand in for you and hold meetings the days you are away." So I walked a little further, and the thought came to my mind that he was not well and it would be difficult for him to stand in for me two days a week. If only he would shorten it to one day a week! He turned to me and said, "Two days a week is not possible for me. I will substitute for you once a week." So I walked with him a little further and the thought of a third thing came to my mind, and he turned to me and gave me explicit information about it.

I heard Abu Abd al-Rahman al-Sulami say that his grandfather, Abu Amr ibn Nujayd, said that Shah al-Kirmani had keen spiritual insight. He did not err. He would say, "Whoever casts down his eyes before forbidden things, restrains his ego from lusts (attraction to pleasure), fills his inner being with continuous attentiveness and his outer being with adherence to the Sunnah, and accustoms himself to eating what is lawful, will make no mistakes with his insight.

Abu 'l- Hasan al-Nuri was asked, "What is the origin of spiritual insight in the one who has it?" He answered, "It comes from the saying of the Most High, '*And I breathed into him [Adam] of My Spirit*' [15:29]. If someone's share of this light is more perfect, his vision is wiser and his judgment based on his insight is truer. Do you not see how the breathing of the Spirit into Adam made it necessary for the angels to prostrate before him? For the Most High said, '*I formed him and I breathed into him of My Spirit, so fall down before him in pros - tration*' [15:29]."

This statement of Abu 'l- Hasan al-Nuri is somewhat difficult, so be careful with it. In this mention of the breathing of the Spirit he was aiming to correct those who say that souls are uncreated. The situation is not as it might occur to the hearts of the weak. That to which this breathing (and union and separation) are properly attributed is liable to influence and alteration, which are signs of the transitoriness of created things. Yet God Glorious and Exalted has chosen the believers for perceptions and lights through which they come to possess insight. In essence, these are forms of the knowledge of God. This is the import of the Prophet's saying, "The believer sees by the light of God"—that is, by a knowledge and inner vision for which God Most High has specially chosen him and by means of which He has distinguished him from others like him. To call these kinds of knowledge and perceptions "lights" is not an innovation, and to describe that process as "breathing" is not reaching far afield. What is intended is one's created nature. Husayn ibn Mansur said, "The man of spiritual insight hits his target with the first shot. He does not turn to interpretation or opinion or calculation."

It is said that the spiritual insight of students is a thought that demands verification, but the insight of gnostics is a verification that demands a reality. Ahmad ibn Asim al-Antaki said, "When you sit with the people of truthfulness, sit with them in truthfulness, for they are the spies of hearts. They will enter and leave your heart without your feeling it." I heard Muhammad ibn al-Husayn say . . . that Abu Jafar al-Haddad said, "Spiritual insight appears as a spontaneous initial thought that nothing can challenge. If contradictions arise, it is a simple thought, an event of the ego."

It is related that Abd Allah ibn Muhammad al-Razi (later of Nishapur), said, "Ibn al-Anbari invested me with a cloak of wool. I saw on Shibli's head an elegant cap that went well with that cloak. I wished to myself that I could have the two of them together. When Shibli stood up after the meeting he turned to me so I followed him, for it was his custom when he wanted me to follow him to turn to me like that. When he went into his house, I went in too. 'Take off the cloak!' he said. I took it off. He folded it and threw the cap on it, then called for fire and burnt the both of them."

Abu Hafs al-Nishapuri said, "It is not for anyone to lay claim to direct spiritual insight, but be careful of the spiritual insight of others. The Prophet said, 'Beware the spiritual insight of the believer.' He did not say, 'Try to practice spiritual insight into people!' How can pretensions to this sort of vision be appropriate for someone who is obliged to be wary of it?"

Abu 'l- Abbas ibn Masruq said, "I went to visit an old

man, one of our companions. I found him in a state of destitution and said to myself, 'How does this shaykh make a living?' 'Put away from you these base thoughts, Abu 'l- Abbas!' he said to me. 'God possesses hidden kindnesses!'"

It is related that al-Zabidi said, "I was in a mosque in Baghdad with a congregation of dervishes. No lawful means of subsistence had presented itself to us for days so I went to al-Khawwas in order to ask him for something. When his eyes fell upon me he said, 'The need for the satisfaction of which you came—does God know of it or not?' 'Of course,' I said. 'Be silent,' he said, 'and do not reveal it to any created being.' So I returned, and after only a short wait, more than we needed was provided for us."

Sahl ibn Abd Allah al-Tustari was in the congregational mosque one day when such fierce heat and discomfort struck the place that a dove fell dead inside. Sahl said, "Shah al-Kirmani has died this very hour. [That is the meaning of this], God willing." So they wrote inquiring about that, and it was just as he said.

Once Abu Abd Allah al-Turughandi—he was one of the great men of his time—traveled to Tus. When he reached Khurr he told his companion, "Buy some bread." The man bought enough for the two of them, but Abu Abd Allah said, "Buy more than that." So his companion deliberately bought enough for ten people. It was as if he did not expect the word of that shaykh to be fulfilled. The man said, "When we climbed the mountain we came upon a group of people who had been bound by thieves. They had not eaten for some time. They begged food from us, and the shaykh said, 'Prepare the table for them.'"

One day I was with Abu Ali al-Daqqaq when there was talk of how Abu Abd al-Rahman al-Sulami would stand up in the spiritual concert just like the dervishes. Abu Ali said, "The likes of him, in his state—perhaps stillness would be more suitable for him." Then in the midst of the gathering he said, "Go to him. You will find him sitting in his library. On top of the books will be a little volume bound in red containing poems of Husayn ibn Mansur al-Hallaj. Take the volume without saying anything to him, and bring it to me." It was midday. I went to see him, and there he was in his library, with the volume placed just as it had been described. When I sat down Abu Abd al-Rahman deduced what had been said. "There used to be someone who forbade that a gnostic should move in the spiritual concert," he remarked. "One day that man was seen alone in his house spinning in circles as if he were trying to bring on an ecstasy. When he was asked about his state, he said, 'A certain spiritual question had been difficult for me. Its meaning became clear. I could not restrain my joy so finally I stood up and turned.' He was told, 'The state [of those you have criticized] is like that.' When I saw the thing that Abu Ali had ordered me to do and saw what he had described to me just as he had said it—and when there came from the tongue of Abu Abd al-Rahman the very thing that he had mentioned—I was confounded. 'How shall I deal with the two of them?' I wondered. Then I thought to myself, 'There is nothing for it but to tell the truth.' 'Abu Ali described this volume to me,' I told him, 'and told me to bring it without asking permission of the shaykh. I am afraid of you, but it is not possible for me to disobey him. To what do you command me?' He took out another volume of the works of Husayn in which was an essay called *Al-Sayhur fi naqd al-duhur*, and said, 'Take this to him and tell him that I am studying the other book and taking some verses from it for my own notebooks.' So I left."

It is related that Hasan al-Haddad said, "I was in the presence of Abu 'l- Qasim al-Munadi while a group of dervishes was with him. He told me, 'Go out and get them something to eat.' I was delighted that he had permitted me to exert myself for the dervishes and bring them something, although he knew of my poverty. 'Take a basket!' he said and I left. When I came to the street of Siyyar I saw a magnificent old man. I greeted him and said, 'A group of dervishes is in such-and-such a place. Do you have anything to give them?' He gave orders and bread and meat and grapes were brought out for me. When I reached the door of the shaykh's house, Abu 'l-Qasim called out to from behind it, 'Return that to the place from which you took it!' So I went back, apologized to the old man and said, 'I did not find them.' I hinted that they had left and gave back the food. Then I went to the market and came across something so I brought that. 'Come in!' said Abu 'l- Qasim. I told him the story. 'Yes,' he said, 'that was Ibn Siyyar, one of the sultan's men [and therefore his wealth, if acquired without right, could be unlawful]. When you come to dervishes with something, bring them the likes of this, not the likes of that!'"

Abu 'l- Husayn al-Qarafi said, "I visited Abu 'l- Khayr al-Tinati. When I was taking leave of him, he went out with me to the door of the mosque and said, 'Abu 'l-Husayn, I know that you do not carry with you any regular sustenance to rely upon but take with you these two apples.' So I took the two of them, put them in my pocket and was happy, for nothing had come my way for three days. I took out one of them and ate it. Then I went to take out the second—and there were both of them together in my pocket! So I would eat of them, and they would keep coming back. But at the gate of Mosul I said to myself, 'They are corrupting my state of trust in God since they have become a known source of sustenance for me.' So I took them both out of my pocket at the same time, looked around, and there was a dervish wrapped in a cloak, saying, 'I crave an apple!' I gave them both to him. When I had covered some distance it occurred to me that the shaykh had actually meant the apples for him.

They had just kept me company on the road. I turned back to the dervish, but I could not find him."

I heard Muhammad ibn al-Husayn say . . . Abu Amr ibn Ulwan said that there was a youth who kept company with Junayd who used to speak people's thoughts. This was mentioned to Junayd, who asked him, "What is this thing that has been said about you?" "Hold something in your mind," he told Junayd. "I am holding it," he said. "You are holding such-and-such a thought." "No!" said Junayd. "Try it a second time," said the youth. So he did. "You are holding such-and-such a thought," the youth said. "No!" "A third time!" The same sort of thing was said. "This is very strange," said the youth. "You are a truthful man, but I know my heart!" "You spoke the truth the first, second, and third times," said Junayd, "but I wanted to test whether your heart would change!"

And I heard him say that Abd Allah ibn Muhammad al-Razi said that Ibn al-Raqqi fell ill. Medicine was brought to him in a cup. He took it and then said, "Something has happened in the country today. I will not eat or drink until I know what it is." Several days after this the news came that the Carmatians had entered Mecca on that day and perpetrated in it their dreadful massacre.

I heard Abu Abd al-Rahman al-Sulami say that Abu Uthman al-Maghribi said that this story was mentioned to Ibn al-Katib. "That's amazing!" he said. "No, it isn't amazing," I told him. "So what is the news of Mecca today?" Abu Ali ibn al-Katib asked me. "It is this," I said. "The Talhiyun and the Bani Hasan are fighting with each other. The Talhiyun are being led by a black man in a red turban. In Mecca today there is a cloud over the whole sacred precinct." So Abu Ali wrote to Mecca, and it was just as I had told him.

It is told that Anas ibn Malik said, "Before I went to see Uthman ibn Affan, in the street I had looked at a woman, gazing at her charms. Uthman said, 'One of you has come in upon me with the marks of fornication clear upon his eyes!' 'Can there be revelation after the Messenger of God?' I exclaimed to him. 'No,' he said, 'but there is enlightenment, proof and insight.'"

Abu Said al-Kharraz said, "I entered the Sacred Mosque and saw a dervish, who wore two Sufi cloaks, begging from people. 'This sort of thing is tiresome for people!' I said to myself. He looked at me and said, '*And know that God knows what is within you, so beware of Him!*' [2:235]' So I asked forgiveness in my secret being, and he called to me, "*And it is He who accepts the repen - tance of His servants*" [42:25].'"

It is related that Ibrahim al-Khawwas said, "I was in Baghdad in the Medina mosque, where there was a con- gregation of dervishes. An elegant young man approached us, sweetly perfumed, showing goodly respect, and with a handsome face. I said to our com- panions, 'It comes to me that he is a Jew!' They were all displeased by this so I went out. The young man went out also, then returned to them. 'What did the shaykh say about me?' he asked. They were ashamed to tell him, but he insisted so they said, 'He said that you were a Jew.' Thereupon he came to me, prostrated before me, and became a Muslim. When asked the reason, he said, 'We find in our books that the insight of a man of real integrity does not err. So I said, 'I will put the Muslims to the test.' I considered them closely and felt that if there were a man of true integrity among them, he would be in this group because they talk of Him. So I dressed myself like one of you. When this shaykh became aware of me and had insight into me, I knew that he was indeed a man of true integrity.' The young man became a great Sufi."

I heard Abu Abd al-Rahman al-Sulami say . . . that Muhammad ibn Dawud said, "We were with al-Jurayri. He asked, 'When the Truth wants to bring about some event in the country, is there any man among you whom

He informs of this before He makes it manifest?' 'No,' we said. 'Then weep for hearts that find out nothing from God Most High!' said he."

Abu Musa al-Daylami said, "I asked Abd al-Rahman ibn Yahya about trust in God. He said, 'Even if you thrust your hand into the mouth of a viper up to the wrist, do not fear anything outside of God along with Him.' So I went out to Abu Yazid to ask him about trust in God. I knocked on his door and he said, 'Isn't there enough for you in the saying of Abd al-Rahman?' 'Open the door!' I cried. 'Don't visit me,' he said. 'I have given you the answer from behind the door.' So I went away. I waited a year, then went to see him again. 'Welcome!' he said, 'Now you have come to me as a visitor.' I was with him for a month. Nothing used to enter my heart without his telling me about it. When I was taking leave of him, I asked, 'Profit me with a lesson.' He said, 'My mother told me that when she was carrying me, if lawful food came near her, her hand would reach out to it, but if there were anything doubtful about it, her hand would hold back.'"

Ibrahim al-Khawwas said, "I traveled into the desert and was besieged by difficulties. So when I reached Mecca a certain amount of spiritual pride took hold of me. Then an old woman called out to me, 'O Ibrahim! I was with you in the desert, but I didn't speak to you because I didn't want to distract your inner being. Cast out of yourself these vain imaginings!'"

It is related that al-Farghani used to go out on the pilgrimage every year. He would pass Nishapur, but he never went in to see Abu Uthman al-Hiri. He said, "One time I did go to see him. I greeted him, and he did not return my greeting. I said to myself, 'A Muslim comes to see him and greets him and he does not give greeting in return?' Abu Uthman said,'The likes of this goes on pilgrimage, leaves his mother behind, and takes no care of her?' I went back to Farghanah and stayed with my

mother until she died. Then I went straight to Abu
Uthman. When I came in he received me and made me
sit down. From then on al-Farghani attended upon Abu
Uthman. He asked of him the job of taking care of his
horse and was entrusted with that duty until the shaykh
died."

Khayr al-Nassaj said, "I was sitting in my house
when it struck me that Junayd was at the door. I denied
what was in my heart, but it came to me a second and a
third time. Finally I went out, and there was Junayd!
'Why didn't you come out at the first thought?' he asked."

Muhammad ibn al-Husayn al-Bistami said, "I went
to see Abu Uthman al-Maghribi, saying to myself,
'Perhaps he will want me to do something.' Abu Uthman
said, 'It isn't enough for people that I accept them—they
want me to ask of them, too!'"

A Sufi said, "I was in Baghdad when it struck me
that al-Murtaish was bringing me fifteen dirhams to buy
a small pot, a rope and sandals, and that I would go into
the desert. There was a knock on the door. I opened it,
and there was al-Murtaish, holding a purse. 'Take this,'
he said. 'O Master, I don't want it!' I protested. 'Why are
you troubling us? How much do you want?' 'Fifteen
dirhams.' 'It is fifteen dirhams,' said he."

Concerning the saying of the Most High, "*Or one who
was dead—we have brought him to life*" [6:122], a Sufi
said, "Someone who was dead of mind, but God Most
High brought him to life with the light of insight, and set
for him the light of divine manifestation and direct
vision—he will not be like someone who walks, uncon-
scious, with the people of unconsciousness." It is said
that when insight becomes sound, its possessor progresses to the level of contemplation.

I heard Abu Abd al-Rahman al-Sulami say . . . that
Abu 'l-Abbas ibn Masruq said that a shaykh approached
them and used to speak to them about Sufism with beautiful words. He possessed a sweet tongue and an excel-

lent mind. In one of his talks he said to them, "Whatever thought strikes you, tell it to me." It struck my heart that he was a Jew. The thought became powerful and unceasing. I mentioned this to Jurayri, and it seemed of great importance to him. 'It is inevitable that I will tell the man about this,' I said to myself. So finally I told him, 'You have urged us, "Whatever thought strikes you, tell it to me."' It has occurred to me that you are a Jew.' He bowed his head in silence for an hour. Then he raised his head and said, 'You have spoken the truth. I testify that there is no god but God and that Muhammad is the Messenger of God! I tried all the schools, and said, "If something is to be found with any group of them, it will be found with these." So I came to you to experiment with you, and you are in the right.' And he made good his Islam."

It is related of Junayd that his teacher, Sari, used to say to him, "Address the people!" Junayd said, "There was shyness in my heart about speaking to people, for I had doubts whether I was worthy of this. One night I saw the Prophet in a dream. It was a Thursday night [preceding the day of congregational prayer, when groups would meet in the mosque for discourse]. 'Address the people!' he said to me. I woke up, and went to Sari's door before morning and knocked on it. 'So you would not attest to our truthfulness until it was told to you!' he said." The next day Junayd sat down with the people in the congregational mosque, and word began to spread that he was holding sessions and giving discourse. So a Christian youth, who was in disguise, stopped by him and asked, "O Shaykh, what is the meaning of the saying of the Messenger of God, 'Fear the spiritual insight of the believer, for he sees with the light of God?' Junayd bowed his head, then raised it and said, 'Surrender to God! The time for your Islam has arrived!' So the youth became a Muslim."

33
ON MORAL CHARACTER (*KHULUQ*)

God Most High has said, *"Verily you [the Prophet] are of a moral character"* [68:4].

Ali ibn Ahmad al-Ahwazi reported . . from Anas that the Messenger of God was asked, "Which of the believers has the most excellent faith?" He replied, "The one who has the best (most moral) character."

Thus moral character is the best of the servant's virtues. In it the substance of humanity is manifest. The real human being, who is masked by his old worn-out garment is made known by his nature. I heard Abu Ali al-Daqqaq say, "God Most High specially distinguished His Prophet as He did but then praised none of his traits the way He praised his character. He said—mighty is He Who spoke—*"Verily you are of the (highest moral) char - acter"* [68:4].

Al-Wasiti said, "God Most High described him as 'of a the highest moral character' because both the worlds were lavished upon him, but he was content with God." Husayn ibn Mansur al-Hallaj said, "It means 'harshness had no effect on you after your acquaintance with the

Truth.'" Abu Said al-Kharraz said, "It means that you possess no concern beyond God Most High." I heard Abu Abd al-Rahman al-Sulami say . . . that al-Kattani said, "Sufism is morality. Whoever surpasses you in morality surpasses you in Sufism." It is related that Ibn Umar said, "If you ever hear me say to a slave, 'God shame you!' bear witness that he is free."

Fudayl said, "Even if a man beautifully performs every act of religious merit, if he has a hen and treats it badly, he is not one of the doers of good." It is said that when Ibn Umar saw one of his slaves performing the prescribed prayer well, he would free him. The slaves were familiar with this side of his character. They used to offer the prescribed prayer well with an eye towards him, and he would set them free. He was advised of this and said, "Anyone who deceives us in God—we let ourselves be deceived by him!"

I heard Muhammad ibn al-Husayn say . . . that Harith al-Muhasibi said, "We are lacking three things: a beautiful face accompanied by chastity, beautiful speech accompanied by trustworthiness and beautiful companionship accompanied by loyalty." And I heard him say that Abd Allah ibn Muhammad al-Razi said, "Character is to count as little what proceeds from you toward Him and to count as great what proceeds from Him toward you."

Ahnaf was asked, "From whom did you learn character?" He said, "From Qays ibn Asim al-Munaqqari." "What out of his character impressed you?" "He was sitting in his house when a serving-woman of his came with a skewer of broiled meat. It dropped from her hand and struck one of his sons, who died. The woman was appalled, but he said, 'Don't be afraid. You are free, for God's sake.'" Shah al-Kirmani said, "The sign of moral character is to hold back from giving offense and to bear burdens."

The Messenger of God said, "If you cannot improve people's condition with your property, improve it with an open face and a moral character." Dhu 'l-Nun al-Misri was asked, "What person has the most troubles?" He replied, "The one who has the worst character." Wahb said, "If someone imitates a good habit for forty days, God will make that good characteristic a part of his nature." Hasan al-Basri remarked about the saying of God Most High, "*And your garment purify*" [74:4], "That means, 'Make your character moral.'"

A hermit had a ewe. One day he saw her with only three legs. "Who has done this to her?" he cried. "I did," said his servant. "Why?" "To make you grieve because of her!" "That you cannot do," he said. "But I will bring grief to the evil one who made you do this. Go! You are free."

Ibrahim ibn Adham was asked, "Have you found any pleasure in this world?" "Yes, on two occasions," he answered. "The first of these was a day when I was sitting and a man came and urinated on me. The second was once when I was sitting and a man came and slapped me." When children saw Uways al-Qarani, they would throw stones at him. He used to say, "If you must do that, throw the little ones so that you don't hit my leg and keep me from offering my prescribed prayers!"

A man reviled Ahnaf Ibn Quys while following him through the streets. When they came close to his quarter he stopped and said, "Noble youth, if there is anything left to say, say it! Otherwise some of the fools of the neighborhood may hear you and answer you back."

Hatim al-Asamm was asked, "Is a man to put up with everyone?" "Yes," he said, "Except himself." It is related that the Commander of the Faithful, Ali ibn Abi Talib called his manservant, who did not answer. He called him a second time and a third, and still he did not answer. So he got up and found him lying down. "Didn't you hear me, boy?" he asked. "Yes, I did." "Then what induced you not to answer me?" "I felt safe from your punishment," the boy said, "so I was lazy." "Go!" Ali cried. "You are free, for God's sake!"

Maruf al-Karkhi went down to the Euphrates to make ablution. He set down his copy of the Koran and its wrappings. A woman came and carried them off. Maruf followed her and said, "O sister, I am Maruf—no harm will come to you. Do you have a son who can read the Koran?" "No," she answered. "Or a husband?" "No." "Then give back my copy and take my robe instead!"

One time thieves entered the house of Abu Abd al-Rahman al-Sulami in Mukabirah. They took whatever they found. I heard one of our companions tell that he had heard Abu Abd al-Rahman say, "I was passing through the market and came across my cloak on someone who had bought it at auction. I turned aside and did not approach him."

I heard Abu Hatim al-Sijistani say . . . that al-Jurayri said, "When I came back from Mecca (may God protect it!), I went immediately to see Junayd to save him the bother of visiting me [since returned pilgrims are customarily honored with visits]. So I gave him greeting and then went home. When I offered the morning prescribed prayer in the mosque, I found that he was with me. He was behind me in the row. "I came to you yesterday so that you would not have to be bothered [with honoring me like this]," I said. "That was your goodness," said he, "and this is your right."

Abu Hafs was asked about moral character. He said, "It is that which God Glorious and Exalted chose for His Prophet in His saying '*Accept forgiveness and enjoin what is good*' [7:199] . . . as the verse runs."

Character, it is said, is to be a friend to people and a stranger to their business. And it is also said that character means to accept without vexation or alarm whatever human cruelty or divine judgment may reach you.

Abu Dharr was at a a fountain watering his camels when a man came up in a hurry and broke the spout. Abu Dharr sat down and then lay prostrate. Asked why he did that, he answered, "The Messenger of God ordered that if a man became angry, he should sit down until it passed off, and if it did not pass, that he should prostrate himself."

It is written in the Gospel, "My servant, remember Me when you are angry. I shall remember you when I am angry." Malik ibn Dinar's wife yelled at him, "Hypocrite!" "O wife," he replied, "You have found a name of mine that all the people of Basra have lost!" Luqman said to his son, "There are three that are only made known by three: the gentleman by anger, the hero by war, and the true brother by need of him."

Prophet Moses prayed, "O my God, I beg of You that what is not in me not be attributed to me." God, glory to Him, revealed, "I do not even do that for Myself—how should I do it for you?" Yahya ibn Ziyad al-Harithi had a bad servant. "Why do you hold onto that boy?" they asked. "To learn forbearance through him," he replied.

It is said that in the saying of the Most High, *"He has granted you His favors complete, outwardly and inward - ly"* [31:20], "outwardly" means a harmonious physical being and "inwardly" means a purified character. Fudayl said, "The company of a good-natured libertine is dearer to me than that of a bad-natured devotee."

Good nature is to bear unpleasant things pleasantly. It is related that Ibrahim ibn Adham went out into the steppe, where a soldier hailed him. "Where is human civilization?" he asked. Ibrahim pointed to a graveyard. The man hit him over the head and wounded him. After he left him, the soldier learned that the man he had met had been Ibrahim ibn Adham, the ascetic of Khorasan. The soldier went back to Ibrahim to apologize. "When you struck me," said Ibrahim, "I asked God Most High to grant you paradise!" "But why?" "I knew that God would compensate me for the blow, and I did not want my share from you to be good, while your share from me was bad."

It is related that a man invited Abu Uthman al-Hiri to be his guest. When Abu Uthman appeared at the door of his house, the man said, "O Master, this is not the time for you to come in! I am so sorry! Go back!" So Abu Uthman went home. When he reached his own house, the man came to him again, saying, "O Master, I am sorry!" and began excusing himself. "Come now," he urged. So Abu Uthman got up and went, but when he reached the door, the man said the same sort of thing he had said the first time. He kept on like this a third and a fourth time, while Abu Uthman went back and forth. After a number of repetitions of this behavior, the man confessed, "O Master, I wanted to put you to the test!" And he began to apologize and praise him. "Do not praise me for a character that one finds in dogs," Abu Uthman said. "When you call a dog, he comes, and when you drive him off, he runs away!"

Abu Uthman was crossing the street at midday when a basin of ashes was thrown on him from a roof. His companions were furious and unleashed their tongues against the one who had thrown them. "Don't say anything!" said Abu Uthman. "If someone deserves to have fire poured upon him and a compromise is reached with ashes, he cannot be angry!"

A dervish came to stay with Jafar ibn Hanzalah, and Jafar served him assiduously. "What a fine man you would be," the dervish would say, "if only you were not a Jew!" "Do not vilify my belief," Jafar said, "when you rely upon it to be served! Ask a cure for yourself and guidance for me."

Abd Allah the tailor had a Magian client for whom he sewed clothes. The man would give him counterfeit dirhams, and Abd Allah would accept them. It so happened that one day Abd Allah left his shop on some business. The man came with the counterfeit coins and presented them to Abd Allah's apprentice, who would not take them. So the Magian gave him real ones. When Abd Allah returned he asked his apprentice, "Where is the Magian's shirt?" The story was recounted to him. "You have done very badly!" he exclaimed. "For a long time he has been dealing with me like this. I have been patient with him and thrown the coins into the river for fear that he would use them to deceive someone other than me!"

Bad character, it is said, narrows the heart of the one who possesses it. There is no room in it for anything but what he wants, just as a narrow room is not big enough for anyone but its owner. Good character means that it makes no difference to you who stands in the prayer row beside you. It is part of your own bad character to let your eyes fall upon the bad character of someone else. The Messenger of God was asked about bad luck, and said, "Bad character."

Abu 'l-Hasan Ali ibn Ahmad al-Ahwazi reported. . . from Abu Hurayra that someone said, "O Messenger of God, pray to God Most High against the polytheists!" He replied, "I was only sent as a mercy; I was not sent as a punishment."

34

ON BOUNTIFULNESS AND GENEROSITY (*JUD* AND *SAKHA*)

God Most High has said, *"And they prefer others over themselves, even if they are destitute"* [59:9].

Ali ibn Ahmad ibn Abdan reported . . . from Ayisha that the Messenger of God said, "The generous person is close to God, close to people, close to paradise, and far from hell, while the miser is far from God, far from people, far from paradise, and close to hell. Someone ignorant of faith who is generous is dearer to God Most High than a stingy devotee."

There is no difference, in Sufi usage, between *jud*, bountifulness, and *sakha*, generosity. However the Truth, glory to Him, is not described with the words *sakha* or *samaha*, magnanimity, for lack of an authoritative text. The real essence of generosity is that one does not find it difficult to give freely.

According to the Sufis, *sakha* is the first degree. *Jud* comes after it, and then *ithar*, preferring others to oneself. Whoever gives a part and keeps a part [of his wealth] possesses *sakha*. Whoever freely distributes most of it, but keeps something for himself possesses *jud*. The one who suffers need but prefers that someone else have enough possesses *ithar*. Thus Abu Ali al-Daqqaq says that Asma ibn Kharijah commented, "I do not like to refuse anyone a need that he has asked of me. If he is noble, I guard his honor, and if he is base, I guard my honor from him."

It is told that Muwarriq al-Ijali used to introduce gifts among his spiritual brothers with great refinement. He would leave a thousand dirhams with them, saying, "Hold onto this until I come back," and then send a message to them, "You have it at your disposal."

A man of Minbaj met a man of Medina and asked where he came from. "From the people of Medina," he replied. "One of your men came to us," said the first. "He was called al-Hakam ibn Abd al-Muttalib and he made us rich." "How?" asked the Medinian. "He didn't go to you with anything but a woolen gown!" "He did not enrich us with property, but he taught us generosity. So our rich gave to our poor until we all became rich."

I heard Abu Ali al-Daqqaq say that when Ghulam al-Khalil slandered the Sufis before the caliph, the caliph ordered that their heads should be cut off. Junayd was protected from this penalty by the study of law, for he used to make juridical decisions in the school of Abu Thawr. As for al-Shahham, al-Raqqam, Nuri, and the rest of the congregation, however, they were arrested. The leather mat was spread for their decapitation. Nuri stepped forward. "Do you know what you are hurrying to?" the executioner asked. "Yes." "Then what makes you impatient?" "I prefer that my friends, rather than myself, should live a little longer."

The executioner was amazed and sent word to the caliph, who turned the prisoners over to a judge who could investigate their state. The judge threw some legal questions at Abu 'l- Husayn al-Nuri. He answered them completely and then began to say, "And beyond this, God has servants who when they stand, stand in God, and when they speak, speak in God . . ." Sayings came, one after the other, that made the judge weep. So the judge sent to the caliph, saying, "If these are heretics, there is no Muslim on the face of the earth."

Ali ibn al-Fudayl ibn Iyad used to buy from neighborhood merchants. "You would find it less expensive in the bazaar," people told him. "But these have settled near us hoping we would bring them profit!" he said.

While Jibalah ibn Suhaym was among his companions, a man sent him a woman servant as a gift. "It is an ugly thing for me to accept her for myself while you are here," he said, "and I don't like singling out one of you while each of you has a right and a respect that is due him. And she will not bear dividing!" They were eighty, and he ordered a handmaiden or a page for each one.

One day Ubaydullah ibn Abi Bakra grew thirsty in the street. He asked for water at the house of a woman. She brought him out a jug, but stood behind the door and said, "Stand away from the door and let one of your serving boys come and take it, for I am an Arab woman, and my servant died some time ago." Ubaydullah drank the water and said to his young servant, "Take her 10,000 dirhams!" "God is supreme! Are you making fun of me?" she exclaimed. "Take her 20,000 dirhams." "May God give me strength!" "Boy, take her 30,000 dirhams!" She shut the door, saying, "Shame on you!" But he brought her 30,000 dirhams. She accepted them, and before long she had many suitors.

Generosity, it is said, is to respond to the first thought. I heard one of the companions of Abu 'l- Hasan al-Bushanji say, "Abu 'l- Hasan al-Bushanji was in retreat. He summoned one of his students and told him, 'Take this shirt off of me and give it to so-and-so.' 'Couldn't you have waited until you came out of retreat?'

he was asked. 'I had no confidence that my state would not be changed by the consequences of withholding this shirt!' said he.

They asked Qays ibn Sad ibn Ubadah, "Have you ever seen anyone more generous than yourself?" "Yes," he said. "In the desert we came upon a woman. Her husband was nearby. 'Two guests have come to us,' she told him. So he brought a she-camel, slaughtered it, and said, 'Help yourself!' "When the next day came, he brought another one and slaughtered it too. 'Help yourself!' he said again. 'But we have not eaten more than a little of what you killed for us yesterday!' we protested. 'I am not going to feed my guests leftovers!' said he. We stayed with him two or three days while there was a rain from heaven, and he acted thus. When we wanted to continue traveling we left a hundred dinars for him in his house, told the woman, 'Apologize to him for us,' and left. It was well into the day when suddenly the man was with us, yelling from behind us, 'Stop, vile riders! You gave me a fee for my hospitality!' When he overtook us, he said, 'Take this, or I will pierce you with this lance of mine!' So we took it. He turned back, reciting,

> To accept a reward for what was given
> Would be sufficient insult to a giver!

I heard Abu Abd al-Rahman al-Sulami say that Abu Abd Allah al-Rudhbari went to the house of one of his students, but found him away, and the door of the house locked. "A Sufi, and his door is locked!" he exclaimed. "Break the lock!" So they broke the lock. He ordered that everything that was found on the premises be conveyed to the market, where they sold it, using the price for whatever was useful at the moment. Then they went and sat in the house. When the master of the place came back, he was incapable of speech. Next his wife came home wearing a cloak. She entered the house and threw down the cloak, saying, "Friends, this is also part of the household goods! Sell it!" "Why have you taken this upon yourself by your own choice?" her husband complained. "Hush!" said she. "A shaykh like this acts openly with us—if he judges against us, shall we keep something that we have withheld from him?"

Bishr ibn al-Harith said, "Even to look at a miser hardens the heart." Qays ibn Sad ibn Ubadah fell sick. He waited a long time for his brethren to come. He asked about them and was told, "They are ashamed because of the debts they owe you." "May God shame money that prevents brothers from visiting!" he cried. Then he ordered the town crier to proclaim, "Whoever owes a debt to Qays is free of it!" By evening his threshold was broken by the number of those who came to see him.

Abd Allah ibn Jafar was told, "You lavish much when you are asked—but you won't ask the slightest thing from those to whom you have given!" "I give my money freely," he said, "but I'm stingy with my mind." Abd Allah ibn Jafar went out to his country estate. He stopped by somebody's palm garden where a young black slave was working. When the boy got his food a dog came into the enclosure and approached him. The boy threw him a piece of bread and he ate it. Then he threw him a second, and a third, and the dog ate those too. Abd Allah ibn Jafar watched this. "Young man, how much of your food meets this fate every day?" he asked. "As you see." "Why do you prefer this dog to yourself?" "This is not dog country," the boy said. "He must have come a great distance out of hunger, and I hate to turn him away." "And how do you fare the day?" "Today I will go hungry." "Am I scolded for too much generosity?" Abd Allah ibn Jafar exclaimed. "This fellow is more generous than I am!" So he bought the youth, the garden and the tools that were in it, then freed the boy and gave it all to him.

A man went to his friend's house and knocked on the door. On coming out to him his friend asked, "For what have you come?" "I am in debt for four hundred dirhams." So the friend went into his house, counted out four hundred dirhams and brought them out to him. Then he went back into the house crying. "Why didn't you make some excuse if the request caused you difficulty?" his wife asked. He said, "I am only crying because I didn't pay any attention to his condition so that he found it necessary to speak to me about this."

Mutrif ibn Sukhayr said, "When one of you wants something from me, write me a note, for I would hate to see the humiliation of need in your face."

A man wanted to do some harm to Abd Allah ibn al-Abbas. He went to the dignitaries of the city and announced to them, "Ibn al-Abbas says to you, 'Come have dinner with me tomorrow!'" They all came, filling the house. "What is this?" he asked, and the thing was related to him. He immediately sent for fruit to be bought and ordered bread, hot dishes, and the matter was set right. When they were finished eating, he asked his retainers, "Do we have this available every day?" "Yes," they told him. "Then let all of these dine with us every day!" he said.

I heard Abu Abd al-Rahman al-Sulami say, "One day Abu Sahl al-Suluki was making ablutions in the courtyard of his house when a man came in and asked him for charity. He had nothing with him. "Be patient until I finish," he said. So the man waited. When Abu Sahl finished his ablutions he told him, "Take this water-bottle and go." The man took it and went. Abu Sahl waited until he knew the man was far away. Then he cried, "A man came and took the water-bottle!" So they walked after him but didn't catch up with him. He only did that because his family used to reproach him about how much he would give away. And I heard him say, "One winter Abu Sahl gave away his robe. He would wear a woman's robe when he went out to teach because he didn't have another. A delegation of notables arrived from Persia that included experts of every sort—leaders among lawyers, theologians, and grammarians. The army commander, Abu 'l- Hasan, sent to him and ordered him to ride out to meet them. So he put on a cloak over that woman's robe and rode. 'He is scorning me before the whole country to ride in a woman's robe!' the commander said. But Abu Sahl engaged the lot of them in scholarly argument, and his discourse triumphed over the discourse of them all in every field. And I heard him say that Abu Sahl would not give anyone anything from his own hand. He would cast it on the ground so that the one who received it would pick it up from there. He used to say, 'This world is of too little importance that for its sake I should see my hand set over the hand of someone else.' The Prophet used to say, 'The hand that is above is better than the hand that is beneath.'"

Abu Marthad was the first of the generous. A poet composed a panegyric in praise of him. "I have nothing to give you," he said, "but take me before the judge and claim 10,000 dirhams. I will confess it. Then have me cast into prison. My family will not let me stay in jail." So the poet did that, and before evening he was given 10,000 dirhams, and Abu Marthad went free.

A man asked alms of Hasan ibn Ali ibn Abu Talib. He gave him 50,000 dirhams and 500 dinars. "Bring a porter to carry it to you," he said. So the man brought a porter and al-Hasan gave him a head scarf, saying, "The porter's fee is on me."

A woman asked Layth ibn Sad for a bowl of honey. He ordered a whole skein of honey for her. Asked about that, he said, "She asked according to the extent of her need, but we gave according to the extent of our charity."

A dervish said, "One morning I prayed in al-Ashath's mosque in Kufah. I was looking for a debtor of mine. When the final salutations of prescribed prayer were made, a suit of clothes and a pair of sandals were placed in front of everyone, and in front of me as well. 'What is this?' I asked, 'Al-Ashath has just returned from Mecca,' I was told, 'and he ordered this for the members of the congregation of his mosque.' 'But I only came looking for someone who owes me money!' I said. 'I don't belong to his congregation.' 'It is for everyone present,' they said."

When al-Shafii's death drew near, he said, "Get so-and-so to give me the funeral ablution." The man was away at the time of the death, but when he came back he was told about this request. So he called for al-Shafii's book of accounts and found outstanding against him a debt of seventy thousand dirhams. He paid it, saying, "This is my ablution for him."

It is said that when al-Shafii went to Mecca from Sana he was carrying 10,000 dinars. "Buy a property," people told him. But he struck a tent outside of Mecca and poured out the dinars, which he gave to everyone who came in to see him, by the handful. When the time of noon prescribed prayer came around, he stood up and tore the cloth of the moneybag, and not a thing remained.

Sari went out one holiday and was greeted by a man of importance. Sari gave him only a short salutation. "But this is a man of stature!" he was told. "I am aware of that," he said, "but it is related through a reliable transmission that when two Muslims meet a hundred mercies are divided between them and ninety go to the friendlier of the two. I wanted the greater number to go to him." The Commander of the Faithful Ali ibn Abi Talib was crying one day. "Why are you weeping?" they asked him. "No guest has come to me for seven days," he replied, "and I am afraid that God Most High has scorned me." It is related that Anas ibn Malik said, "The tithe of the house is that a room in it be used for hospitality."

In regard to the saying of the Most High, *"Has the account of the guests honored by Abraham reached you?"* [51:24], they are called honored because he attended upon them himself, and the guests of the generous are honored by generosity." Ibrahim ibn Junayd said, "It used to be said that there are four things a noble man must not hold himself above, even if he be a prince: rising from his place for his father, waiting upon his guest, serving the learned man who taught him, and asking about what he does not know."

Ibn Abbas commented about the saying of the Most High *"There is no sin upon you whether you eat together or separately"* [24:61], that the Companions used to be distressed when one of them ate by himself, and it was made easier for them by this revelation. Abd Allah ibn Amir ibn Kurayz offered hospitality to a man and entertained him very well. But when the man was leaving, Abd Allah did not send his servants to assist him. Asked about that, Abd Allah said, "They will not help anyone who leaves us." Abd Allah ibn Bakawiya al-Sufi recited, saying that al-Mutanabbi recited to us about this:

If you leave those who have the means to keep you —
They are the ones who are leaving.

Abd Allah ibn al-Mubarak said, "The generosity involved in relinquishing what is in human hands is greater than the generosity involved in giving freely."

A dervish said, "I went to see Bishr ibn al-Harith on a day of extreme cold. He had taken off his clothes and was shivering. 'Abu Nasr,' I said, 'On a day like this people put on more clothes! Why have you removed them?' 'I thought of the poor and what this day is like for them,' he said. 'I do not have the means to help them, but I wanted myself to keep company with them in the cruelty of the cold.'"

I heard Abu Abd al-Rahman al-Sulami say. . . that al-Daqqaq said, "It is not generosity when the one who has gives to the one who has nothing, but it is generosity when the one who has nothing gives to the one who has."

35
ON JEALOUSY (*GHAYRA*)

God Most High has said, "*Say: My Lord has only forbidden indecencies—those of them which are evident and those which are hidden.*" [7:33].

Abu Bakr Muhammad ibn Ahmad ibn Abd al-Mazaki reported . . . from Abd Allah ibn Masud that the Messenger of God said, "No one is more jealous than God Most High and out of His jealousy he has forbidden indecencies—those of them which are evident and those which are hidden."

Ali ibn Ahmad al-Ahwazi reported . . . that Abu Hurayra recounted the Messenger of God saying, "God is jealous and the believer is jealous. God Most High is jealous that the believing servant should approach that which God has forbidden him."

Ghayra is an aversion against admitting the partnership of others (*al-ghayr*). When God, glory to Him, is described as possessing jealousy, it means that it does not please Him for anything else to share with Him in the obedience of the servant, which is due to Him alone.

It is related that the verse "*When the Koran is recited ,We set a veil as a covering between you and those who do not believe*" [17:45] was recited before Sari al-Saqati, Sari said to his companions, "Do you know what this veil is? It is the veil of jealousy, and there is no one more jeal-

241

ous than God Most High." The meaning of his saying, "It is the veil of jealousy" is that God does not make disbelievers privy to the understanding of the truth of religion.

Abu Ali al-Daqqaq said, "The people who are lazy in worshipping the Most High are those whose feet the Truth has bound with the shackles of spiritual failure. He has chosen for them to be distant from Him and delayed their reaching the place of closeness. Because of that, they delay their worship and service."

They recite:

> I am enamored of the one I desire,
> But my wiles are not for the evil eye of outsiders.

And with the same meaning they also say, "The sick one who is not healed is a seeker who is not sought."

I heard Abu Ali say that Abbas al-Zawzani said, "I had a good spiritual beginning and used to know how much distance remained between me and the attainment of my goal, the victory of my intention. One night in a dream it seemed to me that I was rolling down a mountain, though I wanted to arrive at its peak. I was saddened. Sleep overtook me, and I saw someone who said, 'O Abbas, the Truth does not want you to reach what you have been seeking. But He has opened wisdom for your tongue.' When morning came I received inspiration for wise words."

I heard Abu Ali say, "There was a shaykh who had a state and a moment with God Most High. For awhile he was hidden and not seen among the dervishes. When he reappeared after that, the moment that had once come upon him no longer did. He was questioned about it, and said, 'Alas, the veil has fallen!'"

Whenever something happened in the course of a spiritual gathering that disturbed the hearts of the participants, Abu Ali used to say, "This is from the jealousy of the Truth, glory to Him. He wished that whatever flowed from the purity of this moment should not flow upon them."

With this sense they recited:

> She cared for our coming till she looked in the
>   mirror.
> Her lovely face forbade her such concern.
> A Sufi was asked, "Do you want to see Him?"
> "No."
> "Why not?"
> "I deem that beauty to be above the glance of the
> likes of me!"

They recited with this meaning:

> I am envious of my glance at You
> So I cast down my eyes when I look at You.
> I see You pass proudly with all those qualities
> That enthrall me, and I jealously guard You for You.

Shibli was asked, "When will you find rest?" "When I don't see anyone remembering Him!" he said.

I heard Abu Ali discuss the matter of a horseman who came to pledge himself to the Messenger of God. He spoke to him as if he did not recognize him. The Messenger of God spoke to him without identifying himself. "May God grant you long life!" said the bedouin. "Who are you?" The Prophet said, "A man of the Quraysh." One of the Companions present said to the bedouin, "It is enough suffering for you that you do not know your Prophet!"

Abu Ali used to say, "He only said 'A man of the Quraysh' out of jealousy, lest he be obliged to acquaint everybody with who he was. Then God, glory to Him, caused this identification to flow from the tongue of that

244 Sufi Book of Spiritual Ascent

Companion to the bedouin by his saying, "It is enough suffering for you that you do not know your Prophet!"

Some people say that jealousy is a trait of beginners, and that a person who truly affirms the unity bears no witness to jealousy and is not characterized by any preference. He has no authority to judge what takes place in the land. The Truth brings to pass what He requires, as He requires.

I heard Abu Abd al-Rahman al-Sulami say that Abu Uthman al-Maghribi said, "Jealousy is the work of students, not of those who know the realities." And I heard him say . . . that Shibli said, "Jealousy is two jealousies: human jealousy, which is hard upon egos, and divine jealousy, which is hard upon hearts." Shibli also said, "Divine jealousy concerns the breaths lost on what is other than God Most High."

It is rightly said that jealousy is two jealousies: there is the Truth's jealousy of the servant that the servant should not give himself over to created things but withhold himself from them; and the servant's jealousy for the Truth, that he will not give over any of his states and breaths to what is not the Truth. One does not say, "I am jealous of God Most High," but one says, "I am jealous for God." To permit jealousy of God is ignorance that may lead to the abandonment of religion. But jealousy for God makes you hold His rights to be great and purifies your works for His sake.

Know that it is God's custom with His Friends that if they dwell upon what is other than Him or give their attention to something else or cleave to something else in their hearts, He will put that thing into disorder. For He is jealous that their hearts should again be purely His, devoid of whatever they dwelt upon or paid attention or clove to. Thus when Prophet Adam settled down to immortality in paradise, God drove him out of it. And when Prophet Abraham delighted in Prophet Ishmael,

He ordered that the boy be sacrificed. But when
Abraham took his son out of his heart *"and they both
submitted and he threw him down on his forehead"*
[37:103], and he had purified his inner being of him, God
commanded the child's redemption by the substitution of
the sacrificial ram.

I heard Abu Abd al-Rahman al-Sulami say that . . .
Muhammad ibn Hassan said, "While I was wandering
the mountains of Lebanon a man suddenly came across
us—a young man, parched by the hot winds. When he
saw me, he turned and ran. So I followed him, and
asked, 'Give me some advice!' 'Beware!' he said to me.
'He is jealous and does not like seeing anything but
Himself in the heart of His servant!'"

I heard Abu Abd al-Rahman say that Nasrabadhi
said, "The Truth is jealous. Part of the jealousy is that
He he has not left a road to Himself that is other than
Himself." It is told that God, glory to Him, revealed to
one of His prophets, "A certain person needs something
of Me and I also need something from him. If he satisfies
My need, I will satisfy his need."

In his private prayers that Prophet asked, "My God,
how can it be that You have a need?" "His heart has
dwelt upon something other than Me," God revealed.
"Let him empty his heart of it and I will satisfy his
need."

Abu Yazid al-Bistami dreamed of a gathering of the
maidens of paradise and gazed upon them. For days he
was stripped of his state. Then again he saw a group of
them in his dreams. He refused to turn to them, saying,
"You are distractions!"

Rabia al-Adawiyyah fell sick. "What is the reason for
your illness?" she was asked. "My heart looked toward
paradise," she said, "and He has reprimanded me.
Reproof belongs to Him. I shall not return to it."

It is related that Sari said, "For a long time I sought

a man to be a friend. I was passing through some mountains and came upon a gathering of diseased, blind and ailing people. I asked what they were doing. They told me that once a year a man came out there, prayed for them, and they would be healed. So I waited for him to come. He prayed for them,and they were indeed cured. I followed after him and clung to him and told him, 'I have an inner sickness! What is the cure?' 'O Sari,' he said, 'get away from me! For the Most High is jealous to see you find rest in anything other than Him, and you will fall from His eye.'"

There are some Sufis whose jealousy is such that when they see people mentioning the Most High in unconsciousness they are unable to look at that and find it unbearable. I heard Abu Ali al-Daqqaq say, "When the bedouin entered the Prophet's mosque and urinated in it, the Companions fell upon him to throw him out. The bedouin had only displayed bad behavior, but embarrassment overcame the Companions and they were upset when they saw someone who had cast off all decency."

Thus the servant, when he knows the majesty of God's Omnipotence, finds it painful to hear the remembrance of someone who mentions Him in unconsciousness or to see the obedience of someone who does not serve Him with respect. It is related that Abu Bakr al-Shibli had a son by the name of Abu 'l- Hasan who died. His mother, mourning for him, cut off her hair. Shibli went to the baths and shaved off his beard. Everyone who came to him to offer condolences would say, "O Abu Bakr, what is this?" "It is in sympathy with my wife," he would say. But one of them said to him, "Abu Bakr, tell me the real reason that you have done this."

"I knew," he said, "that they would come with their condolences, saying 'May God recompense you' in unconsciousness. So I sacrificed my beard as a ransom for their mentioning God unconsciously."

Nuri heard a man make the call to prescribed prayer and exclaimed, "Slander and deadly poison!" Then he heard a dog barking and cried, "At your service and pleasure!" "This is the abandonment of religion!" people said, "that he should say to a believer in his act of witness 'Slander and deadly poison,' and give the pilgrim's cry of service in reply to the barking of dogs!" Nuri was queried about this. He said, "As for that man, his remembrance of God was the very essence of unconsciousness, and as for the dog, God has said, *'There is nothing that does not glorify His praise'* [17:44]."

One time Shibli was making the call to prescribed prayer, and when he had completed the two acts of witness to the unity of God and the messengership of Muhammad, he said, "Were it not that You had commanded me, I would not mention together with You anyone other than You!"

A man heard another man use the common exclamation, "God is greater!" He told him, "I wish you would hold Him to be greater than that!" I heard one of the dervishes say that Abu 'l- Hasan al-Khazafani said, "There is no god but God" from the depths of the heart— "Muhammad is the Messenger of God" from the behind the earlobe!

Someone who looked at the outward aspect of this expression might imagine that it devalues the divine law. It is not the way that it might occur to him. But in reality, importance given to others is trivial in comparison with the omnipotence of the Truth.

36
ON SAINTHOOD (*WILAYA*)

G od Most High said, "*The Friends of God—no fear is upon them, nor do they grieve*" [10:62].

Hamzah ibn Yusuf al-Sahmi reported . . . from Ayisha that the Prophet said that God Most High said, "Whoever harms a friend of Mine has declared war upon Me. The servant has no means to approach Me equal to the performance of what I have made his duty. The servant will not stop drawing close to me through voluntary devotions until I love him. I do not hesitate in anything that I do as I hesitate in taking the soul of My believing servant because he hates death, and I hate to trouble him, but it is necessary for him."

The word *wali*, "saint," "Friend of God," has two etymological senses. The first assigns the word the meaning of a passive participle. The *wali* is then the person of whose affairs God, glory to Him, takes charge. God Most High has said, "*He has charge over the doers of good*" [7:196]. God does not leave such a person with his own ego for even a moment. He Himself takes care of him."

The second sense assigns the word the meaning of an intensive active participle. In this sense the *wali* takes the service and worship of God into his care, so that his service flows uninterruptedly without any disobedience intervening. Both of these descriptions are necessary for a *wali* to be truly a *wali*—his discharge of the rights due to God Most High through close study and full performance and God's continual protection of him in joy and sorrow. It is part of the definition of being a saint that one be protected, just as it is part of the definition of being a prophet that one be made incapable of sin. And anyone who objects to the statement that obedience to the religious law is required of a saint is mistaken and deceived.

I heard Abu Ali al-Daqqaq say that Abu Yazid al-Bistami went to see someone who had been described as a saint. When he arrived at the man's mosque, Abu Yazid sat and waited for him to come out. The man came out and spit in the direction of the mosque. Abu Yazid left without greeting him. "The man is not trustworthy regarding a point of behavior of the divine law," Abu Yazid said. "How shall he be trustworthy regarding the secrets of the Truth?"

The Sufis differ over whether or not it is possible for the saint to know he is a saint. Some of them say that is not possible. According to them, a saint looks upon himself with an eye that sees his own smallness. When any sort of miraculous grace appears to him, he is afraid that it may be a test of deception. He is constantly filled with fear—the fear of falling from where he is, of his end becoming the opposite of his current state. Those who take this position hold that one of the conditions of sainthood is the carrying out of one's duty until the end.

In this section many stories of the saints have been met with, and a countless number of Sufi shaykhs have held this opinion. If we were to occupy ourselves with recounting what they said, we would exceed the bounds of brevity. Of the shaykhs whom we have met personally, Abu Bakr ibn Furak took this point of view.

Some Sufis say that it is possible for the saint to know he is a saint, and that carrying out one's duty to

the end is not a condition for the actualization of sainthood now. Given that this faithfulness at death is a
defining characteristic of sainthood, a saint might still
be chosen by God for the grace of knowing that his final
state is secure for we must admit the possibility of the
miracles granted to the saints. No matter how the saint
may fear his end, his actual state of awe, magnification,
and glory is more effective and perfect. Hearts find more
peace in a little bit of awe and glorification than in a lot
of fear. And [if uncertainty about one's end is a necessity
for sainthood], why did the Prophet say, "Ten of my
Companions are in paradise?" The ten undoubtedly
believed the Messenger of God spoke the truth and knew
the safety of their end. That knowledge could not have
nullified their state.

One of the conditions for a proper understanding of
prophethood is an awareness of the nature of prophetic
miracles. To know the reality of the special graces granted the saints is a part of this awareness. If a saint saw
such graces manifested upon him, he would have to be
able to distinguish between them and other sorts of
events. And when he saw them, he would know that his
current state was true. Therefore it is possible that he
could know that in the end he would remain in the same
condition, for the knowledge would be a grace granted to
him, and to speak of the miraculous graces granted the
saints is sound religion.

Many Sufi stories suggest this view is correct. We
shall recount some of them in the section on the miracles
of the saints, if God so wills. Among the shaykhs whom
we have met, Abu Ali al-Daqqaq takes this point of view.
Ibrahim ibn Adham asked a man, "Would you like to be
a Friend of God?" "Yes," he said. "Do not concern yourself
with anything of this world or the next, but devote yourself to God Most High. Turn your face toward Him so
that He will turn His face toward you and befriend you."
Yahya ibn Muadh said, characterizing the saints,

"They are servants who, after suffering, have been clothed in intimacy with God Most High and who have embraced ease after struggle through their attainment of the station of Friendship."

I heard Abu Abd al-Rahman al-Sulami say . . . that Abu Yazid said, "The saints of God Most High are God's brides. Brides are not seen except by members of the family. They are secluded with Him behind the curtain of intimacy. They are not seen by anyone of this world or the next."

I heard Abu Bakr al-Saydalani, who was a righteous man, say, "Many times I rebuilt the marker at the grave of Abu Bakr al-Tamastani in the cemetery at Hira and wrote his name upon it. The marker was torn up and stolen! Nothing like that happened to any of the other graves. This astonished me so I asked Abu Ali al-Daqqaq about it one day. He said, "That shaykh preferred secrecy in this world. With the marker that you made, you wanted to make his grave known. The Truth, glory to Him, chose to hide his grave just as he had preferred to veil himself."

Abu Uthman al-Maghribi said, "The saint may be famous, but he is not dazzled." I heard Abu Abd al-Rahman al-Sulami say that al-Nasrabadhi said, "The saints ask for nothing—their state is only waning and extinction." He also heard him say, "The end of saintship is the beginning of prophethood."

Sahl ibn Abd Allah said, "The saint is he whose acts are continuously in harmony with God's will." Yahya ibn Muadh said, "The saint does not act for show and is not a hypocrite. There are so few friends with such character!"

Abu Ali al-Juzjani said, "The saint has passed away from his own state and abides in the contemplation of the Truth. God takes charge of the governance of his life, and the lights of this care continuously fall upon him. He possesses no information about himself and no home with what is other than God."

Abu Yazid said, "The worldly destinies assigned the saints, together with their explanations, come from four divine Names. The support of every party of them derives from one of these four. They are: 'the First,' 'the Last,' 'the Outer,' 'the Inner.' When a saint passes away from these after having known them intimately, he is perfect and complete. Whoever draws a share from God's Name 'the Outer' takes as his portion the wonders of divine Omnipotence. Whoever draws a share from God's Name 'the Inner' takes as his portion the divine lights that shine upon souls. Whoever draws a share from God's Name 'the First' is occupied with what preceded Creation, and whoever draws a share from God's Name 'the Last' has been stationed with what will come to pass. Each receives knowledge according to what he can bear, except the one of whom the Truth, in His goodness, has taken charge. That one He supports through Himself."

This saying of Abu Yazid's points to the elite of God's servants who have progressed beyond these categories. There are no consequences for them to remember, no origins for them to think upon, no calamities for them to be captured by. Thus those who have entered into the truth are erased from the qualities of created beings. As God Most High has said, "*You would reckon them awake, while they are asleep*" [18:17].

Yahya ibn Muadh said, "The saint is the sweet herb of God Most High in the earth. The truthful smell him and his fragrance reaches their hearts so that they yearn for their Lord and increase their worship according to their different characters."

Al-Wasiti was asked, "How is the saint nourished in his sainthood?" He said, "In the beginning, through his devotions. In his maturity, through God's concealing the graces He has bestowed upon him. Then God draws him to the qualities and attributes destined for him and makes him taste the pleasure of living every moment for God's sake."

It is said that the saint has three signs: he is occupied with God, he flees to God, and he cares for God. Al-Kharraz said, "When God Most High wants to befriend one of His servants, He opens for him the door of His remembrance. When remembrance gives him delight, He opens for him the door of closeness and in that way raises him to the circles of intimacy. Then he seats him upon the throne of the recognition of unity. Then removes the veil from him and causes him to enter the house of singularity. Then He reveals to him the divine Majesty and Grandeur. When his sight rests upon that Majesty and Grandeur, he loses himself. At that time the servant becomes crippled, annihilated, and falls under the protection of God, and he is freed from the pretenses of his ego."

I heard Muhammad ibn al-Husayn say . . . that Abu Turab al-Nakhshabi said, "When the heart is fond of turning away from God, its speech is the vilification of the Friends of God."

The Sufis say that one of the traits of the saint is that he has no fear. Fear is the anticipation of something hated coming about in the future or the anxiety that something liked will pass away in the future, but the saint is the son of his moment. He has no future that he should be fearful of anything. And just as he has no fear ,he has no hope because hope is the expectation that something liked will come about or that something hated will be taken away, and that also refers to a second moment. Thus also he has no grief, for grief comes of the difficulty of the heart. Someone who is in the radiance of contentment and the soothing coolness of harmony with the divine will—how should he grieve? God Most High has said, "The Friends of God—no fear is upon them, nor do they grieve."

37
ON SUPPLICATION (*DUA*)

God Most High said, "*Call upon your Lord humbly and secretly*" [7:55], and He said, "*Your Lord says, 'Call upon Me; I will answer you*" [40:60].

Abu Ali ibn Ahmad ibn Abdan reported . . . from Anas ibn Malik that the Messenger of God said, "Supplication is the core of worship." *Dua*, supplication, is the key of need, the comforter of the distressed, the refuge of the destitute, the breath of relief for those who are in want. God Glorious and Exalted has condemned a people who abandoned such prayer, saying "*And they close their hands*" [9:67]—that is, "They do not stretch them toward Us, asking." Sahl ibn Abd Allah al-Tustari said, "God Most High created the Creation and said, 'Confide in Me, and if you do not, then look toward Me, and if you do not, then listen to Me, and if you do not, then be at My door, and if you are not, then lay upon Me what you need of Me.'"

I heard Abu Ali al-Daqqaq say that Sahl ibn Abd Allah said, "The prayer that is closest to being answered is the prayer expressed in one's state. 'The prayer expressed in one's state,' means that the one who prays is in absolute need and has no other recourse.

I heard Hamzah ibn Yusuf al-Sahmi say that Abu Abd Allah al-Makanisi said he was with Junayd when a

woman came to them and said, "Pray to God that He
return my son to me. I have a son who is lost." "Go away,
and be patient," he said. She left. Again she came back
and said the same thing to him. "Go away and be
patient," Junayd told her. So she went away but later
came back. She did this many times, while Junayd said
to her, "Be patient." Finally she said to him, "Enough of
patience! I have no more capacity for it. Pray for me!" "If
things are as you say," Junayd said, "then go home. Your
son has returned." So she left and found him. Later she
came back to thank the shaykh. "How did you know
that?" they asked Junayd. Said he: "God Most High said,
'Or, Who answers the distressed one when he calls upon
Him, and removes the evil . . . ?' [27:62]."

People differ over whether it is better to ask things
in prayer or to keep silent and be satisfied with one's lot.
Some say that to ask is in itself an act of worship—the
Prophet said "Supplication is the core of worship"—and
to perform an act of worship is better than to abandon it.
Moreover, supplication is the right of God Most High
over His servants. Even if God does not accept the servant's supplications and the servant does not receive the
thing he wants, still he is performing his duty in ren-
dering the right of his Lord. For supplication is the manifestation of the need proper to servanthood. Abu Hazim
al-Araj said, "Being forbidden to ask would be harder on
me than being refused an answer."

Another party says that silence and indifference to
whatever happens is the more perfect course, and that
satisfaction with what God has already chosen is superi-
or. Thus al-Wasiti said, "To prefer what has been coming
to you since before time began is better for you than to
resist what is happening now. The Prophet gave news
that God Most High said, 'If My remembrance distracts
someone from asking things of Me, I will give him more
than I give those who ask.'"

Yet another group says that the servant should have supplication on his tongue and satisfaction in his heart so that he brings both sides of matter together. The best opinion is that situations vary. In some states supplication is better than silence so that supplication is the best behavior, while in other states silence is better than supplication so that silence is the best behavior. This is something that can only be understood in the moment, for the knowledge of the moment only comes to exist in that moment. If someone finds an indication for supplication in his heart, then supplication is most suitable for him. If he finds there an indication for silence, then silence is most suitable for him.

It is correctly said that the servant must not forget to look to his Lord when he supplicates. Then he must observe his own state. If he finds that the supplication is increasing the openness of his heart, supplication is better for him. But if something like a rebuke or a tightening comes over his heart at the moment of supplication, then it is better for him to give up the petition at that time. If he finds neither an increase of openness nor the occurrence of a rebuke, then supplicating or giving it up are at that point alike. If the thing that governs him at that moment is religious knowledge, then supplication is better because of its being an act of worship. If the thing that governs him at that moment is divine realization and spiritual state and silence, then silence is better.

It is correctly said that in the case of things that are the rightful lot of a Muslim or that involve some service to the Truth, asking is better. When supplication involves asking something for one's lower self, silence is more perfect.

According to a transmitted hadith, "When a servant is supplicating God and God loves that servant, He says, 'O Gabriel, delay My servant's need, for I love to hear his voice.' And when a servant is supplicating God and God is angry at that servant, He says, 'O Gabriel, satisfy My servant's need, for I hate to hear his voice!'"

It is related that Yahya ibn Said al-Qattan saw the Truth, glory to Him, in a dream and said, "My God, how often have I supplicated You and You have not answered me!" He said, "O Yahya, it is because I love to hear your voice."

The Prophet said, "By Him in Whose hand is my life, the servant will supplicate God Most High while God is angry with him, and God will turn away from him. Again he will supplicate, and God will turn away and again he will supplicate, and God will turn away. Then again he will supplicate, and God Most High will say to the angels, 'My servant refuses to call upon anything other than Me so I have answered him.'"

Abu 'l-Husayn Ali ibn Muhammad ibn Abd Allah ibn Bushran of Baghdad reported . . . from Anas ibn Malik, "There was a man who had made an arrangement with the Messenger of God to trade between Damascus and Medina and between Medina and Damascus. Placing his trust in God Almighty and Glorious, he would not have the caravans accompanied by guards. He said that he was coming from Damascus intending to go to Medina when suddenly a brigand on horseback appeared and shouted, 'Halt, halt!' So the merchant stopped and said to him, "Your business is with my property so let me go free.' 'The property is my property anyway,' said the brigand. 'I want your life!' 'What do you want with my life?' the merchant asked him. 'Your business is the merchandise. Let me go free!' But the brigand replied to him with the same speech as before. So the merchant said, 'Wait until I perform ablution and a prescribed prayer and call upon my Lord.' 'Do what has occurred to you,' said the thief. So the merchant stood up, performed ablution and offered four cycles of prescribed prayer. Then he raised his hands to heaven and said in his supplication, "O

Loving One, O Loving One, O Owner of the Glorious
Throne, Beginner of things and Returner of everything
to its proper state, constant Doer of what He wills—I ask
You through the light of Your Countenance that floods
the pillars of Your Throne, through Your Omnipotence by
which You have total power over Your Creation, and
through Your Mercy which encompasses everything—
there is no god but You—O Granter of help, help me!
(three times).' When he had finished his prayer, suddenly there appeared a rider upon a grey horse wearing
green garments and holding in his hand a spear of light!
When the thief saw the rider, he left the merchant and
began to edge toward him. But when he had drawn close,
the horseman charged the thief and pierced him with a
stab that threw him away from his horse. Then he came
to the merchant and said, 'Rise and kill him!' 'Who are
you?' the merchant asked him. 'I never killed anyone in
my life, and his death is not sweet to me!' The rider went
up to the brigand and killed him. Then he came to the
merchant and said, 'Know that I am an angel of the third
heaven. When you prayed the first time, we heard the
doors of heaven shake and said, "Something is happening!" When you prayed the second time, the doors of
heaven opened with sparks like flames of fire. Then
when you prayed the third time, Gabriel descended to us
from the height of heaven and cried, 'Who is for this man
in distress?' Then I prayed to my Lord that He assign me
to kill the one who threatened you. And know, O Servant
of God, that whoever offers this supplication of yours in
any difficulty, any danger, any calamity, God Most High
will liberate him from it and help him.' So the merchant
proceeded safe and sound until he entered Medina,
where he went to the Prophet, told him the story and
told him the supplication. The Prophet said to him, 'God
Almighty and Glorious has instilled in you those
Beautiful Names of His which, when you call upon Him

by them, He answers, and when you ask of Him by them, He gives.'"

Part of the conduct proper to supplication is presence of heart—that you are not inattentive while you supplicate. It is related that the Prophet said, "God Most High will not answer the supplication of a servant whose heart is heedless."

Another one of the conditions of supplication is that your food be lawful. The Prophet said to Sad, "Earn your livelihood lawfully so that your supplication will be answered." It has been said that supplication is the key of need, and the teeth of that key are lawful morsels.

Yahya ibn Muadh used to supplicate, "My God, how can I supplicate You while I am disobedient? And how can I not supplicate You while You are the Generous One?"

Prophet Moses passed by a man who was supplicating and imploring. "My God," Prophet Moses said, "If his need were in my hand, I would satisfy it!" God Most High revealed to him, "I am more compassionate toward him than you are, but he has a herd of sheep, and while he is calling upon Me, his heart is with his sheep! I do not answer a servant who calls upon Me while his heart is with something else." So Prophet Moses recounted this to the man, who then devoted his heart completely to God Most High and his need was satisfied. Someone asked Jafar al-Sadiq, "Why is it that when we supplicate we are not answered?" "Because you are calling upon someone whom you do not know!" he said.

I heard Abu Ali al-Daqqaq say, "An illness appeared in Yaqub ibn al-Layth for which the physicians could find no cure. They told him, 'In your domain is a righteous man named Sahl ibn Abd Allah al-Tustari. If he supplicates for you, perhaps God will answer him.'" So he summoned Sahl and said, "Supplicate God Almighty and Glorious for me." "And how will he answer my prayer on your behalf," said Sahl, "while the victims of oppression are in your prisons?" Yaqub freed everyone whom he was holding. Sahl prayed, "My God, as You have shown him the humiliation of disobedience, show him also the dignity of obedience and remove this from him." And he was cured. Yaqub sent money to Sahl, but Sahl refused to accept it. "Why didn't you take it and distribute it among the dervishes?" he was asked. He looked toward some desert pebbles. Suddenly they were jewels! "Does someone who has been granted the likes of this," he asked his companions, "stand in need of the money of Yaqub ibn al-Layth?"

Salih al-Murri often would say, "Someone who applies himself to knocking at the door is on the verge of having it opened." Rabia asked him, "How long are you going to keep on saying this? When has the door ever been closed that one needs to seek for it to be opened?" "An ignorant shaykh," said Salih, "and a woman who knows!"

I heard Abu Abd al-Rahman al-Sulami say . . . that Sari al-Saqati said, "I was present at one of Maruf al-Karkhi's meetings when a man stood up and said, 'Abu Mahfuz, pray to God Most High that my purse be returned to me! It was stolen, and there were 1,000 dinars in it!'" Maruf was silent. The man reiterated what he had said. Maruf remained silent, and the man repeated it again. Finally Maruf said, "What shall I say? Shall I say, 'That which You have removed from Your prophets and sincere friends, give it back to him?'" "Just supplicate God Most High for me!" the man said. Maruf supplicated, "O God, give him whatever is good for him."

It is related that al-Layth said, "I saw Uqbah ibn Nafi blind and later I saw him with his vision. 'By what means did God return your sight?' I asked him. 'A visitation in my dreams,' he told me. 'It was said, "Say: O Near One, O Answerer, O Hearer of prayers, O You Who are Gracious toward what You will, restore to me my sight!" I said it and God Glorious and Exalted gave me back my vision.'"

I heard Abu Ali al-Daqqaq say, "When I first returned to Nishapur from Merv, I developed pain in my eyes. For a period of some days I could not sleep. One morning I was lying awake when I heard a voice say to me, *'Isn't God sufficient for His servants?'* [39:36]. So I understood and the inflammation left me. The pain immediately disappeared. Pain in my eyes has not troubled me since then."

It is related that Muhammad ibn Khuzaymah said, "When Ahmad ibn Hanbal died, I was in Alexandria. I was grieved. Then I saw him in a dream. He was strutting! 'O Abu Abd Allah,' I said, 'What kind of a bearing is this?' 'It is the bearing of the servants in the House of Peace,' said he. 'What has God Glorious and Exalted done with you?' I asked. 'He forgave me, set a crown on my head, sandals of gold on my feet and said, "Ahmad, this is for saying that the Koran is My speech." Then He said, "Ahmad, call upon Me with those supplications that came to you from Sufyan al-Thawri and that you used to supplicate with in the lower world." So I supplicated, 'O Lord of everything, by Your power over everything, forgive me everything and don't ask me about anything!' "O Ahmad," He said, "this is paradise. Enter it!" So I went in.'"

A young man clung to the drapery of the Kabah and said, "My God, You have no partner to influence You nor any minister to be bribed. If I have obeyed You, it is through Your grace, and the praise belongs to You. If I have disobeyed You, it is through my ignorance, and the argument against me is Yours. For the sureness of Your argument against me and the disruption of my argument before You, there is no help but that You forgive me!" A voice from nowhere was heard to say, "The noble youth is freed from the fire!"

It is said that the point of supplication is that it manifests need before the Most High. Otherwise, the Lord does what He wills. The supplication of ordinary people, it is said, is made with words. The supplication of ascetics is made with actions. The supplication of the gnostics is made with states. The best supplication is that which provokes sadness.

A Sufi said, "If you ask God Most High for something you need and it comes easily, then ask Him after that for paradise. Maybe it is your day to be answered!" The tongues of novices, it is said, utter supplications, but the tongues of the gnostics are mute.

Al-Wasiti was asked to supplicate. He said, "I am afraid that if I supplicate, I will be told, 'You have asked Us for what was already yours according to Us. You have doubted Us!' Or else, 'You have asked Us for what does not belong to you, according to Us. You have behaved badly toward Us! If you had remained content, in time We would have brought things to pass so that you would have been satisfied.'"

It is reported that Abd Allah ibn Munazil said, "For fifty years I have asked nothing in supplication, nor have I wanted anyone to supplicate for me." Supplication, it is said, is the ladder of sinners. Supplication is communication. As long as communication continues, the business is still beautiful.

It is said that the tongue of sinners is their supplications. I heard Abu Ali al-Daqqaq say, "When the sinner cries, he is in contact with God Glorious and Exalted." And with this sense they recited:

The tears of the youth spell out what he has hidden,
And his sighs show forth what his heart conceals.
A Sufi said, "Prayer is to give up sinning."

Prayer is the voice of yearning for the Beloved.
Permission to pray is better for the servant than
receiving the gift.

Al-Kattani said, "God Most High never opens the
tongue of the believer to ask for pardon without opening
also the door of forgiveness."
It is said that supplication makes one be present
with God, while receiving the gift makes one go away. To
stand at the door is more perfect than to go elsewhere.
Supplication is to speak personally to the Truth with the
tongue of shame. The prerequisite of asking in supplication is to abide with God's destiny in contentment. How
can you be waiting for an answer to your supplication
when you have blocked its road with sin? Someone asked
a dervish, "Supplicate for me." He replied, "It is enough
foreignness to your Lord that you set a mediator
between yourself and Him!"
I heard Hamzah ibn Yusuf al-Sahmi say that. . . Abd
al-Rahman ibn Ahmad said, "A woman came to Taqi ibn
Mukhallad and said, 'My son has been captured by the
Byzantines. My only property is a little house that I cannot sell. Could you direct me to someone who would ransom him with something? I know neither day nor night,
sleep nor rest!' 'Yes,' he told her. 'Go back home until I
look into his affairs, God willing.' The shaykh bowed his
head, and his lips moved. We waited some time. The
woman came back, and with her was her son. She began
to pray for the shaykh, and said, 'My son has returned
safe and sound, and he has a story to tell you.' Her son
said, 'I was in the hands of one of the Byzantine kings
together with a group of other prisoners. He had a man
who would set us to work every day. He used to send us
out into the desert to labor and then bring us back. We
were in chains. While we were leaving work after sunset
with the official who would oversee us, the shackle on

my foot opened and fell onto the ground. He described the day and hour, and it agreed with the time when the woman had come to us and the shaykh had prayed. So the overseer pounced on me and yelled at me, 'You have broken the chain!' 'No,' I told him. 'It fell from my foot.' He was amazed and summoned his companion. They summoned the blacksmith, who set a new shackle on me. But when I walked a few steps, it fell from my foot again. They were astounded by the affair so they called their monks. 'Do you have a mother?' they asked me. 'Yes,' I said. 'Her supplication has attained an answer and God Almighty and Glorious has set you free,' they said. 'It is not possible for us to keep you captive.' So they provisioned me and sent to accompany me someone who could lead me to the borders of the Muslims."

38
ON SPIRITUAL POVERTY
(*FAQR*)

God Most High has said, "*Charity is for the poor who are confined in the way of God. They cannot go about in the land. The ignorant man thinks them to be rich on account of their abstaining from beg - ging. You can recognize them by their mark—they beg not of people importunately. And whatever good thing you spend, surely God is Knower of it*" [2:273].

Abu Abd Allah al-Husayn ibn Shuja ibn al-Husayn ibn Musa al-Bazzaz in Baghdad reported. . . through Abu Hurayra from the Prophet, "The poor will enter paradise 500 years before the rich: that is half a celestial day."

Abu Bakr Muhammad ibn Ahmad ibn Abd al-Hiri reported in Baghdad . . . from Abd Allah, "The Messenger of God said, 'The utterly poor one is not the one who goes from door to door for a morsel or two, or a date or two.' 'Who is the utterly poor one, O Messenger of God?' they asked. 'The one who cannot find what would free him of need and who is ashamed to beg from people so no one notices him to give him alms.'"

The meaning of his saying, "They are ashamed to beg from people" is that they are ashamed before God Most

High, not ashamed before the people. Poverty is the badge of the saints, the adornment of the pure, and the state the Truth chooses for His elect among the pious and the prophets. The poor are the cream of God's servants, the repositories of His secrets amidst His creation. Through them the Truth maintains the creation, and by the strength of blessing they accumulate He expands its sustenance.

According to the report that has reached us from the Prophet, on the day of judgment, the poor who are full of patience will be the close companions of God Most High. Abu Abd al-Rahman al-Sulami reported . . . from Umar ibn al-Khattab that the Messenger of God said, "Everything has a key. The key of paradise is the love of the wretched and the patient poor. They will be the close companions of God Most High on the day of judgment."

A man gave Ibrahim ibn Adham 10,000 dirhams, but he refused to accept them. "You want to erase my name from the register of the poor with 10,000 dirhams!" he exclaimed. "I won't have it!" Muadh al-Nasfi said, "God Most High will not destroy a people, even though they continue in their evil practices, as long as they do not humiliate and abase the poor."

If the poor man had no merit beyond his wish and desire that God should grant abundance to Muslims and that prices should be low—because he needs to buy while the rich man needs to sell—it would be enough for him. Such are the common run of the poor. What then must be the state of their elect?

I heard Abu Abd al-Rahman al-Sulami say . . . that when Yahya ibn Muadh was asked about poverty, he said, "Its essence is that the servant is not enriched except by God, and its form is the lack of all means whatsoever." And I heard him say . . . that Ibrahim al-Qassar said, "Poverty is a gown bequeathed by satisfaction in God when the servant has made that a reality." A poor dervish arrived from Zuzan to see Abu Ali al-Daqqaq in the year 394 or 395 AH [1004 or 1005 AD]. He was wearing a worn-out haircloth robe and a haircloth hat. Jokingly, one of the company asked him, "How much did you pay for that robe?" "I bought it for the price of this world," he said, "and I have been offered the next world for it—but I wouldn't sell!"

I heard Abu Ali al-Daqqaq say, "A poor dervish stood up in a Sufi gathering to ask for charity. 'I have gone hungry for three days,' said he. A shaykh who was there called out, 'You lie! Poverty is God's secret. He is not going to entrust His secret to somebody who will carry it to anyone he feels like!'

I heard Muhammad ibn al-Husayn say . . . that Hamdun al-Qassar said, "When satan and his armies get together, nothing makes them happier than three things: a believing man who has killed another believer, a man who dies in unbelief, and a heart in which there is fear of poverty. And I heard him say . . . that Junayd said, "O company of the poor! You know God. You give honor to God—see how you will fare with God when you are alone with Him!"

I heard Abu Abd al-Rahman al-Sulami say . . . that Junayd was asked which is more perfect, the state of being in need of God or the state of being enriched by Him. He said, "If the state of poverty before God is sound, if the state of wealth through God is sound, and if wealth through God is properly the perfection of independence from the world that He grants, then it cannot be asked, 'Which is more perfect, poverty or wealth!' For these are two states neither of which is complete without the other." And I heard him say . . . that Ruwaym, when asked about the quality of the poor dervish, said, "Giving oneself over to the decisions of God Most High." It is said that the character of the poor dervish is three things: protecting his secret, performing his obligations, and guarding his poverty.

Abu Said al-Kharraz was asked, "What keeps the kindness of the rich from reaching the poor?" He answered, "Either that which is in the hands of the rich is not good or God has not accepted them for service or the poor have been intended for trial."

It is told that God Almighty and Glorious revealed to Prophet Moses, "When you see the poor, inquire after them as you inquire after the rich. If you will not do it, then put everything that I have taught you under the dust!"

It is related that Abu Darda said, "I would rather fall from the top of a castle and be shattered to bits than to sit with wealth. For I heard the Messenger of God say, 'Beware of sitting with the dead!' And when it was asked, 'O Messenger of God, who are the dead?' he said, 'The rich.'"

They complained to Rabi ibn Haytham, "The prices have gone beyond bounds!" "We are too insignificant to God that he should make us go hungry," he replied. "It is only His friends that He keeps hungry." Ibrahim ibn Adham said, "We sought poverty and met with riches. Most people seek riches and meet with poverty."

I heard Muhammad ibn al-Husayn say . . . that al-Husayn ibn Ulluyah said that Yahya ibn Muadh was asked, "What is poverty?" He answered, "Fear of poverty." He was asked, "What is wealth?" He answered, "Security coming from God Most High."

And I heard him say . . . that Ibn al-Karini said, "The genuine poor man is on guard against wealth for fear that wealth will overtake him and spoil his poverty, just as the rich man is on guard against poverty for fear that it will overtake him and spoil his wealth." Abu Hafs was asked, "With what does the poor man approach his Lord?" He said, "The poor man has nothing with which to approach his Lord except his poverty."

God Most High revealed to Prophet Moses, "Would you like to have the equivalent of all the good deeds of all of humanity together on the day of judgment?" "Yes!" said he. "Visit the sick and rid the clothes of the poor of lice!" So Prophet Moses established for himself a week every month to circulate among the poor, cleanse their clothes of lice and visit the sick.

Sahl ibn Abd Allah al-Tustari said, "Five things come from the essence of the self: a poor person who appears rich, a hungry person who appears satisfied, the sad who appear happy, a man who is at enmity with another man but shows him affection, and a man who fasts during the day and supplicates during the night without showing weakness!" Bishr ibn al-Harith said, "The best of stations is to hold firmly to patience in poverty until the grave." Dhu 'l-Nun said, "The sign of God's displeasure with His servant is the servant's fear of poverty."

Shibli said, "The lowliest sign of true poverty is this: if someone owned the whole world and spent it in a day and then thought, 'I should have kept one day's sustenance!' — his poverty would not be genuine."

I heard Abu Ali al-Daqqaq say, "People talk about poverty and wealth. They ask which of the two is better? As far as I am concerned, the best thing is for a person to be given what is sufficient to him and then be preserved in it."

I heard Muhammad ibn al-Husayn say . . . that Abu Muhammad ibn Ya Sin said that Ibn al-Jalla was asked about poverty. He remained silent until he had gone off by himself and then shortly returned. He said, "I had four pennies on me and I was ashamed before God Almighty and Glorious to speak on poverty. So I went and got rid of them." Then he sat down and talked about poverty. And I heard him say . . . that Ibrahim ibn al-Muwallid said that he asked Ibn al-Jalla, "When does the dervish become worthy to be called poor?" He said,

"When no remnant of poverty remains." "How is that?" I asked again. "If a dervish possesses poverty, he is not poor. When poverty does not belong to him, he is truly poor."

Poverty is sound, it is said, when the poor man seeks no wealth but in the One of whom he is in need. Abd Allah ibn al-Mubarak said, "To appear rich while being poor is better than poverty."

I heard Muhammad ibn Abd Allah al-Sufi say . . . that Bunnan al-Misri said, "I was sitting across from a young man in Mecca when a fellow came and brought the youth a purse of dirhams, setting it down in front of him. 'I have no need of it,' he said. 'Distribute it among the poor.' Yet when evening came I saw him in the valley searching for something to eat. 'If only you had left yourself something out of what you had,' I said. 'But I didn't know that I would live until this moment!' said he."

I heard Abu Abd al-Rahman al-Sulami say . . . that Abu Hafs said, "The best connection between the servant and his Lord is to be in continuous need of Him in all circumstances, to attach oneself to the Sunnah in all acts, and to seek one's livelihood in a lawful way." And I heard him say . . . that al-Murtaish said, "The poor dervish's aspiration must not run ahead of where he sets his feet." And I heard him say . . . that Abu Ali al-Rudhbari said, "In their time, they were four."

One would not accept anything from the brethren or from the sultan. That was Yusuf ibn Asbat, who inherited 70,000 dirhams from his father and did not take a thing from it, but used to work with his hands, weaving palm leaves. Another would receive from brethren and the sultan both. That was Abu Ishaq al-Fazari. What he would get from the brethren he would distribute among contemplatives who had withdrawn from the world, and what he got from the sultan he would give out to the needy of the people of Tarsus. The third would take from the brethren but not from the sultan. That was Abd Allah ibn al-Mubarak, who used to accept things from the brothers and give things in return. The fourth used to take from the sultan but not from the brethren. That was Mukhallid ibn al-Husayn. He used to say, "The sultan is not doing a favor, but the brothers would be doing a favor."

I heard Abu Ali al-Daqqaq say, "It has come in a hadith, 'Whoever humbles himself to a rich man on account of his wealth has lost two-thirds of his religion.'" It is like that because a man is heart, tongue and ego. When he has humbled his tongue and his ego before a rich man, two-thirds of his religion have gone. If he were to believe in that man's superiority in his heart as he abased himself in ego and tongue, all of his religion would have left."

It is said, "The poor man in his poverty should hold on to at least four things: a knowledge that governs him, a scrupulousness that restrains him, a certainty that carries him, and a remembrance that makes him intimate with his Lord." Whoever wants poverty because of the nobility of poverty dies a poor man, but whoever wants poverty so that he may occupy himself with God Most High dies rich. Al-Muzayyin said, "The roads reaching to God were more than the stars of the sky and not one of them remains except the road of poverty, the soundest road."

I heard Muhammad ibn al-Husayn say. . . that Nuri said, "The poor dervish's quality is to keep silent when he has nothing and to give to others when he has something." And I heard him say . . . that when asked about the essence of poverty, Shibli said, "It is that the servant is not enriched by anything except God Almighty and Glorious." And I heard him say that Mansur ibn Khalaf al-Maghribi said that Abu Sahl al-Khashshab al-Kabir said to him, "Poverty: poverty and abasement." He said,

"No, rather poverty and honor." Mansur said, "Poverty and the dust." He said, "No, rather poverty and a throne."

I heard Abu Ali al-Daqqaq say, "I was asked about the meaning of the saying of the Prophet, 'Poverty is close to unbelief.' I answered thus, 'The ruination and opposite of a thing is commensurate with its virtue and scope. The more it is in itself excellent, the more its ruination and opposite are defective. Thus with faith— since it is the noblest of personal qualities, its opposite is the worst, unbelief. And since the danger attached to poverty is disbelief in God, this indicates that it is the noblest of conditions.'"

I heard Abu Abd al-Rahman al-Sulami say . . . that al-Murtaish said that Junayd said, "When you encounter a poor dervish, show him kindness. Do not show him your knowledge because kindness makes him intimate with you, but knowledge will make him a stranger." "Abu 'l- Qasim," I asked him, "Is the poor dervish then alienated by knowledge?" "Yes," he told me. "If the poor one is sincere in his poverty and you set your knowledge before him, it will melt just as lead melts in a fire." And I heard him say that. . . Muzaffar al-Qirmisini said. "The poor one is he who has no need of God."

Abu 'l- Qasim said, "This expression contains the deepest mystery for someone who hears it without awareness of the aim of the Sufis. The speaker is only alluding to the falling away of all objects of desire, the absence of individual choice, and satisfaction with whatever the Truth, glory to Him, might send."

Ibn Khafif said, "Poverty is lack of possessions and exiting the realm controlled by attributes." Abu Hafs said, "Poverty is not appropriate for anybody until giving is dearer to him than receiving. It is not generosity for someone who has to give to someone who lacks. It is only generosity for someone who lacks to give to someone who has."

I heard Muhammad ibn al-Husayn say . . . that Ibn al-Jalla said, "If humility were not an honor due to God, it would be the right of the poor dervish to swagger when he walks." Yusuf ibn Asbat said, "For forty years I have not owned anything except two shirts."

A Sufi said, "I had a vision that the day of judgment had come. It was announced, 'Malik ibn Dinar and Muhammad ibn Wasi, enter paradise!' I looked to see which of them would go first, and it was Muhammad ibn Wasi who preceded. I asked the cause of his precedence and was told, 'It is because he had one shirt, and Malik had two!'"

Muhammad al-Musuhi said, "The poor dervish is he who does not see himself as in need of means." Sahl ibn Abd Allah was asked, "When will the poor dervish find rest?" He replied, "When he cannot visualize for himself any other moment than the one he is in."

People were discussing wealth and poverty before Yahya ibn Muadh. He commented, "Neither poverty nor wealth will be weighed tomorrow, only patience and gratitude. It is said, 'Be thankful and be patient.'"

It is told that God Most High revealed to one of the prophets, "If you want to know the degree of My satisfaction with you, look at how far the poor are satisfied with you." Abu Bakr al-Zaqqaq said, "Whoever is not accompanied by the fear of God in his poverty eats what is totally unlawful." In the gatherings of Sufyan al-Thawri, it is said, the poor were treated like princes.

I heard Abu Abd al-Rahman al-Sulami say . . . that Abu Bakr ibn Tahir said, "One of the principles of the poor dervish is that he should have no desire for this world. And if he does, if it is inescapable, then his desire must not exceed what is sufficient for him."

Abu Abd al-Rahman al-Sulami recited what . . .
Ahmad ibn Ata recited to some dervishes, "They ask,
'Tomorrow is a holiday. What will you wear?' I say, 'The
robe of honor of a cupbearer whose love is deep
draughts.'"

Poverty and patience—these are my two garments.
Under them is a heart
That sees its darling holidays and days of prayer.
The most fitting apparel is that given by the Beloved
On the day of visitations, in garments that are robes
of honor!
If You are not there, my hope, all life is just
    mourning
A holiday when You are not mine is merely an event.
    (It is said that these are verses of Abu Ali al-
Rudhbari.)

When questioned about the genuine poor one, Abu
Bakr al-Misri said, "One who does not possess and is not
so inclined." Dhu 'l- Nun al-Misri said, "Continual need
of God, though one mixes with the world, is dearer to me
than continual purity together with spiritual pride." I
heard Abu Abd Allah al-Shirazi say . . . that Abu Abd
Allah al-Husri said, "For twenty years Abu Jafar al-
Haddad worked each day for one dinar, distributed it to
the poor, and fasted. Between sunset and night prayer
he would go and seek alms for himself at the public
gates."
    I heard Muhammad ibn al-Husayn say . . . that Nuri
said, "The characteristic of the poor dervish is silence
when he has nothing and free giving and preference for
others when he has something." And I heard him say . .
. that Muhammad ibn Ali al-Kattani said, "When we
were in Mecca there was a spiritual warrior who wore
old rags who would neither visit us nor keep company
with us. Love for him came into my heart. Two hundred

dirhams reached me from a lawful source. I took them to him, set them by the side of his prayer mat, and said, 'This has come to me lawfully: spend it on your affairs.' He looked at me askance. Then he revealed what had been hidden from me. 'I bought this sitting with God Most High by giving up 70,000 dinars free of profit and loss,' he told me. 'And you want to dupe me out of it with these!' He got up and scattered them. I sat picking them up off the ground. I never saw the like of his dignity when he passed by nor the like of my humiliation while I gathered them up. Abu Abd Allah ibn Khafif said, "For forty years I did not own enough to pay the alms due at the end of Ramadan, though I received a warm welcome from high and low."

I heard Abu Abd Allah ibn Bakawiya al-Sufi say that he heard Ibn Khafif say that he heard Abu Ahmad al-Saghir said, "Abu Abd Allah ibn Khafif was asked what was to be said about a poor dervish who went hungry for three days, and after the three days passed went out and begged the amount that would suffice him. He said, "It should be said about him that he was exhausted. Eat and be silent! If a poor dervish were to enter this door, he would shame the lot of you!"

I heard Muhammad ibn al-Husayn say . . . that al-Duqqi was asked what constituted bad behavior toward God in the states of poor dervishes. He said, "It is their falling from spiritual reality back to indirect religious knowledge." And I heard him say . . . Khayr al-Nassaj said, "I entered a certain mosque. In it was a poor dervish. When he saw me, he attached himself to me. 'O Shaykh,' he said, 'turn to me with sympathy, for my affliction is great!' 'What is it?' I asked. 'I have lost trouble,' he said, 'and have grown strong in well-being.' I looked and saw that he had been given some alms." And I heard him say that Muhammad ibn Muhammad ibn Ahmad said that Abu Bakr al-Warraq said, 'Happy is the dervish who is poor in this world and the next.' Asked about this, he explained, 'The sultan does not seek taxes from him in this world, and the Sovereign shall not seek an accounting from him in the next!'"

39
ON SUFISM (*TASAWWUF*)

Purity, *safa*, is praised by every tongue; its opposite, impurity, is condemned.

I heard Abd Allah ibn Yusuf al-Ispahani report . . . that Abu Juhayfah, "The Messenger of God came out to us with his color changed. He said, 'The earth's purity has gone and only impurity remains. Death, today, is a blessing for every Muslim.'" Thereafter this title came to be widely applied to this group so that a person might be called *sufi*—its plural being *sufiyya*. Someone who is attempting to reach this level is called *mutasawwif*—in plural, *mutasawwifa*.

In respect of Arabic philology, there is no other word in the Arabic language to be drawn from the name *sufi*. The most obvious one would be that it resembles a descriptive surname, as if someone were to say, "He is of wool." Then *tasawwaf* could be said to mean "he wears wool," just as *taqammasa* means "he wears a shirt." That is one possibility. But the Sufis are not distinguished by the wearing of wool!

Some say the Sufis are named from their relation to the bench (*suffa*) of the mosque of the Messenger of God. But the attributive name derived from *suffa* does not come anywhere near to being *sufi*. Others say that the

279

name is derived from purity, *safa*. But to derive *sufi* from
safa is a long stretch according to the rules of the language. Then there is the proposition that the name
comes from the word "rank," *saff*, because the hearts of
the Sufis are, as it were, in the first rank. The meaning
is sound, but the language does not permit such a deriv-
ative adjective from *saff*. However, this group is certainly too famous to have to be defined by a linguistic model
or vindicated by means of a derivation.

Many people have discussed "What is the meaning of
Sufism?" and "Who is a Sufi?," each one expressing what
most struck him. A close examination of all this material would take us far from our aim of brevity. Here we will
mention only some of the statements on this topic, with
the aim of fostering understanding, if God Most High so
wills.

I heard Muhammad ibn Ahmad ibn Yahya al-Sufi say
. . . that Abu Muhammad al-Jurayri was asked about
Sufism and said, "Sufism means to take on every sublime moral characteristic from the life of the Prophet
and to leave behind every lowly one."

I heard Abd al-Rahman ibn Yusuf al-Ispahani say . .
. that when questioned about Sufism, Junayd said, "To
be a Sufi means that the Truth causes you to die to yourself and to live through Him." I heard Abu Abd Rahman
al-Sulami say . . . that when asked about the Sufi, al-
Husayn ibn Mansur al-Hallaj said, "The Sufi is a person
whose essence is one. No one admits him, and he admits
no one." And I heard him say . . . that Abu Hamzah al-
Baghdadi said, "The sign of the genuine Sufi is that he
is poor, after having been rich, abased after having been
honored, hidden, after having been famous. The sign of
the false Sufi is that he has worldly wealth, after having
been poor is honored after having been abased, and
becomes famous after having been obscure."

Amr ibn Uthman al-Makki was asked about Sufism.

He said, "It is that the servant be engaged at every moment in what is best for him at that moment." Muhammad ibn Ali al-Qassab said, "Sufism is noble traits manifested at a noble time in a noble individual among noble people." Sumnun, asked about Sufism, said, "Sufism means that you own nothing and nothing owns you." Ruwaym answered, "It means giving the self over to God Most High for whatever He wants of it." Junayd answered, "It means that you are together with God Most High, without other attachments."

I heard Abd Allah ibn Yusuf al-Ispahani say . . . that Ruwaym ibn Ahmad al-Baghdadi said, "Sufism is founded on three traits: clinging to spiritual poverty and the need of God; confirming oneself in generosity and concern for others; abandoning resistance to God's will and [abandoning] personal preference."

Maruf al-Karkhi said, "Sufism is to seize the realities and despair of what is in the hands of creatures." Hamdun al-Qassar said, "Keep company with the Sufis. With them the ugly person has all sorts of excuses!" Asked about the people of Sufism, Al-Kharraz said, "People who are made to give until they are exhilarated, who are blocked and frustrated until they lose themselves, who then are summoned away from intimate secrets—why, weep for us!"

Junayd said, "Sufism is force without compromise. The Sufis are people of one household. No outsider enters among them. Sufism is a remembrance of God and a uniting of parts, an ecstasy and a listening to guidance, an individual work and an emulation of the Prophet. The Sufi is like the earth. Every ugly thing is cast upon it, yet nothing grows out of it but what is pleasant. The Sufi is like the earth upon which walk the righteous and the libertine alike or like the cloud that shades everything or like the rain that gives everything drink. When you see a Sufi whose outward aspect is wealthy, know that his inner aspect is in ruins."

Sahl ibn Abd Allah al-Tustari said, "The Sufi is one whose blood may be shed with impunity and whose property is open to all." Nuri said, "The characteristic of the Sufi is to keep silent when he has nothing and to prefer others over himself when he has something." Kattani said, "Sufism is morality. Whoever is superior to you in morality is superior to you in Sufism."

Abu Ali al-Rudhbari said, "Sufism is to stay at the door of the Beloved even if you are driven away." He also said, "It is the purity of nearness to God after the impurity of distance from Him." It is said, "The most repulsive of all repulsive things is a stingy Sufi." And, "Sufism is an empty palm and a good heart." Shibli said, "Sufism is to sit with God without concerns." Abu Mansur said, "The Sufi is a pointer from God Most High while the rest of Creation are pointers to God Most High."

Shibli said. "The Sufi is cut off from the creation and put in contact with the Truth. He has said [to Moses], *'I have attached you to Myself'* [20:41].God severs the Sufi from everything else, then says to him, *'You shall never see Me'* [7:143]! The Sufis are children in the lap of the Truth. Sufism is scorching lightning. Sufism is to be protected against seeing the universe."

Ruwaym said, "Sufis do not disappear due to the virtue of their correcting each other. When they become reconciled to the way they are, there is no good in them." al-Jurayri said, "Sufism is self-observation and holding fast to right behavior." Al-Muzayyin said, "Sufism is yielding to the Truth." Abu Turab al-Nakhshabi said, "The Sufi is polluted by nothing and purifies everything." The Sufi, it is said, is he whom no search wearies nor any cause upsets.

I heard Abu Hatim al-Sijistani say . . . that Dhu 'l-Nun al-Misri was asked about the Sufis. He said, "They are a people who prefer God over everything and whom

God prefers over everything." Al-Wasiti said, "The Sufis have hints. Then these become actions. Then nothing remains but sorrows!"

Nuri, questioned about the Sufi, said, "He is the one who listens to the spiritual concert and prefers lawful means." I heard Abu Hatim al-Sijistani say that Abu Nasr al-Sarraj said, "Al-Husri was asked, 'In your view, who is a Sufi?' He replied, 'He whom the earth does not bear nor the heavens shade.'"

This points to the state of *mahw*, erasure from the world. It is said that the Sufi is one who, if he meets with two states or two characteristics that are both good, will choose the better of the two.

Shibli was asked, "Why are the Sufis called by that name?" He answered, "Because of the last remaining remnant of their egos. If not for that, no name would attach to them!"

I heard Abu Hatim al-Sijistani say . . . that Ibn al-Jalla was asked, "What is the meaning of calling someone a Sufi?" He said, "We will not recognize this person by the condition of his formal learning. We will recognize that someone who is poor, stripped of means, who is with God Most High and without worldly place, but whom the Truth, glory to Him, does not prevent from the knowledge of every place, is to be called 'a Sufi'."

A dervish said, "Sufism is falling from dignity and blackness of face in this world and the next!" Abu Yaqub al-Mazabili said, "Sufism is a state in which the hallmarks of humanity melt away." Abu 'l-Hasan al-Sirwani said, "The Sufi is someone who is concerned with inner spiritual conditions as well as outer devotional exercises."

I heard Abu Ali al-Daqqaq say, "The best thing that has been said on this topic is the statement of the one who said, 'This is a path that is only suitable for people whose souls God has used to sweep away their dunghills.'"

In reference to this, he said one day, "If the poor dervish had nothing but a soul and he laid it before the dogs of this gate, no dog would look at it." Abu Sahl al-Suluki said, "Sufism is the resistance to resistance." Al-Husri said, "The Sufi is not to be found after his nonexistence and does not cease to exist after he has come to be."

There is some ambiguity in this. The meaning of his statement, "He is not to be found after his nonexistence," is that when the calamities of his nature have passed away, those calamities do not return. His statement, "He does not cease to exist after he has come to be," means that when he is occupied with the Truth he does not collapse, like the rest of creation, for the events of life do not affect him.

The Sufi, it is said, is the one who has lost himself in what he has glimpsed of the Truth. And it is said, "The Sufi's will is overpowered by direct divine action, but he is veiled by the conduct proper to servanthood." And, "The Sufi is not altered, but if he is altered, he is not polluted."

I heard Abu Abd al-Rahman al-Sulami say . . . that al-Kharraz said, "I was in the mosque of Kairouan one Friday, the day of congregational prescribed prayer, when I saw a man passing among the ranks, saying, "Be charitable to me! I used to be a Sufi, but I was weak. I gave him some money, but he said, 'Go away; for shame! That is not the thing for this problem!' And he would not accept it."

40

ON MODEL BEHAVIOR (*ADAB*)

God Almighty and Glorious has said, "*The sight [of the Prophet, at the time of his Ascension], did not deviate nor overstep the bounds*" [53:17]. This is said to mean, "He maintained the conduct proper to the Divine Presence."

The Most High also said, "*Save yourselves and your families from the fire*" [66:6]. According to the commentary of Ibn Abbas, this means, "Teach them the stipulations of the divine law and refined behavior."

Ali ibn Ahmad al-Ahwazi informed us . . . from Ayisha that the Prophet said, "The child owes it to his parent to make good his name, his upbringing, and his education in conduct." It is related that Said ibn al-Musayyib said, "Whoever does not know what rights God Almighty and Glorious has over him and has not been educated in His command and prohibition is cut off from right behavior." It is reported that the Prophet said, "God Almighty and Glorious had educated me in refined behavior and made good my education."

The essence of *adab*, the most beautiful and fitting, refined behavior, is the gathering together of all good traits. The *adib*, the refined person, is he in whom are gathered all these good characteristics. From this is taken the word *maduba*, banquet, a name for the coming together [of such people].

I heard Abu Ali al-Daqqaq say, "Through his obedience the servant attains to paradise. Through refined conduct in obedience he attains to God. I also heard him say, "I saw someone who, during the prescribed prayer before God, wanted to stretch his hand to his nose to remove something that was in it. His hand was seized!"

He could only have been hinting that it was himself because it is not possible for a human being to know that someone else's hand was seized. Abu Ali used never to lean on anything. One day when he was at a gathering, I saw that he was without any support. I wanted to put a pillow behind his back. He drew a little away from the pillow, and I imagined that he was wary of it because there was neither a dervish robe nor a prayer carpet over it. But he said, "I do not want to lean." After this I marveled at his state, for in fact he never did lean on anything.

I heard Abu Hatim al-Sijistani say . . . that al-Jalajili al-Basri said, "For the testimony of unity (*tawhid*) to be in force, faith is prerequisite, for whoever has no faith cannot testify to the unity. For faith to be in force the divine law is prerequisite, for whoever does not hold to the divine law has no faith and cannot testify to the unity. For the divine law to be in force refined conduct is prerequisite, for whoever has not refined his conduct cannot hold to the divine law, has no faith, and cannot testify to the unity.

Ibn Ata said, "*Adab*, refined behavior, is to hold fast to the commendable things." When asked, "What is the meaning of this?" he replied, "It means that you behave properly toward God both in secret and in public. If you are like that, you are a man of refined culture even if you are a foreigner." Then he recited:

When she conversed, her speech was all graciousness,
And when she kept silent, her silence was all fair.

Muhammad ibn al-Husayn informed us . . . that Abd
Allah al-Jurayri said, "For twenty years, in my times of
sitting in solitude, I have not stretched out my feet. It is
better to act beautifully toward God." I heard Abu Ali al-
Daqqaq say, "If someone keeps company with kings and
lacks refined behavior, his ignorance will consign him to
death!"

It is related that Ibn Sirin was asked, "What way of
behaving brings one closest to God Most High?" He
replied, "Realization of His Lordship, work in obedience
to Him, praise to Him in happy times, and patience in
times of trouble."

Yahya ibn Muadh said, "When the gnostic abandons
his courtesy in the presence of the One he knows, he has
been ruined like all the rest of the spiritually ruined."

I heard Abu Ali say, "To abandon good conduct brings
about expulsion. Someone who behaves badly upon the
carpet of contemplation is sent out to the gate, and
someone who behaves badly at the gate is sent out to
look after the animals."

Hasan al-Basri was asked, "People have got hold of
much knowledge of forms of refinement. What will give
them profit and bring them to union later?" "Acquiring
knowledge in religion," he said, "renouncing this world,
and understanding the rights of God over you."

Yahya ibn Muadh said, "Whoever is educated in the
conduct of God Most High joins the people who love God
Most High." Sahl said, "The Sufis are those who seek
help from God, for the sake of God's business and persevere with God's forms of conduct."

It is related that Ibn al-Mubarak said, "We have
greater need of a little bit of refinement than of a lot of
knowledge." I heard Muhammad ibn al-Husayn say . . .

that ibn al-Mubarak said, "We sought for right conduct once the teachers of right conduct had left us."

It is said that if one has three traits, one is never a stranger. They are avoiding doubters, behaving well, and restraining oneself from causing harm. On this topic, Abu Abd Allah al-Maghribi recited this to us:

> Three things adorn the stranger far from home:
> First, fine conduct, second, fine character,
> Third, leaving doubters alone.

When Abu Hafs entered Baghdad, Junayd said to him, "You have trained your companions to the conduct of sultans!" "Beautiful outward behavior is the model for beautiful inward behavior," Abu Hafs told him.

Abd Allah ibn al-Mubarak said, "Refined behavior is to the gnostic what repentance is to the beginner." I heard Mansur ibn Khalaf al-Maghribi say, "A dervish was addressed, 'O uncultured one!'" 'I am not uncultured!' he said. 'Why, who has taught you culture?' they asked. 'The Sufis taught me!' said he.

I heard Abu Hatim al-Sijistani say that Abu 'l- Nasr al-Tusi al-Sarraj said, "People have three levels of refinement. For the people of this world, refinement largely consists of eloquent speech and rhetoric, along with the memorization of sciences, of the names of kings, and of the poetry of the Arabs. For the people of the next world, refinement largely consists of training the ego and disciplining the body, preserving the limits of the law and abandoning desires. For the elite, refinement largely consists of cleansing the heart of vices, guarding inner secrets, being faithful to one's promises, protecting the present, not turning aside in thought along with refined behavior in the stations of the search, in the moments of presence with God, and in the stages of closeness to God."

It is told that Sahl ibn Abd Allah al-Tustari said, "Whoever overpowers his ego through refining conduct is serving God with sincerity." The perfection of refined conduct, it is said, is not unimpaired except in the prophets and the possessors of true integrity. Abd Allah ibn al-Mubarak said, "People have had much to say about fine conduct. As for us, we say that it is the real understanding of the ego."

Shibli said, "To be carefree about speaking with the Truth, glory to Him, is to abandon right conduct." Dhu 'l-Nun al-Misri said, "The culture of the gnostic is above all other culture, for it is the One he knows Who is the educator of his heart."

A Sufi said, "The Truth, glory to Him, said, 'When I sustain someone with My names and attributes, I attach him to right or refined conduct. When I show someone part of the reality of My Essence, I attach him to his own destruction. Choose whichever of the two you will: refinement (*adab*) or destruction (`atab)!'"

One day while he was with his companions Ibn Ata stretched out his feet. "Not putting emphasis upon one's refined behavior is itself considered refined behavior among the people who have attained refinement," said he. A hadith has been related that testifies to this story. The Prophet had Abu Bakr and Umar with him. Then Uthman entered, and he covered up his leg, saying, "Shall I not be ashamed before a man in front of whom the angels are ashamed?" He was pointing out that even though he held the modesty of Uthman in great esteem, the affection that existed between himself, Abu Bakr and Umar had been more pure. It is with nearly this meaning that they recited:

I act with restraint and modesty,
But sitting with loyal and generous men
I open myself spontaneously

And say what I say without reticence.

Junayd said, "When love is sound, the rules of behavior are dropped." Abu Uthman al-Hiri said, "When love is sound, attachment to good behavior in the lover is assured." Nuri said, "Whoever has not been educated for the present, his present is disaster!" Dhu 'l- Nun al-Misri said, "When the student abandons the exercise of refined behavior, he returns whence he came."

I heard Abu Ali al-Daqqaq discuss God's saying, ". . . *Job, when he called to His Lord, 'Trouble has touched me, and You are the Most Merciful of the Merciful'* [21:83]." He said, "Because Job maintained the correct refinement of address [and would not presume to tell his Lord what to do], he did not say, 'Have mercy upon me!' For the same reason Jesus said, *'If You punish them, they are Your servants'* [5:121]. Jesus also said, *'Had I said it, You would have known it'* [5:121]. Because he was aware of the conduct proper to the divine presence, he could not insult divine Omniscience by saying, 'I did not say it.'"

I heard Muhammad ibn Abd Allah al-Sufi say . . . Junayd said, "A righteous man came to me one Friday and asked, 'Would you send along with me a poor dervish who would bring happiness to my house and eat something with me?' I looked around and saw that among those present was a poor dervish in whom the signs of need were visible. So I extended him the invitation and told him, 'Go with this gentleman and bring him happiness.' So he went. But it was not long before the man came back to me and said, 'O Abu 'l-Qasim, that poor man ate nothing but a mouthful and left!' 'Perhaps you said some rough word to him,' I suggested. 'I said nothing!' he assured me. I looked around and saw that the poor dervish was back again sitting with me! 'Why did you not complete his happiness?' I asked him. 'O

Master,' he told me, 'I left Kufa and came to Baghdad without anything to eat, but I hated the idea that because of need, bad behavior should appear from me in your presence. When you gave me the invitation, I was happy because it originated with you. So I went, but I had no heart for it. When I sat at his table, he set a meal before me and told me, "Eat, for it is dearer to me than 10,000 dirhams!" When I heard that from him, I knew that his aspiration was low, and I shied away from eating his food.' 'Did I not say to you that you had behaved badly toward him?' I said. 'Abu 'l- Qasim, I repent!' he cried. So I asked the dervish to go with him and make him happy."

41

ON GNOSIS (*MARIFA BILLAH*)

God Most High said, "*And they honor not God with the honor due Him*" [6:91]. According to commentary, this means, "They do not know God as He deserves to be known."

Abd al-Rahman ibn Muhammad ibn Abd Allah al-Adl related . . . from Ayisha that the Messenger of God said, "The support of a house is its foundation, and the support of religion is the direct knowledge of God Most High, certainty, and the taming intellect." I asked, "By my father and mother, what is the taming intellect?" "Abstinence from disobeying God and eagerness in obeying God," he said.

Marifa—understanding, realization, true familiarity—in the language of scholars means *ilm*, knowledge. Thus every realization is a form of knowledge and every knowledge is a form of realization. Everyone learned in God knows Him and everyone who knows Him is learned. But according to the Sufis, *marifa* is the trait of someone who knows the Truth in His names and attributes and then bears witness to the divine in all his actions.

The gnostic is purified of base characteristics and the disasters of his nature. He stands patiently at the door of God and remains secluded in his heart. He enjoys the good graces of God and corroborates Him in all of his states. He has cut off the whims of his own self. He does not permit a thought in his heart that would summon to other than God. He becomes a stranger to the creation and is liberated from the catastrophes of his ego. He is cleansed of attachments and distractions and in his secret being is always conversing with God Most High. His every glance returns to God Most High. The Truth inspires him with the understanding of His secrets—the secrets of the course of His Omnipotence. That is why such a person is called an *arif*, a gnostic, and his state is called *marifa,* direct knowledge.

In general, it is to the measure of one's alienation from one's own ego that one attains direct knowledge of one's Lord. Each of the shaykhs who has spoken of direct knowledge has discussed what has happened to him and hinted at what he has found in his own experience.

I heard Abu Ali al-Daqqaq say, "One of the tokens of the realization of God is the achievement of deep awe and reverence for God. If someone's realization increases, his awe increases." And I heard him say, "Realization requires stillness of heart, just as learning requires outward quiet. If someone's realization increases, his tranquility increases."

I heard Abu Abd al-Rahman al-Sulami say . . . that Shibli said, "The gnostic has no worldly attachment. The lover has no complaint of his Beloved. The servant has no pretension. The one who fears God has no rest. No one has any escape from God."

And I heard him say . . . that Shibli, when asked about realization, said, "Its beginning is God Most High, and its end is endless." And I heard him say . . . that Abu Hafs al-Haddad said, "Since I came to know God, neither truth nor falsehood has entered my heart."

What Abu Hafs has here expressed is somewhat ambiguous. Its greatest implication is that among the

Sufis, direct divine knowledge requires that the servant be absent from himself and so overwhelmed by the remembrance of God that he witnesses only God Almighty and Glorious. He refers to nothing outside of God.

When events occur to an ordinary intelligent person or he has some kind of experience, he refers to his own heart, his own thoughts and recollections. The gnostic refers only to his Lord. Since he is occupied only with his Lord, he cannot turn to his heart. How shall meaning enter the heart of a person who no longer possesses one? There is a difference between someone who lives through his heart and someone who lives through his Lord.

Abu Yazid al-Bistami was asked about realization. He quoted, "*Kings, when they enter a city, ruin it, and make the high among its people to be low.*' [27:34]" This is the meaning hinted at by Abu Hafs.

Abu Yazid also said, "People have states, but the gnostic has no state. His form has been erased and his identity annihilated in the identity of Another. All trace of him has vanished into the traces of Another."

Al-Wasiti observed, "While the servant is satisfied with God and in need of God, direct knowledge of God is not appropriate for him." What al-Wasiti means is that this satisfaction and need are signs of the servant's sobriety and the persistence of his own form. Both traits pertain to the servant. The gnostic, however, is effaced in the One he knows. And how could this be—that someone should be overcome by God's existence or drowned in His vision—while the servant has not reached a state of being in which he is kept from the perception of any trait that might be called his own?

Thus al-Wasiti also stated, "He who knows God Most High is stopped short—rather, he is struck dumb and subdued." The Prophet said, "I cannot count the praises due to You." Such are the qualities of those who hit the far target, but those who have descended from this limit have spoken about realization and at length.

Muhammad ibn al-Husayn related . . . that Ahmad ibn Asim al-Antaki said, "He who knows God best fears Him most."

A Sufi said, "He who knows God Most High tires of his own continuing existence, and the world with all its breadth becomes narrow for him." It is said, "When someone knows God, his livelihood is serene, and life is sweet to him. Everything honors him. The fear of created things leaves him, and he is intimate with God Most High. The fear of worldly things leaves the one who knows God. He does without union and separation. Realization produces shame and the glorification of God, just as affirming the unity (*tawhid*) produces satisfaction with His will and surrender to Him."

Ruwaym said, "To the gnostic, divine knowledge is a mirror. When he looks into it, his Lord appears to him."

Dhu 'l- Nun al-Misri said, "The spirits of the prophets raced in the arena of divine knowledge, and the spirit of our Prophet was first to the fountain of union." Dhu 'l-Nun al-Misri also said, "The company of the gnostic is like the company of God Most High. He will tolerate your ways and be gentle to you because he is qualified with the qualities of God."

Ibn Yazdanyar was asked, "When does the gnostic see the Truth?" He said, "When the witness appears but things witnessed disappear, when the senses depart and sincerity vanishes."

Husayn ibn Mansur al-Hallaj said, "When the servant reaches the stage of direct knowledge, God inspires his thoughts and protects his inmost being from fabricating any thought but the truth." And he said, "The mark of the gnostic is that he is empty of this world and the next."

Sahl ibn Abd Allah al-Tustari remarked, "The goal of realization is two things: perplexity and amazement." I heard Muhammad ibn al-Husayn say . . . that Dhu 'l-Nun al-Misri said, "The person who knows God Most High best is the one who is most amazed in Him." And I heard him say . . . that Abu Umar al-Antaki said, "A man mentioned to Junayd, 'Some esotericists say that abandoning all action is the door of righteousness and fear of God.' Junayd said, 'This is the speech of people who talk of dropping religious works. To me this is very grave. Someone who steals or commits adultery is in a better state than whoever says this. The gnostics receive their works from God Most High and return with them to Him. If I were to live for a 1,000 years, I would not diminish the works of goodness by an atom's weight.'"

Someone asked Abu Yazid, "Through what thing did you find this realization?" He replied, "Through an empty belly and a naked body." Abu Yaqub al-Nahrajuri said, "I asked Abu Yaqub al-Susi, 'Does the gnostic lament over anything but God?' He answered, 'Does he see anything else that he should lament over it?' I asked, 'With what eye does he look at things?' He answered, 'With the eye of annihilation and passing away.'" Abu Yazid said, "The gnostic is a bird, the ascetic a wayfarer." "The gnostic's eye weeps," they say, "but his heart laughs."

Junayd said, "The gnostic is not really a gnostic until he is like the earth upon which walk righteous and wicked alike or like the clouds which shade everything or like the rain which gives water to the loved and the unloved." Yahya ibn Muadh commented, "The gnostic goes forth from this world with two goals yet unfulfilled: his weeping over himself and his praise for his Lord."

Abu Yazid said, "People only reach realization by squandering what is theirs and holding fast to what is His." I heard Abu Abd al-Rahman al-Sulami say . . . that

Yusuf ibn Ali said, "The gnostic is not truly a gnostic until if he were given a kingdom like Solomon's, it would not distract him from God for the blink of an eye." And I heard him say . . . that Ibn Ata said, "Direct knowledge has three pillars: awe, shame, and intimacy."

I also heard him say . . . that Yusuf ibn al-Husayn said, "Dhu 'l-Nun al-Misri was asked, 'How do you know your Lord?' He replied, 'I know my Lord by my Lord. Were it not for my Lord, I would not know my Lord.'"

"The learned man imitates examples," it is said, "but the gnostic receives living guidance." The gnostic gives no attention to anything but God," Shibli remarked. "He does not speak of anything else for even a sentence and sees no protector for himself but God Most High." They say that the gnostic is friendly with the remembrance of God but estranged from His creation, dependent upon God but independent of His creation, abased before God but exalted over His creation. Abu 'l- Tayyib al-Samiri said, "Direct knowledge is the Truth's approach to people's inward hearts by means of lights." Is is said that the gnostic is more than what he talks about, while the scholar is less than what he talks about.

Abu Sulayman al-Darani said, "God Most High reveals to the gnostic lying upon his bed more than He reveals to anyone else standing in prayer." Junayd said, "The gnostic: God speaks from his inner being, while he himself is silent."

Dhu 'l- Nun said, "Everything has a punishment and the punishment for the gnostic is to be cut off from the remembrance of God." I heard Abu Hatim al-Sijistani say . . . that Ruwaym said, "The hypocrisy of gnostics is better than the sincerity of students." Abu Bakr al-Warraq observed, "The gnostic's silence is more profitable to him, but his speaking is sweeter and more delicious." Dhu 'l-Nun said, "Ascetics are the kings of the next world, but they are the poor among the gnostics."

Junayd was asked about the gnostic. He replied, "The color of the water is the color of the vessel." (That is, the gnostic is under the rule of his immediate state.)

Asked about the gnostic, Abu Yazid said, "Sleeping he sees nothing but God. Waking he sees nothing but God. He conforms to nothing but God. He studies nothing but God."

I heard Muhammad ibn al-Husayn say that he heard Abd Allah ibn Muhammad al-Dimashqi say that one of the shaykhs was asked, "By what means do you know God Most High?" He replied, "By means of a flash signaling news gathered by an established discernment and an utterance coming forth from a lost and ruined tongue." (The shaykh is hinting at a manifest ecstasy and giving word of a hidden secret. He is himself insofar as he is manifested and something else insofar as he is hidden). Thus they recited:

> I spoke without any speech that was speech.
> That speech was Your expression — or it's manifes-
>   tation in speech.
> You showed Yourself to hide me. While You were
>   hidden from me
> You made lightning flash upon me, and lightning
> made me speak.

And I heard him say. . . that al-Jurayri said that Abu Turab al-Nakhshabi was asked about the character of the gnostic. He said, "The gnostic is polluted by nothing and purifies everything." And I heard him say that Abu Uthman al-Maghribi said, "The lights of knowledge shine upon the gnostic, and with them he sees the wonders of the unseen. I also heard him say that Abu Ali al-Daqqaq said, "The gnostic is drowned in the seas of realization. As one of them said, 'Divine knowledge is plunging waves: they ebb and flow.'"

Yahya ibn Muadh was asked about the gnostic and replied, "He is a man existent, separate." Another time he said, "He exists and yet is separate." Dhu 'l-Nun said, "The gnostic has three marks: the light of his realization does not extinguish the light of his moral care; he does not believe any piece of esoteric knowledge that is contradicted by an exoteric rule; the many blessings of God upon him do not move him to tear the veils of God's forbidden things."

Direct knowledge is not attributed to the gnostic by people who seek the next world, they say. How then should it be attributed to him by people who seek this one? Abu Said al-Kharraz said, "Realization proceeds from a generous eye and the expenditure of effort."

I heard Muhammad ibn al-Husayn say. . . that Jafar said that Junayd was asked about the saying of Dhu 'l-Nun al-Misri describing the gnostic, "He was here, but he left." He commented, "The gnostic is not held back by any one state from any other state. No station veils him from roaming freely among the stations. When he is with the people of any place, he finds in it the same things that they find. While he is there he articulates that place's qualities so that its people may profit." And I heard him say. . . that Muhammad ibn al-Fadl said, "Direct knowledge is the life of the heart with God Most High." I also heard him say. . . that al-Kattani said, "Abu Said al-Kharraz was asked, 'Does the gnostic come to a state that turns him away from weeping?' He said, 'Yes. Weeping belongs to the time of their journey to God. When they dismount at the realities of closeness, and through His goodness, they taste the flavor of union, weeping passes away from them.'

42

ON LOVE (*MAHABBA*)

God Almighty and Glorious said, "*O you who believe, if anyone among you turns back from His religion—God will bring a people whom He loves and who love Him*" [5:54].

Abu Naim Abd al-Malik ibn al-Husayn reported. . . from Abu Hurayra that the Messenger of God said, "Whoever loves to meet God, God loves to meet him. Whoever does not love to meet God, God does not love to meet him." Abu 'l-Husayn Ali ibn Ahmad ibn Abdan reported. . . from Anas ibn Malik that the Messenger heard from Gabriel that his Lord said, "Whoever humiliates a friend of Mine has declared war upon Me. I do not hesitate in anything that I do as I hesitate in taking the soul of My believing servant who hates death, and I hate to trouble him—but it must be. My servant does not come close to Me with anything that is dearer to Me than the performance of the things that I have made his duty. My servant will not stop coming close to Me with extra devotions until I love him, and when I love him I become his hearing and his sight and his hand and his support."

Ali ibn Ahmad ibn Abdan reported . . . from Abu Hurayra that the Prophet said, "When God Almighty and Glorious loves the servant, He says to Gabriel, "O Gabriel, I love so-and-so. You love him too." So Gabriel loves him. Then Gabriel calls to all the heavenly folk, 'God Most High loves so-and-so. You love him too!' So all the denizens of the heavens love him, and they prepare a welcome for him in the earth. When God hates the servant, he says, 'What is wrong with you?' It seems that in His displeasure He says nothing more than that."

Love is a noble condition that the Truth has acknowledged to the servant. He has informed the servant of the existence of His love. The Truth, glory to Him, may be described as loving the servant, and the servant may be described as loving the Truth.

In scholarly usage, love, *mahabba*, means will, *irada*, but the Sufis do not mean will when they speak of love. For human will does not connect to the Eternal—unless one understands it as the will to draw close to Him and glorify Him. We shall mention here just a fraction of the examination of this subject, if God Most High so wills.

The love of the Truth—glory to Him—for the servant is His will to bestow special blessings upon that servant. Just so, His mercy is also His will to bless, but mercy is more particular than will, and love is more particular than mercy. For the will of God Most High, when it brings reward and blessing to the servant, is called mercy. And when that will selects the servant for closeness and exalted states, it is called love. God's will is a single attribute, but through the variety of aims to which it attaches itself, it takes on different names. When it concerns punishment, it is called anger. When it concerns general blessings, it is called mercy. When it concerns special blessings, it is called love.

One party holds that God's love for the servant means His praise and beautiful approval. The meaning of His love, in that case, comes back to His speech—and His speech is eternal. Another party holds that God's love for the servant is one of the attributes of action. It is then a special virtue through which the servant encounters God and a special state to which he ascends. As one holding this view has said, "God's mercy to the servant is a blessing that accompanies him." A party of our respected forebears simply said that God's love is one of the divine attributes related in hadith so they permitted the use of the expression but refrained from commenting upon it.

As for traits in excess of this—the well-known attributes of human love, such as sympathizing with the beloved object and seeking to be intimate with it or the creaturely state the lover experiences when with his beloved—the Eternal, glory to Him, is exalted above all that.

If we turn to the love of the servant for God, it is a condition found in the servant's heart that is too fine and subtle to be expressed. This condition moves him to the glorification of God, the preference for God's good pleasure above all else, a lack of patience away from Him, a passionate excitement about Him, and an inability to rest anywhere short of Him. It shows itself in the existence of a desire to draw close to Him through continuously remembering Him within the heart. The servant's love for God contains no sympathetic identification and lays no claim to possessing the Beloved. How should it? For the reality of His Absolute nature is hallowed beyond being overtaken, perceived or comprehended. The lover, drowned in the Beloved, is closer to Him than he would be if he could be said to possess the Beloved.

Love cannot be described with any clearer attribute or defined with a more understandable definition than to say that it is love. One makes a close study of what has been said about it in order to resolve ambiguities. When this abstruseness and obscurity pass away, the need to immerse oneself in the explanation of statements can be dropped. People have offered a great many explanations of love, including discussions of its linguistic roots.

Some say that *hubb*, love, is a name for purity of affection, because the bedouins when speaking of the pure whiteness and regularity of someone's teeth use the expression *habab al-asnan*. Others say that since *hubab* is a word for the excess water that results from a heavy rain, *mahabba* came to mean the heart's boiling and stirring with the thirst and excitement of meeting the Beloved. Still others say the word is derived from *habab al-ma*, the greater part of a body of water, because love is the object of most of the heart's concerns. Another derivation draws the word from necessity and fixity, for one says *ahabba al-baghir* of a camel that kneels and refuses to stand. In just this way the lover's heart refuses to leave the remembrance of his Beloved. *Hubb* is also said to come from *hibb*, an earring. The poet says:

> The snake showed its flicking tongue at the place of
> his earring;
> Stealthily listening to secrets.

The earring is called *hibb* either because of its clinging to the ear or because of its jangling sound; both of these meanings are acceptable [as original associations] for love.

Other derivations are from *habb* [the plural of *habba*], bread, and *habbat al-qalb*, the heart's blood, meaning the thing that sustains it. So love would be called *hubb* from the name of its location. *Habb* and *hubb* are said to be like *amr* and *umr*, [synonyms, both of which mean "lifetime"]. *Hubb* is also said to be taken from *hibbah,* the seeds of desert plants, and so named because it is the kernel of life, just as a seed is the kernel of vegetation. *Hubb* is also the name of the four planks upon which one sets a jar. Love is then called *hubb* because it supports everything that comes from the beloved, whether it be humiliating or exalting.

Again, the name of love comes from that *hubb* which is a vessel that contains water. The vessel holds what is in it, but has no room for anything but what fills it. Like this, when the heart is full of love, it has no space for anything but the Beloved.

As for the sayings of the shaykhs, they have said that love is the perpetual inclination of the enraptured heart; preference for the Beloved over every friend; harmony with the Beloved in what is seen and what is unseen; the effacement of the attributes of the lover and the affirmation of the essence of the Beloved; the heart's agreement with the wishes of the Lord; the fear of abandoning reverence together with established service.

Abu Yazid al-Bistami said, "Love is to count it as little when a great deal comes from yourself and to count it as much when a little bit comes from your Beloved." Sahl al-Tustari said, "Love is to embrace obedience and leave disobedience." Junayd, asked about love, said, "It is to enter into the attributes of the Beloved in exchange for the attributes of the lover."

Junayd was indicating the state of being overwhelmed by the remembrance of the Beloved until nothing can dominate the lover's heart except the recollection of the attributes of the Beloved. Then everything that pertains to the traits of the ego and the very sense of it is forgotten.

Abu Ali al-Rudhbari said, "Love is harmony." Abu Abd Allah al-Qurayshi said, "The essence of love is to give all of yourself to the one you love so that nothing of yourself remains to you." Shibli said, "Love is called love because it erases from the heart everything except the Beloved." Ibn Ata said, "Love is to always be blameworthy."

I heard Abu Ali al-Daqqaq say, "Love is a delight,and occasions of reality are an amazement." And I heard him say, "Passionate desire (*ishq*) means to exceed the bounds in love. The Truth, glory to Him, cannot be described as exceeding bounds and so passion is not attributed to Him. And if all of the loves of all of creation converged in one person, that love would not reach the degree of love that is due to the Truth—so it cannot be said that a servant exceeds the bounds in the love of God."

So passion cannot be attributed to the Truth and cannot be attributed to the servant in his love of the Truth. Thus passion is disqualified. It is not possible in the description of the Truth. It does not proceed from the Truth to the servant nor proceed from the servant to the Truth.

I heard Abu Abd al-Rahman al-Sulami say . . . that Shibli said, "Love means you are jealous that anyone else like you should love the Beloved." And I heard him say . . . that Ibn Ata, when asked about love, said, "Love's branches are planted in the heart and bear fruit according to one's mind." And I heard him say that al-Nasrabadhi said, "There is a love that demands the sparing of blood, and there is a love that demands the spilling of blood." I also heard him say . . . that Sumnun said, "The lovers of God Most High have carried off the honors in this world and the next; for the Prophet said, 'A man is together with the one he loves'— so they are together with God Most High."

Yahya ibn Muadh said, "The essence of love is not decreased by harshness or increased by kindness." And he said, "That person is not truthful who claims to love God yet does not respect the limits He has set." Junayd said, "When love is sound, the rules of behavior fall away." With this meaning Abu Ali recited:

When people's love is pure, their ties are constant
Speeches of praise sound ugly.

He used to say, "You don't see a kindly father showing elaborate respect when he talks to his son. People
may stand on ceremony when they address a man, but
his father just calls him by name." Al-Kattani said,
"Love is to prefer the beloved to oneself."

I heard Muhammad ibn al-Husayn say that . . .
Bundar ibn al-Husayn said, "Majnun ibn Amir was seen
in a dream. He was asked, "What did God do with you?"
He replied, "He forgave me and set me as evidence
against the lovers."

Abu Yaqub al-Susi said, "The essence of love is that
the servant forgets what he has received from God and
forgets what he needs from Him." Husayn ibn al-Mansur
said, "The essence of love is that you stand with your
Beloved stripped of your attributes."

I heard Abu Abd al-Rahman al-Sulami say that
Nasrabadhi was told, "People say you have not experienced love." He said, "People have spoken the truth, but
I have their griefs and in that I am inflamed." And I
heard him say that Nasrabadhi said, "Love is to avoid
solace in every circumstance." Then he recited:

One whose passion is prolonged tastes a kind
     of forgetting
But I taste no forgetfulness of Layla.
The closest I came to union with her
Consisted of wishes that did not come true,
     passing like a lightning flash.

Muhammad ibn al-Fadl said, "Love means that every
love falls from the heart except the love of the Beloved."

Junayd said, "Love is an excess of attraction without
fulfillment." Love, it is said, is a disturbance of hearts
occasioned by the beloved. And it is said to be a trial
imposed upon the inmost heart by the object of one's
desire.

Ibn Ata recited:

I planted a branch of desire for the people of love.
No one before me knew what desire was.
As a branch it came to leaf. It ripened as the
    infatuation of youth
Then bitterness was born to me from the sweet fruit.
The desire of all of the lovers, every one—
If they look for its history, that is its origin.
It is said that the beginning of love is deception, and
    its end is slaughter.

I heard Abu Ali say (concerning the meaning of the saying of the Prophet, "'Your love of a thing makes you blind and deaf). It makes you blind to all but the Beloved out of jealousy and to the Beloved out of awe." Then he recited:

When what appears to me is His Grandeur
I turn back as if I had not arrived.

I heard Abu Abd al-Rahman al-Sulami say . . . that Harith al-Muhasibi said, "Love is your attraction to a thing with your entire being; then your preference for it over your own self, your soul, and your possessions; then your harmony with it privately and publicly; then your knowledge that you have fallen short in the love of it." And I heard him say . . . that Sari said, "Love between two is not sound until the one says to the other, "O I!"

Shibli said, "The lover is destroyed if he keeps silent. The Knower is destroyed if he does not keep silent." It is said:

Love is a fire in the heart that burns all but the wish
    of the Beloved."
Love is to spend all effort while the Beloved does
    what He wills."

Nuri said, "Love tears veils and reveals secrets." Abu Yaqub al-Susi said, "Love is not sound until one leaves off seeing love and, instead, sees the Beloved through the annihilation of the knowledge of love." Jafar said that Junayd said, "Sari gave me a scrap of paper and said, 'This is better for you than 700 stories or traditions of the Companions.' On it was written:

When I claimed to love, she said, "You lie to me!
"How should I see your limbs still clothed in flesh?
"It isn't love till your heart cleaves to your guts,
"And you waste away past answering any caller—
"You waste away till no desire remains
"But an eye to cry with and a secret shared!"

Ibn Masruq said, "I saw Sumnun speak about love; every lamp in the mosque shattered." I heard Muhammad ibn al-Husayn say . . . that Ibrahim ibn Fatik said, "Sumnun was seated in the mosque discoursing upon love when a little bird came in. It came closer and closer to him never stopping its approach, until it was sitting upon his hand. Then it struck its beak upon the earth until the blood flowed and it died." Junayd said, 'Every love pertains to an object. When the object vanishes, that love vanishes.'"

Shibli, it is told, was committed to an asylum. A number of people went to see him. "Who are you?" he asked. "We are people who love you, Abu Bakr," they replied. He began to throw stones at them, and they ran away. "If you claim to love me," he called, "then you should be patient under my trial!"

Shibli recited:

O Generous Lord, the love of You
    never ends inside me.
O You who take sleep from my eyes
You know what has happened to me.

I heard Abu Abd al-Rahman al-Sulami say . . . that Ali ibn Ubayd said, "Yahya ibn Muadh wrote to Abu Yazid, 'I am intoxicated with how much I have drunk from the cup of love.' Abu Yazid wrote back to him, 'Someone else has drunk the oceans of the heavens and the earth and his thirst is not yet quenched. His tongue is hanging out and he is asking, "Is there any more?"'

They recited:

> I'm amazed at someone who says, "I've remembered
>   my darling."
> Have I ever forgotten, that I should have to
>   remember?
> I die remembering You, then come back to life.
> Were it not for my good thought of You, I would not
>   have revived.
> Desire's object lives when I die to desire.
> How many times have I lived for you, how many
>   times died?
> I drink love, glass after glass.
> The glass is not empty. My thirst is not sated.

God Most High revealed to Jesus, "When I look upon the heart of a servant and do not find in it the love of this world or the next, I fill it with the love of Me." I saw in the handwriting of Abu Ali al-Daqqaq, in an inspired book, "My servant, I love you as a right due to you. So love Me as is My right." Abd Allah ibn al-Mubarak said, "Whoever is given something of love and has not been given the same amount of fear is deceived." Love, it is said, is that which obliterates all trace of you. Love is said to be a drunkenness from which one never recovers except through seeing the Beloved. And the drunkenness that then comes of that vision cannot be described. They recite:

> The people grew drunk from passing the cup,

But the One who passed it made them drunker still.

Abu Ali al-Daqqaq often recited:

I have two intoxications; the regretful have but one.
The thing by which I am distinguished from them is
One.

Ibn Ata said, "Love is to perish continuously." Abu Ali
had a woman servant named Fayruz whom he used to
love because she would often wait upon him. I heard him
say, "One day Fayruz was bothering me and speaking
sharply to me. Abu 'l-Hasan al-Qari said, 'Why are you
troubling this shaykh?' She replied, 'Because I love
him!'"

Yahya ibn Muadh said, "A mustard seed's worth of
love is dearer to me than seventy years of loveless worship." A young man looked down over the people gathered on the festival day and said:

Whoever dies of love, let him die thus.
There is no good in love without death!
Then he cast himself from a high terrace and fell
down dead.

It is told that a Hindu loved a maidservant. She
moved away and the man went out to say farewell. Tears
fell from one of his eyes but not the other. For eighty-four
years he kept shut the eye that did not weep. He would
not open it in order to punish it for not crying over the
departure of his beloved. With this meaning they recited:

My one eye wept on the morn of departure.
The other was miserly toward us with tears.
I punished the tear-miser by closing it tight
On the day when we met again.

A Sufi said, "We were discussing love among ourselves in the presence of Dhu 'l- Nun al-Misri. He said,
'Drop this topic. The lower self cannot hear of it and so
it pretends to it.' Then he began to recite:

Fear and sadness best befit the sinner when he
worships.
Love is for the pious and the purified of filth.

Yahya ibn Muadh said, "Whoever spreads talk of love
among those not suited for it is an impostor in what he
claims." It is said that a man claimed to have been totally overcome by the love of a particular person. "How can
that be?" the youth asked him. "My brother here has a
handsomer face than I and a more perfect beauty!" The
man raised his head to see and the youth threw him off
the balcony upon which they were standing. "That is the
reward of whoever pretends to love me but looks at
someone else!" said he.

Sumnun used to give love priority over inner knowledge, but most of the shaykhs have given inner knowledge priority over love. Among those who know the true
meanings of things, love means to be overwhelmed with
delight, while inner knowledge means to bear witness
with wonder and to lose oneself in awe.

Abu Bakr al-Kattani said, "The topic of love arose in
Mecca during the pilgrimage season, and all the shaykhs
were talking about it. Junayd was the youngest present.
'Share with us what you know about it, O Iraqi!' the others urged. "He cast down his head, and his eyes were full
of tears. He said, 'There is a servant who has left himself
behind, who is attached to the remembrance of his Lord,
who is steadfast in performing the duties due Him, who
looks to Him in his heart, a heart burning with the lights
of His Essence. God has purified the draught he has

drunk from the cup of His love. The All-Powerful has raised for him the veils of the unseen. If he discourses, it is through God. If he speaks privately, it is from God. If he moves, it is by the order of God. If he keeps still, it is together with God. He is by God, for God, with God.' The shaykhs wept and said, 'There is nothing to be said beyond this. May God grant you strength, O Crown of the Knowers!'"

God Most High revealed to Prophet David, "O David, I have forbidden My love to enter hearts while the love of something else is in them." Hamzah ibn Yusuf al-Sahmi related that . . . Abu Abbas, the servant of al-Fudayl ibn Iyad, said, "Fudayl suffered from retention of the urine. He raised his hands and prayed, 'My God, by my love for You, unless You relieve me of this, I won't go away until I am cured!' [grammar dubious—might be 'I won't leave till I'm worn out!']."

Love, they say, is to prefer the other above oneself. Thus the wife of Pharaoh's minister, when her love for Joseph became great, said, *"I tried to tempt him, but he is surely one of the truthful"* [12:51]. In the beginning, though, she had said, *"What should be the requital of one who wished to do evil to your wife, except imprisonment or a painful punishment?"* [12:25]. In the beginning she attributed the sin to him, but in the end she admitted the treachery was hers.

I heard Abu Ali say that it is related that Abu Said al-Kharraz said, "I saw the Prophet in a dream and said, 'Messenger of God, forgive me! Loving God has distracted me from loving you.' He replied, 'O blessed one, whoever loves God Most High loves me.'" In her private prayers, Rabia asked, "My God, would You burn in the fire a heart that loves You?" A voice from the unseen replied, "We would not do such a thing. Do not think bad thoughts about Us!"

The word for love, *hubb*, is made of two letters, "h"

and "b." This is said to indicate that whoever loves must leave behind both soul (*ruh*, symbolized by its final letter) and body (*badan*, symbolized by its initial letter).

In summary, the Sufis have said that love, overall, is harmony, and that the strongest form of harmony is the harmony of the heart. Love requires the absence of all discord. The lover is always together with his Beloved. Thus we have received the following hadith: Abu Bakr ibn Furak reported . . . that Abu Musa al-Ashari said, "The Prophet was asked, 'If a man loves a people, will he not overtake and join them?' The Prophet answered, 'A man is with the one he loves.'"

I heard Abu Abd al-Rahman al-Sulami say . . . that Abu Hafs said, "Most corruption of states comes from three things: the dissoluteness of gnostics, the faithlessness of lovers, and the dishonesty of seekers."

Abu Uthman said, "The dissoluteness of gnostics means freeing their glances, tongues, and hearing to follow worldly causes and benefits. The faithlessness of lovers means their choosing their own whims over the pleasure of God Almighty and Glorious in whatever they encounter. The dishonesty of seekers means their being occupied with the remembrance and vision of people to the exclusion of the remembrance of God." And I heard him say . . . that Abu Ali Mumshad ibn Said al-Ukbari said, "Inside the dome of Solomon's temple, a male swallow courted a female swallow. She refused to have anything to do with him. He asked her, 'Why do you reject me? If you wished, I would pull down this dome on top of Solomon!' Prophet Solomon summoned the bird to him. "What is the meaning of this?" he demanded. "O Prophet of God," pleaded the bird, "lovers are not to blame for the things they say!" "You have spoken the truth!" said the king.

43
ON LONGING (*SHAWQ*)

God Almighty and Glorious said, "*Whoever hopes to meet his Lord—God has delayed the meeting*" [29:5].

Ali ibn Ahmad ibn Abdan al-Ahwazi reported . . . that al-Saib said, "Ammar ibn Yasir prayed with us. He made the prayer short. 'You have made a simple prayer, Abu Yaqzan!' I exclaimed. 'That is not my doing,' he replied. 'I have prayed to God with prayers that I heard from the Messenger of God. Once when he stood up after finishing his private prayer, a man who was there at the time followed him and asked him what he had said. He told him, "My God, by Your knowledge of the unseen and Your power over the Creation, make me live the life You know to be best for me. Make me die the death You know to be best for me. My God, I ask You for the middle course between wealth and poverty. I ask You for a blessing that does not diminish and a comfort that is unbroken. I ask You for satisfaction after Your judgment and ease of existence after death. I ask to look upon Your Generous Face, and for the longing to meet You without painful distress, without misleading trials. My God, adorn us with the adornment of faith. My God, make us leaders of the well-guided."'

Longing, *shawq*, is the heart's excitement to meet the

Beloved. One's longing is to the extent of one's love.
I heard Abu Ali al-Daqqaq discriminate between
longing, *shawq*, and passionate desire, *ishtiyaq*. He said:
Longing is quieted by meeting and seeing the Beloved,
but passionate desire does not cease with the meeting.
With this sense they recited:

> The glance turns not away from Him when He is
> seen
> Save to come back ardently to Him.

I heard Abu Abd al-Rahman al-Sulami say that al-
Nasrabadhi said, "Every person has some share of longing, but not everyone has a share of passionate desire.
Whoever enters into the state of ardent yearning wan-
ders distracted in it until no trace of him remains to be
seen." It is said that Ahmad ibn Hamid al-Aswad went
to Abd Allah ibn Munazil and said, "I saw in a dream
that you will die in a year. Are you ready to go?" "Have
you delayed us for so long a time?" Abd Allah ibn
Munazil cried. "How shall I manage to live for a whole
year? I feel so close to that verse I heard from al-Thaqafi
(that is, Abu Ali):

> O you who complain of desire because the
> separation from Him has been long,
> Be patient in your illness. You shall meet your
> Beloved tomorrow.

Abu Uthman said, "The sign of longing is to love
death with ease." Yahya ibn Muadh said, "The sign of
longing is the weaning of the body away from lusts." I
heard Abu Ali al-Daqqaq say, "One day Prophet David
went out into the desert alone. God Most High revealed
to him, "How is it that I see you solitary, O David?" "My
God," he replied, "Longing to meet You possesses my
heart and comes between me and the society of men."

God Most High revealed, "Return to them. If you guide one servant who has strayed to Me, I will put your name on the Guarded Tablet as a great sage."

An old woman, it is told, went out to meet a relative who had arrived after a long journey. All of her people were showing great joy, but the old lady wept. They asked her, "Why are you crying?" and she replied, "The arrival of this young man reminds me of the day of arrival before God Most High."

Ibn Ata was asked about longing and said, "The burning of guts, the blazing of hearts, the laceration of livers!" Then they asked him which was higher, longing or love. He said, "Love—because longing is born of it."

A Sufi said, "Longing is a flame generated in the folds of the bowels and produced by separation. If there is meeting, that flame is extinguished. When what dominates one's inmost being is the witnessing of the Beloved, longing does not befall one." A dervish was asked, "Do you yearn?" "No," said he. "Longing is only for someone absent. He is here!"

I heard Abu Ali al-Daqqaq say, concerning God's word, "*And I hastened to You, my Lord, to please You*" [20:84]. The meaning of this is, "Out of longing for You." It is veiled by the expression "good pleasure."

And I heard him say, "One of the signs of longing is to wish for death when everything is going well. Thus Prophet Joseph did not say, "Take me to You!" when he was cast into the well nor when he was put into prison. But when his parents came to him and his brothers fell down prostrate before him, and wealth and dominion were his, then he said, "*Take me to You in full submis - sion*" [12: 101]. With this sense the Sufis recited:

> We have the most perfect of joys,
> But only with you will joy be complete.
> Our joy is shame, people of love,

Since you are absent, though we are here.

They also recited:

Whom does the new holiday bring joy?
I've found no joy in it.
My happiness would be perfect
Were my Beloved here with me.

Ibn Khafif said, "Longing is the heart's finding rest in ecstasy and the love of that meeting with God that takes place through closeness to Him." Abu Yazid said, "God has servants who, if He veiled them from seeing Him in paradise, would seek rescue from paradise the way that the people of hell seek rescue from the fire."

Muhammad ibn Abd Allah al-Sufi reported . . . that al-Husayn al-Ansari said, "In a dream it seemed to me that the day of judgment had come. There was a person standing under the Throne of God. The Truth said, "O My angels, who is this?" "God knows best!" they replied. He said, "This is Maruf al-Karkhi, drunken with My love. He will not recover except by meeting with Me."

In another relation of a dream like this it is said, "This is Maruf al-Karkhi. He left the world out of yearning for God so God Almighty and Glorious permits that he look upon Him." Faris said, "The hearts of those full of ardent yearning are illuminated with the light of God Most High. When their yearning is awakened, that light illumines all that exists between heaven and earth. God displays them to His angels, and says, "These are they who passionately desire Me. I call you to witness that I desire them more!"

I heard Abu Ali al-Daqqaq comment on the prayer of the Prophet, "I ask You for the longing to meet You." Longing had a hundred parts. Ninety-nine of them were given to him and one part was distributed among the people. But he wanted that one part to be his also, out of jealousy that there should be even a fragment of longing for anyone else. The longing felt by people who are close to God is more complete than that felt by those who are still veiled. If those who yearn for God sip at the sweetness of death when it comes, it is because they have been shown that the comfort of meeting Him is sweeter than honey.

I heard Muhammad ibn al-Husayn say . . . that Sari said, "Longing, when it is thoroughly actualized, is the greater station for a gnostic. When he attains longing, he becomes oblivious to whatever might turn him away from the object of his longing."

Abu Uthman al-Hiri commented on the divine words, *"God has delayed the meeting"* [29:5], saying, "This is a consolation for those who yearn for Him. It means, 'I know your desire for Me has overcome you, while I have put off the meeting with you until its appointed time. But soon you will reach the One Whom you desire.'"

It is told that God Most High revealed to Prophet David, "Tell the young men of Israel, 'Do not occupy yourselves with anything but Me. I am yearning for you—what sort of coarse behavior is this?'" It is also said that God Almighty and Glorious revealed to Prophet David, "If those who oppose Me knew how I watch over them, knew of My friendship toward them and My longing for them, they would abandon their disobedience and die out of longing for Me—though I have cut their connection to My love! O David, if this is My wish for people who oppose Me, what then shall be My wish for people who turn to Me?"

It is written in the Torah, "We set yearning in you, but you have not yearned. We set fear in you, but you have not feared. We set mourning in you, but you have not mourned."

I heard Abu Ali al-Daqqaq say, "Shuayb wept until he

went blind, so God Almighty and Glorious returned his vision to him. Again he wept until he went blind, and again God returned his sight. A third time he wept until he was blinded." God Most High revealed to him, "If this weeping were for paradise, I would ensure it to you. If it were on account of hell, I would secure you from it." "No," said Shuayb. "It is out of desire for You." God revealed, "Since it is for the sake of that, I have appointed you My prophet, one who shall speak to Me over ten years."

They say everything yearns for the one who yearns for God. It comes in a hadith: "Paradise longs for three: Ali, Ammar, and Salman." I heard Abu Ali say that one of the shaykhs said, "I entered into longing and all things longed for me, but I was free of all of them." I heard Abu Abd al-Rahman al-Sulami say . . . that Malik ibn Dinar said, "I read in the Torah, 'I set yearning in you, but you did not yearn. I played for you, but you did not dance.'" I heard Muhammad ibn Abd Allah al-Sufi say that Muhammad ibn Farhan said, "Junayd was asked, 'Why does the lover cry when he meets the Beloved?'"

He replied, "That is only out of joy, and out of ecstasy from the intensity of the longing for Him. "I have heard that once two brothers' embraced. One of them exclaimed, 'O, what longing!' "The other one cried, 'O, what bliss!'"

SELECTED BIBLIOGRAPHY

Abdel-Kader, Ali Hassan. *The Life, Personality and Writings of Al-Junayd*. E. J. W. Gibb Memorial Series, New Series 22. London: Luzac G Co., 1976.

Cambridge History of Islam. 4 vols. Cambridge: Cambridge University Press, 1970. Vol. la: The Central Lands from Pre-Islamic Times to the first World War, edited by P.M. Holt, Ann K.S. Lambton, and Bernard Lewis.

Cambridge History of Iran. 6 vols. Cambridge: Cambridge University Press, 1968. Vol. 4: The Period from the Arab Invasion to the Saljuks, edited by R.N. Frye. "Religion in the Saljuq Period," by A. Bausani. Vol. 5: The Saljuq and Mongol Periods, edited by J.A. Boyle. Sufism," by S.H. Nasr.

Gatje, H. *The Quran and Its Exegesis. Selected 'Texts and Modern Muslim Interpretation*. Translated by A. T. Welch. Berkeley and Los Angles: University of California Press, 1976.

Gilsenan, Michael. *Recognizing Islam*. New York: Pantheon Books, 1982.

Goldziher, Ignaz. *Introduction to Islamic Theology and Law*. Translated by Andras and Ruth Hamori. Introduction and additional notes by Bernard Lewis. Princeton: Princeton University Press, 1981.

Graham, William. *Divine Word and Prophetic Word In Early Islam*. The Hague: Mouton, 1977.

Hodgson, Marshall. *The Venture of Islam: Conscience and History in a World Civilization*, 3 vols. Chicago and London: University of Chicago Press, 1974.

al-Hujwiri, Ali b. Uthman al-Jullabi. *Kashf al-Mahjub of Al-Hujwiri: The Oldest Persian Treatise on Sufism*.Translated by Reynold R. Nicholson. E.J.W. Gibb Memorial Series 17. London: Luzac, new ed., 1976.

Islam Ansiclopedisi. Istanbul: Milli Egitim Basimevi, 1977. "Kusheyri" by Ahmad Ates.

al-Kalabadhi, Abu Bakr. *The Doctrine of the Sufis*.Translated by A. J. Arberry. Cambridge: Cambridge University Press, paperback ed., 1977.

I

INDEX TO QURANIC VERSES

A